JEKKA'S HERB COOKBOOK

JEKKA'S HERB COOKBOOK

Jekka McVicar

FIREFLY BOOKS

A FIREFLY BOOK

Published by Firefly Books Ltd. 2011

First printing

Publisher Cataloging-in-Publication Data (U.S.)
McVicar, Jekka.
    Jekka's herb cookbook / Jekka McVicar ; illustrated by Hanna McVicar.
[352] p. : col. ill. ;   cm.
Includes index.
Summary: This book discusses 50 culinary herbs, which range from well-known herbs
such as parsley, to exotic ones such as curry leaf. Each chapter is dedicated to an herb,
explaining how the herb is grown, it's benefits and varieties, as well as recipes to cook
with each herb. The aim is to illustrate a wide range of herbs, and how they can be
combined and used in a variety of dishes.
ISBN-13: 978-1-55407-814-1
ISBN-10: 1-55407-814-8
1. Cooking (Herbs). I. McVicar, Hanna. II. Title.
641.657 dc22   TX819.H4M385 2011

Library and Archives Canada Cataloguing in Publication
McVicar, Jekka
          Jekka's herb cookbook / Jekka McVicar ; Hannah
McVicar, illustrator.
Includes index.
ISBN-13: 978-1-55407-814-1
ISBN-10: 1-55407-814-8
          1. Cooking (Herbs). 2. Herbs. I. McVicar, Hannah II. Title.
TX819.H4M43 2010   641.6'57   C2010-905900-X

Published in the United States by
Firefly Books (U.S.) Inc.
P.O. Box 1338, Ellicott Station
Buffalo, New York 14205

Published in Canada by
Firefly Books Ltd.
66 Leek Crescent
Richmond Hill, Ontario L4B 1H1

Printed in China

Dedicated to

my grandmother, Ruth,

my mother, Clare,

and

my daughter, Hannah

CONTENTS

FOREWORD

I've known the lovely Jekka for many years now and she is passionate about many things in life, but especially herbs. Without fail, each time I see her I learn something new about these wonderful plants. Jekka believes herbs are one of the best things in the world, and after listening to her rave about their many benefits you can't help but agree with her.

Not only does she know loads about growing, cooking and storing herbs, she is also full of good information about how they can make you feel. I have no doubt that if more people were into growing and cooking their own herbs on a regular basis we'd be well on our way to having a happier and healthier country.

Jekka really is the herb queen of England in my books, yet she doesn't just know about the herbs we commonly enjoy in this country; she also knows about herbs from all around the world. If you're a foodie geek like me, you'll always find yourself ordering the newcomers to the ever-increasing collection at her farm.

In this day and age, varieties of herbs we used to think of as quite exotic are readily available in our local supermarkets. What's exciting and clever about what Jekka has done with this book is that she's focused on a "hit-list"– her top 50 cooking herbs of all time – and gives you delicious and exciting ways of using them. If you use herbs on a regular basis, you'll have tastier food and be a healthier person. I have no doubt you'll enjoy them and find Jekka's many practical hints and tips incredibly useful, as I have done over the years. Her book is a great start to finding serious solutions to good, exciting eating.

Jamie Oliver

INTRODUCTION

My passion for herbs has evolved over 50 years – it started before I went to school. My mother, who was a keen grower of herbs and vegetables, to the extent that we were self-sufficient, had an herb bed that contained more than 25 different herbs. There were lemon thyme, French tarragon, dill, horseradish and spearmint, to name but a few. She was always bottling, preserving and baking. She taught me which mint to pick to make mint sauce and then how to prepare it, and for a number of years this was my special contribution to the Sunday meal. When I was at school, I had a garden plot where I grew salad vegetables, including purslane and rather awful radishes that I proudly brought home for the family to eat.

When I started work, I was working in television – often on short contracts – and in between jobs I ended up working at Tumbler's Bottom Herb Farm. I thought I knew a lot about herbs, thanks to my mother's garden, but soon realized I knew nothing. I became fascinated by the different varieties of herbs at the farm, and with this burgeoning knowledge and access to new plants, my personal herb garden in Bristol expanded rapidly. It was from this garden that the idea for Jekka's Herb Farm originated. I was at home with my two small children one day when a girlfriend came around and asked if she could have some French tarragon. I told her to help herself, and it dawned on me that she could not buy it anywhere, yet I could grow it. Within a few months my husband and I had converted our small back garden into a mini organic herb farm and had started to supply local grocers and a garden center with organic culinary potherbs. Within a year I needed more space as it was becoming difficult to keep up with demand, so we moved the farm to our present site in south Gloucestershire. The business grew from there, and in the early 1990s we started exhibiting organic culinary and medicinal herbs at the Royal Horticultural Society (RHS) flower shows, where we have now been awarded more than 60 RHS gold medals. There are currently more than 650 different species of herb being grown at the farm, which we supply to our customers, mainly via mail order.

My interest in herbs is ever increasing and I am particularly fascinated by their incredible versatility. Herbs have long been a part of our history, yet we often remain wary of utilizing them to their full potential. Not only do herbs impart flavor, aroma and texture to cooking, they are also beneficial to our diet and have medicinal and even household uses. It is well documented, for example, that thyme contains antiseptic oils that counteract decay and contamination, sage contains a natural preservative that

prolongs the shelf life of food and aniseed-flavored herbs such as French tarragon help the digestion of fatty foods.

In this book I have limited myself to talking about my top 50 culinary herbs. These range from the well-loved and well-known parsley and rosemary to the more exotic curry leaf and Vietnamese coriander. All the herbs chosen are ones that I grow on my herb farm and have used for many years in the kitchen. There is a chapter devoted to each herb, and within it you will learn how that herb is grown, its culinary benefits and what different varieties are available before discovering the recipes that I hope will entice you to cook with it. I have also included sections titled "Excess Bay," "Exess Dill," etc., because there are times of the year when you may have a glut of a specific herb and no idea how to preserve or harvest it for the winter months. My aim is to illustrate the wide range of herbs now available, how you can combine different herbs and how they can be used, not only in savory dishes but also to make delightful desserts.

The recipes in this book are inspired by my love and enjoyment of food. I am a passionate cook and always experimenting with how to incorporate new herbs and flavors into my dishes. Over the years I have discovered that one of the enormous benefits of cooking with herbs is their amazing ability to enhance dishes: they can transform a cheap cut of meat, stretch a sauce for pasta and add a new dimension to vegetables, eggs or just about anything! I have also drawn inspiration from friends and, above all, my family. I grew up surrounded by marvelous home cooks and as a result this book is infused with four generations of passion and talent. My grandmother Ruth Lowinsky wrote cookbooks from 1930 to 1950 and she inspired me to write my own; my mother, Clare, kept detailed handwritten notes of her recipes and encouraged my love of cooking; and my daughter, Hannah, who I am proud to say has inherited my love of food and cooking, has filled this book with her beautiful illustrations. (In doing so she is also following a family tradition, as my grandfather Thomas Lowinsky illustrated my grandmother's original cookbooks.) And finally, a number of professional chefs – Jamie Oliver, Heston Blumenthal, Michael Caines and Rick Stein, to name a few – have found their way to the farm over the years and have been enthused by the herbs we grow. They too have motivated me to try new ways of cooking with herbs.

I hope that this book will inspire you to both grow and cook with herbs and to enjoy the pleasure of these remarkable plants.

General Recipe Notes

Produce

Having been an organic herb farmer for over 25 years, it goes without saying that I prefer to use organic and locally grown or raised produce in all my recipes, but I leave the choice up to you.

Herbs – in all the recipes I use fresh herbs; if you are using dried, please halve the quantities I have given, as dried herbs have a stronger and more intense flavor.

Eggs – unless otherwise stated, eggs are medium. Where possible, use organic free-range eggs.

Milk – I use reduced-fat (2%) or 1% milk.

Butter – I always use unsalted butter, and organic where possible. You can always add salt, but you can never take it away.

Sugar – sugar is granulated unless otherwise specified.

Fish – during my lifetime the depletion in fish stocks has been staggering. I try, where possible, to source fish that has been ethically farmed or caught, and such fish are now becoming more easily available.

Making preserves, jams, jellies or chutneys

Making preserves is a wonderful way of conserving the harvest for use throughout the winter months. However, it is important to follow a few simple rules when preserving foods, because botulism (a bacterial infection) can be very dangerous. Botulism can be difficult to detect as the bacteria are often found in minute quantities. Homemade preserves that are made without vinegar, salt or preservatives are more susceptible to bacteria as they lack the acidity that stops the bacteria's development.

So, to avoid complications,

* Choose only fresh, unblemished fruit, vegetables and/or herbs.
* Storage jars or bottles must be thoroughly cleaned, sterilized (see page 12) and dried.
* The lids or tops of the storage jars should be new or lined with waxed paper and fit tightly.
* Clean cutlery should always be used when extracting the contents from the jars.
* Once opened, the jars should be kept in a cool, dark place or stored in the fridge and consumed fairly quickly. If at any time the contents of the jar look or smell suspicious, throw them out or compost them.

How to sterilize jars and bottles

While there are a number of methods you can use to do this, I prefer to use either of the following:

❀ Preheat the oven to its lowest setting. Wash the jars and bottles and their tops well in hot, soapy water, rinse, then place them in the oven for at least 15 to 20 minutes prior to use. Remove the jars or bottles from the oven and fill, cover, or cool them, according to your recipe.

❀ Wash the jars or bottles in hot, soapy water, rinse and leave to drain. Fill a large pan with cold water, immerse the jars or bottles in the water, bring to a boil and simmer for 10 to 15 minutes. Remove the jars or bottles from the water using clean tongs, drain until fully dry, then fill.

How to peel tomatoes

Place the washed tomatoes in a bowl. Bring a kettle to a boil, pour the boiling water over the tomatoes, covering them completely, and leave for 3 to 4 minutes. Gently tip the tomatoes into a colander to drain. Taking care, since the tomatoes are hot, use a sharp-tipped knife to make a small nick in the skin; then it should peel off easily.

The sauce below can be enhanced by adding the herb of your choice, according to what best suits the dish you are serving it with. It can be sieved if you want a smooth sauce.

Some useful basic recipes

BASIC TOMATO SAUCE

Serves 2

2 tbsp (30 ml) unsalted butter
1 tbsp (15 ml) olive oil
1 small onion, finely sliced
1 clove garlic, crushed
½ lb (250 g) fresh tomatoes, peeled
(see above) and finely sliced, or
14-oz (398 ml) can of chopped
Italian tomatoes
½ tsp (2 ml) soft brown sugar
Salt and freshly ground black pepper

In a pan or frying pan, melt the butter and the oil. When just bubbling, add the onion and cook gently until its flesh is translucent. Add the garlic and cook for a further minute, then add the tomatoes, sugar and salt and pepper to taste.

CHICKEN STOCK

Makes 1 quart (1 L)

1 chicken carcass (raw or cooked)
with giblets, washed
1 large onion, quartered
1 large carrot, scraped and cut into 4
1 tsp (5 ml) salt
Bouquet garni (see page 40)
2 qt (2 L) cold water (or 1 qt/1 L if
using a pressure cooker)

Break up the carcass and put it in a large saucepan or a pressure cooker (this is not only a great eco way to cook, as it uses less power and half the amount of water, it is also so much faster than simmering in a pot for hours). Add all the other ingredients and bring to a boil, uncovered. Using a slotted spoon, remove any scum that rises to the surface.

Put on the lid, reduce the heat and simmer very slowly for 1½ hours, or if using a pressure cooker, follow the manufacturer's instructions to bring the cooker to high pressure (15 lb) for 45 minutes, then reduce the pressure slowly.

Strain the stock into a large bowl and leave to cool. When cold, remove the fat. Keep in the fridge and use within 3 days.

VEGETABLE STOCK

Makes 1½ quarts (1.5 L)

2 large onions, sliced
4 large carrots, scraped and sliced
2 oz (50 g) rutabaga or turnip,
peeled and sliced
1 leek, sliced and washed
Bouquet garni (see page 40)
1 tsp (5 ml) salt
4 peppercorns
3 qt (2.8 L) cold water (or 1½ qt
/1.5 L if using a pressure cooker)

Put all the ingredients into a large saucepan and bring to a boil, uncovered. Using a slotted spoon, remove any scum that rises to the surface.

Put on the lid, reduce the heat and simmer for 1 hour. If using a pressure cooker, follow the manufacturer's instructions to bring the cooker to high pressure (15 lb) for 15 minutes, then reduce the pressure slowly.

Strain the stock into a large bowl and leave to cool. Once cold, refrigerate and use within 3 days.

ANGELICA

(also known as Root of the Holy Ghost, European Angelica)
Angelica archangelica

My earliest memory of this herb is picking off the sugary translucent green pieces from my birthday trifle and reserving them for eating last. These were the candied stems of angelica that were traditionally used to decorate cakes and, on very special occasions, trifles. (Trifles just have to be the best "leftover dessert," so I have included a favorite version of this typically English dish on page 18.) Stems of angelica are not the only part worth eating; the leaves have a unique flavor that combines well with many fruit and vegetable dishes.

Description

Once angelica goes to flower it is absolutely stunning; it is one of the best architectural plants you can grow, giving great structure to an herb garden. The sweet honey scent of the flowers is lovely too, especially when it catches an early summer's warm breeze. This is an interesting herb because, if it is growing happily, it will not die until it has flowered and set seed (the horticultural name for this is monocarpic), usually living for two to four years. Its final height, when in flower, is a magnificent 8 feet (2.5 m). The greenish white, sweetly scented flowers form in large, round clusters in the late spring to early summer of the second or third year. The large, deeply divided bright green leaves around the base of the plant decrease in size around the stem. They emit the smell of sweet muscatel when crushed or, if you have a powerful sense of smell, something like gin – it is one of the main ingredients of the spirit.

Raise this plant from seed sown in the autumn in small pots or modules. In the early stages, make sure seedlings and plants do not dry out. Plant out in the following spring in deep, moist soil, as angelica prefers to have its roots in the shade and its flowers in the sun. Because it is very tall when in flower, though, you should choose your site carefully: place it toward the back of a border or in the center of the garden. If it is grown in an exposed windy site you may need to stake the plant when it goes into flower to stop the stems from breaking. It is not an ideal plant for a pot because of its size.

History in cooking

Throughout history angelica has been used as a vegetable. In Greenland, Sweden and Finland the young shoots are blanched and used in soups and stews. Traditionally it has been used to flavor many drinks, including absinthe and anisette vermouth, as well as the aforementioned gin, where it is combined with juniper. If you are an enthusiastic forager, please be aware that you do need to know what you are looking for, as angelica has been mistaken for hemlock (*Conium maculatum*), which is extremely poisonous. Unlike angelica, hemlock has a foul smell when the leaves are crushed, the white flowers form flat clusters, and it has purple spots on its stems.

Harvesting and uses

Leaves

Pick young leaves to use fresh in late spring to early summer, while still soft. Their flavor is dry with a slightly bitter tang and a hint of aniseed and should be used sparingly – a little is good, a lot is not. It is ideal in salads, blanched as a spring vegetable or used as flavoring in soups and stews. When stewed with fruit such as gooseberries or rhubarb, angelica reduces the tartness of the fruit and by so doing cuts down the amount of sugar needed to sweeten the dish. When using the leaves in this way, it is a good idea to tie them up with a piece of string, tightly enough so they don't drift off into the fruit and can be easily removed once the fruit is cooked; if you leave the bunch in when serving the dish, the flavor of the leaves will overpower the fruit.

Flowers

Pick the small green flower as soon as you see it opening in late spring to early summer in the second or third year of the plant's life. These sweetly scented flowers also have a warm, slightly aniseed flavor. Add to fruit salads, cordials, cream cheese, crème fraîche and fruit sorbets.

Stems

Cut the stems of second-year growth before the flower head forms in early summer. Young, tender stems can be steamed as a vegetable, candied or used to make jam (see my recipe on page 21).

The stems need to be boiled, peeled, then boiled again before starting the cooking process. Alternatively, they can be peeled, then soaked in brine (a solution of 3 tbsp (45 ml) of salt per 1 qt/1 L of boiling water) for 12 hours before steaming.

Seeds

Harvest seed heads in late summer and early autumn of the second and third year, as soon as the seeds turn from pale green to pale brown and start to fall. They have an aromatic musky flavor and are excellent in soups, eggs and custards.

Roots

Dig up second-year growth in late spring to early summer before the plant runs to flower. The roots can be used medicinally to treat digestive ailments; traditionally, though, these were eaten as a root vegetable. I have tried it and was not enamored with the flavor or the texture – it was rather stringy and tasted of anise and gin.

| Properties | Angelica leaves and stems are considered appetite stimulants. They are also high in potassium and magnesium. |

Other varieties

Wild Angelica, Ground Ash, Jack-Jump-About
Angelica sylvestris
Tall, hardy monocarpic herb with umbels of flowers in summer, which are white and often tinged with pink, sitting atop stems that often have a purple tinge. The large lower leaves are narrow and sharply toothed and the roots are thick and gray on the outside. The plant is native throughout North America and Europe. It is often found growing in moist fields and hedgerows. Harvesting is carried out in September; young leaves can be used as an aromatic herb in salads and the seeds are used by confectioners in pastry.

American Angelica, Bellyache Root, High Angelica
Angelica atropurpurea
Tall, hardy monocarpic herb with white to greenish white flowers from early to midsummer. The mid-green leaves are large and the roots are purple. The whole plant has a powerful odor when fresh. It is found growing wild in fields and damp places in Canada and the northeastern and north-central states of the US. It is used in the same way as *Angelica archangelica*.

Alexanders, Maceron
Smyrnium olusatrum
Tall, hardy monocarpic herb with large, broad clusters of green to yellow small flowers in late spring and early summer. The mid-green wide, oval leaves, when crushed, are highly aromatic with a pleasant scent. It can be found growing wild in Europe, especially along the coast on cliffs, rocks and damp sand dunes. The young leaves can be used in the same way as angelica. In France it was historically considered an important vegetable.

ANGELICA AND APPLE SNOW TRIFLE

This delicious trifle is made with lots of fruit but is not too heavy at the end of a meal, as it is lightened with egg whites. The angelica leaves reduce the tartness of the fruit, making the fruit flavor more predominant, but they should be removed before adding the egg whites, otherwise their flavor will overpower the dessert.

My mom always made this trifle as a birthday treat, serving it with candles in the meringues.

Warning There can be an increased risk of salmonella poisoning when eating raw or lightly cooked eggs. Pregnant women, the elderly and young children should take particular care, and such dishes are not recommended. If you are concerned, this dessert can be made omitting the egg whites, but it will be heavier.

Serves 8

1½ lb (750 g) Granny Smith apples, peeled, cored and sliced
2½ cups (100 g) young small angelica leaves, left whole and tied with string for easy removal
6 tbsp (90 ml) fruit (superfine) sugar
1 cup (250 ml) dates, pitted
7 tbsp (105 ml) apple juice, plus another 2–4 tbsp (30–60 ml) for soaking the ladyfingers
6 ladyfingers
2 tbsp (30 ml) calvados (optional)
3 egg whites
Baby meringues
Powdered (icing) sugar, for dusting
Pieces of candied angelica stems (see page 20), to decorate

Put the apples in a medium-sized saucepan with the angelica leaves, sugar and 7 tbsp (105 ml) of water. Bring to a boil, cover and cook over low heat for about 10 minutes, stirring halfway through, until the apples collapse into a mush.

Remove the angelica leaves. Purée the apples in a blender or food processor, transfer to a bowl and leave to cool.

Place the dates and apple juice in the food processor and process until puréed but not too smooth. Cover the base of an 8-inch (20 cm) dessert bowl with the ladyfingers, sugared side down. Sprinkle with either a mixture of 2 tbsp (30 ml) of apple juice and 2 tbsp (30 ml) calvados or just 4 tbsp (60 ml) of apple juice, if you prefer. Spread the date purée on top.

Whisk the egg whites until stiff and fold into the cooled apple purée. Pour this over the trifle base and decorate with meringues. Cover and chill for at least half a day. If you make this a day in advance, decorate with the meringues closer to the serving time.

Dust with powdered sugar and scatter the candied angelica stems on top before serving.

BRAISED LETTUCE AND ANGELICA FLOWERS

My grandmother often cooked lettuces. This is one of her recipes that I have adapted. The use of angelica flowers, with their lightly sweet, aromatic flavor, complements the lettuce and is a wonderful contrast to the saltiness of the bacon.

This makes a lovely light supper when served with crusty homemade bread.

Serves 2–4

4 firm round lettuces, either romaine or Little Gem
Butter, for greasing
4 slices Canadian (back) bacon
1 carrot, finely chopped
1 onion, finely sliced
1 tbsp (15 ml) angelica flowers, removed from stems
1¼ cups (300 ml) strong chicken or vegetable stock (homemade if possible, see page 13)
1 tbsp (15 ml) chopped parsley, to garnish

Wash the lettuces well and remove any loose or damaged outer leaves before placing them, whole, in a large saucepan. Cover with cold water and bring to a boil. Immediately remove from the heat, strain and rinse under cold running water. Shake off as much water as possible and dry on paper towels.

Preheat the oven to 350°F (180°C). Grease an ovenproof dish and line the bottom with the slices of bacon. Sprinkle on the carrot, the onion and half of the angelica flowers. Fold under the tops of the outer lettuce leaves to make neat parcels and place them on top of the onion and carrot mixture. Pour the stock over and cover with waxed paper. Cook in the oven for 45 minutes.

Lift out the lettuces and arrange on plates or a large serving dish. Reduce the stock, bacon and vegetable mixture in which they were cooked and pour over the lettuces. Sprinkle with chopped parsley and the remaining angelica flowers.

ANGELICA AND GOOSEBERRY COMPOTE

When I dined at my great-aunt's house, she always produced a cartload of desserts; two would be a fruit compote of some sort. One of her great tips was to add a good-sized handful of angelica leaves when cooking gooseberries, not only to reduce the tartness of the fruit but also because the muscatel flavor of the leaves cuts through the acidity of the gooseberries. You can adjust these measurements to meet your needs and personal tastes. Serve with homemade yogurt or crème fraîche with a little nutmeg grated on top.

Serves 6–8

2 lb (900 g) gooseberries, topped and tailed
5½ cups (225 g) angelica leaves, tightly tied up with string
Juice and peel of 1 orange
⅔ cup (150 ml) cold water
¼ cup (60 ml) fruit (superfine) sugar

Combine all the ingredients in a large saucepan and gently cook until the fruit is tender. Once it is cooked, remove the angelica leaves and orange peel and discard.

Excess angelica

Candied angelica stems

Making candied angelica stems can take time, but it is worth it, for they taste delicious. The reason for the many washes is to make the stems tender and palatable. This is a traditional recipe; the candied stems can be used on many desserts and cakes as decoration or as added crunch, for example, in a fruit fool.

Warning Wear a long-sleeved shirt when picking the angelica stems, as they contain furanocoumarins, which are toxic chemicals produced by the plant and which may cause skin irritation and allergic reactions.

Some second-year stems (use as many as you want, but do not be overambitious)
Granulated sugar (equal in measure to the cooked angelica stems; see recipe)
Water
1 tsp (5 ml) baking soda
Fruit (superfine) sugar or granulated sugar, for dusting

Choose sturdy, succulent green stems, not pale or weak ones or any that are colored purple. Remove all leaves, then cut the stems into 3- to 5-inch (8–13 cm) lengths. Place them in a saucepan with just enough water to cover. Simmer the stems until tender, approximately 25 to 45 minutes, depending on the thickness of the stems. Drain, return to the pan, cover with cold water and bring to a boil for 5 minutes. Remove from the heat, drain and peel off the outside skin.

Return the stems to the pan and add enough water to cover and the baking soda. Bring to a boil again and count to 5. Remove from the heat, drain immediately and allow to cool.

When cool, weigh the angelica stems and add an equal amount of granulated sugar. Place the sugar and angelica in a covered dish, mix gently and leave in a cool place for 2 days. After this time the sugar will have dissolved to make a syrup.

Preheat the oven to its lowest setting. Put the stems and their syrup in a saucepan and slowly bring to a boil again. Turn the heat down to a simmer and cook, stirring occasionally, until the angelica stems have a clear green color and are rather translucent.

When the clarity and color have been achieved, drain again, discarding all the liquid. Sprinkle on as much fruit (superfine) sugar as will cling to the angelica. Put the angelica in the oven to dry (about 1½ to 2 hours) – if it is not thoroughly dry it will become moldy later.

Store the dried candied angelica stems between pieces of waxed paper in an airtight container for up to 3 months.

Angelica jam

This is a great way to preserve angelica, especially if you do not have the time or patience to candy the stems. I have often been asked to describe the flavor and the best description I can come up with is "gin on toast"!

Makes 3–4 lb (1.3–1.8 kg)

Angelica stems (enough to make 2 lb/900 g cooked weight)
3½ cups (875 ml) granulated sugar
1¾ cups (425 ml) water
Juice and peel of 1 lemon

Choose young, tender stems from 2-year-old plants for this jam. Remove all leaves, then cut the stems into lengths that will fit into your saucepan. Fill the pan with water, bring to a boil and add the stems. Return to a boil then lower the heat to a simmer. Cook until the stems are tender, about 25 to 45 minutes depending on the thickness of the stems. Drain.

Fill the saucepan with fresh cold water and leave the stems to soak overnight (at least 12 hours). Drain, and throw away the water. If you have used mature stems they may need to be peeled, so do so now. Weigh the stems, and for every 2 lb (900 g) of angelica stems you will need 3½ cups (875 ml) of sugar.

Cut the cooked stems into bite-sized pieces and add them to a large pan. (I use a preserving kettle, which is a very worthwhile investment if you often make chutneys, jams and jellies.) Add the sugar and the water and cook over very low heat, stirring constantly until the sugar is dissolved. Add the lemon juice and peel, bring to a boil and boil rapidly until the setting point is reached.

To tell when the setting point has been reached, either use a sugar thermometer (the setting point being 200°F/110°C) or put a little jam on a chilled saucer – as it cools the jam should begin to set and will wrinkle slightly when you draw your finger across it.

Cool slightly before pouring into warm, sterilized jars (see page 12), cover and seal immediately. This will keep for a year in sealed jars. Once the jar is opened, store in the fridge and use within 4 weeks.

ANISE HYSSOP

(also known as Giant Hyssop, Blue Giant, Hyssop, Fennel Hyssop, Fragrant Giant Hyssop, Mexican Hyssop)
Agastache foeniculum (Pursh) Kuntze

Interestingly, there are few references in cookbooks or dedicated herb books to this most attractive, underused herb, other than the fact that it is a native of North America and eastern Asia, where it was originally used in teas to treat fevers and as a food seasoning. Personally, I rate this herb highly not only for being another useful culinary herb that combines well with many dishes, but also for the fact that it looks wonderful in the garden.

Description

This short-lived, eye-catching herb is a delight, with its striking blue-purple spikes that flower throughout the summer and attract bees and butterflies. It is a herbaceous herb that dies back into the ground in winter and reappears in the spring.

It can be raised from seed sown under protection in spring or from cuttings taken from non-flowering shoots in midsummer. Plant seedlings out in the late spring when the soil has started to warm up and there is no threat of frosts. Ideally, plant anise hyssop in a sunny position in rich, moist soil; however, it will adapt to most soils with the exception of those that are very dry. Anise hyssop also happily adapts to being grown in a large container.

History in cooking

Historically *Agastache foeniculum* was used by Native Americans and *Agastache rugosa* has been used for thousands of years in Chinese medicine. The few references to food that I can find are always about herbal teas in the United States and marinades and fish in Asia.

Harvesting and uses

Leaves

The leaves have a lovely warm, minty/anise flavor that works well with fish, chicken, vegetables, desserts, sauces and teas. The young leaves should be picked from early to midsummer for use fresh and for preserving. The leaves can be frozen, whole or chopped, or made into oils, vinegars, butters or sauce (see page 27).

Flowers

The flowers are best used fresh, but this is not a problem, as the herb flowers for most of the summer until early autumn, giving plenty of opportunities to gather them as they open. They can be pulled from the flowering spikes without having to remove the whole stem, thereby preserving the look of the plant.

Stems:

Stems are best cut in early summer; left any later they become tough and stringy. Cut them down to 1½ to 2½ inches (4–6 cm) from the ground and the plant will respond by producing new bushy growth. The stems are great for using as skewers for barbecuing vegetables or alternatively for placing on top of the barbeque rack, onto which you can then place the fish.

Properties

Anise hyssop is a member of the mint family and as such has rather similar medicinal and digestive properties. It is reputedly an appetite stimulant and it is also said that the volatile oils in this plant, which give it its minty liquorice flavor, are a beneficial digestive. I have also found over the years that if you want a slightly more herby/liquorice flavor in a recipe that uses mint, anise hyssop makes an excellent substitute for it.

Other varieties

Korean Mint, Huo Xiang
Agastache rugosa
Short-lived perennial herb with lovely mauve-purple flower spikes in summer. Distinctly minty-scented mid-green oval, pointed leaves that can be used in culinary dishes. Makes a good tea for hangovers!

ANISE HYSSOP AND APPLE SALAD

When I first started growing this herb, I simply used it in salads. This was one of my first recipes, and one that I have developed and updated over the years. The warm flavor of the anise combined with the sweetness of apple and the cool, slightly bitter flavor of lettuce really stimulates the taste buds.

Serves 4

1 cucumber
Salt
2 eating apples
½ iceberg lettuce, sliced
½ head bok choy or napa cabbage, sliced
1 Belgian endive, sliced
1 tbsp (15 ml) finely chopped anise hyssop leaves
5 anise hyssop flower spikes, individual flowers removed

For the dressing
3 tbsp (45 ml) basil olive oil (see page 36; or use a plain light olive oil)
1 tbsp (15 ml) balsamic vinegar

Peel the cucumber (if you want to be fancy, leave alternate stripes of skin). Slice thinly, then sprinkle salt over the cucumber and leave for at least 1 hour. Wash the salt off under cold water and drain.

Core and slice the apples – there is no need to peel them. Mix together the sliced apple, iceberg lettuce, bok choy, endive, cucumber and anise hyssop leaves. Toss in the flowers, reserving a few for scattering over the finished salad.

Make the dressing by mixing together the ingredients. Pour over the salad and then toss. Scatter the remaining flowers over the salad and serve.

ANISE HYSSOP SORBET WITH CRYSTALLIZED ANISE HYSSOP LEAVES

As a form of food, sorbet is brilliant. The Romans ate it between each course to clear the palate and also to act as a digestive. The lovely minty/anise flavor of anise hyssop leaves combines well with melon, especially Galia (see opposite). Crystallizing the leaves as decoration makes this dessert extra special; the added texture complements both the sorbet and the melon.

This whole dessert can be made a few days in advance, so it is ideal if you are planning a large meal or are very busy.

Warning There can be an increased risk of salmonella poisoning when eating raw or lightly cooked eggs. Pregnant women, the elderly and young children should take particular care, and such dishes are not recommended.

Serves 4–6

For the crystallized anise hyssop leaves

12 or 24 even-sized anise hyssop leaves

2 egg whites

1 tbsp (15 ml) fruit (superfine) sugar

1¾ cups (425 ml) water

1¼ cups (300 ml) granulated sugar

1 lemon

1 large handful anise hyssop leaves (young ones have a stronger anise flavor)

First make the crystallized anise hyssop leaves, as these need to be made the day before serving. Remove any stalks from the leaves and make sure they are clean and patted dry on paper towels. Lightly whisk the egg whites and use some to brush each leaf on both sides. Reserve the remaining egg white for making the sorbet. Sprinkle each leaf with fruit sugar, lay them gently on a baking sheet lined with waxed paper and leave in a warm, dry place for 12 hours.

Put the water and sugar in a small saucepan over low heat, stirring all the time until the sugar is dissolved. Peel a strip of lemon zest and add it to the pan. Bring to a boil, reduce the heat and simmer for 5 minutes. Remove from the heat and allow to cool for a few minutes.

Chop the anise hyssop leaves and place them in a bowl with the juice of the lemon. Pour the hot, but not boiling, sugar syrup onto the leaves and lemon juice. Set aside to allow the flavors to infuse, until the syrup is cold.

Strain the syrup into another bowl and place in the freezer for about 2 hours, until it starts to crystallize and become mushy. Whisk the remaining egg white until stiff, fold into the half-frozen syrup and return to the freezer for a minimum of 4 hours before serving.

MELON WITH ANISE HYSSOP SORBET

1 ripe melon, preferably Galia
1 recipe Anise Hyssop Sorbet (see page 26)

Cut the melon into 4 to 6 pieces (depending on the number of guests you are feeding) and remove the seeds. If you wish to be delicate, cut the flesh so that it can be easily removed from the skin, or, if you are like me, leave it for the guests to attack with gusto.

Place the melon pieces on individual serving plates, put a spoonful of sorbet into the middle of each piece, and decorate with the crystallized leaves.

Excess anise hyssop

It is often said that culinary accidents are sometimes the best. This recipe was one I came across purely by chance. I wanted to make mint sauce to go with lamb chops, but for some reason, when I went onto the farm I became distracted and picked anise hyssop instead. On returning to my kitchen I noticed my mistake but thought it would make a nice change. It certainly did, so if you have a glut of this herb this is a wonderful way of preserving and using these leaves.

Anise hyssop sauce
This sauce goes well with cold or hot lamb and cold pork.

1 bunch anise hyssop
Fruit (superfine) sugar (enough to cover the leaves when chopped)
Balsamic vinegar

Remove the anise hyssop leaves from the stalks and chop them very finely. Add the sugar and keep chopping – this way the oils and flavors of the anise hyssop are amalgamated into the sugar.
Once you are happy that it is all combined, transfer the anise hyssop and sugar to a small bowl. Stir in enough vinegar to just make it runny. Check the sweetness and add extra sugar if required. This will keep in a sealed jar or bottle in the fridge for up to a week. Stir well before use. If the vinegar starts to evaporate, add a little more.

BASIL

(also known as Sweet Basil, Genovese Basil)
Ocimum basilicum

I think basil could merit a complete book on its own; it is an herb that never ceases to amaze me, from its culinary appeal to its astounding medicinal properties. When I started herb farming, over three decades ago, this was an herb I was told to use sparingly, as the flavor could be overpowering; looking back I think we were just unsure how to use basil, as it was such a new herb to us. Of course, now it is used prolifically in the kitchen, and I myself use it liberally in many dishes from pasta to custards, teas, salads and sauces. It is one of the must-have culinary delights that can transform a meal into a feast.

Description

The most popular basil, sweet basil (*Ocimum basilicum*), has clusters of small, white tubular flowers in summer and green oval, pointed leaves that have a wonderful smell when crushed.

Basil, in the majority of cases, is an annual herb, meaning that it lasts only one year in the garden or in a pot, and for this reason it needs to be raised from seed each season. Sow the seeds under protection in early spring and outside, direct into the ground, in late spring or early summer, when the soil is warm to the touch and risk of frost has passed. Choose a well-drained, fertile soil in a sunny, warm situation with a bit of shelter from the midday sun.

This herb is ideal for growing in containers, especially in cool temperate climates, as that gives the flexibility of being able to easily bring it under cover and provide it with protection from inclement weather and slugs. When growing in containers, use a soil-based potting compost.

Basil is a good companion plant; it repels white flies, aphids, tomato hornworms, asparagus beetles and fruit flies, and also, if kept in a pot on your windowsill, flies from the kitchen.

History in cooking

Before becoming king of the kitchen, this herb was steeped in history and folklore. You can find different forms of basil growing throughout the world, and as I researched its properties I found that each culture uses it differently. Thousands of years ago basil was used by the ancient Egyptians to clear poisons from the body. There is a wonderful folk story that is said to originate from the ancient Greeks, who believed that if you wanted to grow intensely strong, fragrant basil, you should shout and swear as you sow the seed! In India the use of this herb dates back over 1,000 years; it is considered a sacred herb and is used medicinally as a detoxifier and a heart medicine. In the 17th century, Nicholas Culpeper, the famous herbalist, wrote of basil's uncompromising if unpredictable appeal: "it either makes enemies or gains lovers, but there is no in-between."

Harvesting and uses

Leaves

In cool climates the leaves are available from late spring until late summer; in warm climates they can be available all year round. The leaves have a wonderful spicy, minty flavor that is good with tomatoes, lemon, fish, chicken, pasta, pizza, marinades, salads, dressings and teas. A word of warning, though: the flavor can be ruined if the leaves are cooked for too long, so it is best to add basil to warm dishes at the end of cooking, when the heat will release its flavor and aroma. It is an herb that is favored in many international cuisines, notably Mediterranean cooking, and in Thailand and other countries the leaves are added to soups and fish dishes. However, the leaves are rarely used in Indian cooking; more often they are used to make herbal teas, usually combined with other herb seeds or simply with tea leaves to make a refreshing drink.

The leaves do not freeze well, as they become slimy when thawed, so the best preserving methods for use in the home are in oils, vinegars, butters or sauces (see pages 35 and 36).

Flowers

The flowers are best used fresh from the plant throughout the summer months. Gently pull each one away from the flower spikes before adding to the dish. They are very good with salads, both savory and sweet, and jellies, especially with fruit such as pears or figs.

Properties

Basil is a member of the renowned mint family, which, when used in cooking, stimulates digestion and is a beneficial antioxidant. Medicinally it is used to treat bronchitis, colds, fevers and stress; the juice of the leaves is used for skin complaints, and the essential oil extracted from it is used to treat ear infections and as an insect repellent. Current research has shown that basil has the ability to reduce blood sugar levels, and it is used in the treatment of some types of diabetes.

Other varieties

African Blue Basil
Ocimum 'African Blue'
Lovely dark purple-blue oval, highly scented leaves that have a very fruity flavor. This basil is a perennial in its country of origin.

Cinnamon Basil
Ocimum basilicum 'Cinnamon'
Olive green-brown oval, pointed, slightly serrated leaves that have a very spicy flavor. Lovely in stir-fry dishes.

Dark Opal Basil, Purple Basil
Ocimum basilicum var. *purpurascens* 'Dark Opal'
Dark purple oval, pointed leaves that have a very spicy, warm flavor.
Great added to rice and pastas, not only for its clove-scented flavor
but also as a stunning color contrast.

Greek Basil
Ocimum minimum 'Greek'
Small green oval, pointed leaves. In Greece pots of basil are placed
on gateposts as a sign of welcome or on tables to keep flies away.
These small leaves are lovely with tomatoes.

Holy Basil, Tulsi
Ocimum tenuiflorum
Hairy and slightly serrated leaves that have a very pungent scent and
flavor. Tulsi is often added to Thai dishes.

Lemon Basil
Ocimum x *citriodorum*
These wonderful lemon-flavored leaves make the best salad dressing.
They are also great for making sorbets and other desserts.

Lettuce Leaf Basil
Ocimum basilicum 'Napolitano'
Large, bright green textured, crinkled oval leaves. Good for pasta
sauces and for making pesto and basil oil (see page 36).

Mrs. Burns Basil
Ocimum basilicum 'Mrs. Burns'
Green oval, intensely lemon-scented and -flavored leaves. Great with
fish, chicken, rice and pasta, and also for making dressings and sauces.

Thai Basil
Ocimum basilicum 'Horapha'
Attractive oval mulberry-tinted leaves that have an anise scent and
flavor. Essential in Thai cooking.

SWEET BASIL GNOCCHI

To be honest, once you have eaten homemade gnocchi you will be inspired not only by the flavor but also by how easy they are to make. Adding the basil to the gnocchi rather than the sauce means its flavor comes through separately rather than being absorbed or overpowered by other ingredients in the sauce.

Serves 4–6

For the sauce
14-oz. (398 ml) can chopped tomatoes
1 shallot, finely chopped
2 cloves garlic, finely chopped
1 rosemary sprig, 2 thyme sprigs, or a couple of bay leaves
Salt and freshly ground black pepper
Pinch of sugar (optional)

For the gnocchi
1 lb (500 g) boiling potatoes (red or Yukon Gold), peeled and diced
6 tbsp (90 ml) sweet basil leaves, finely chopped
2 cups (500 ml) all-purpose flour
Salt and freshly ground black pepper
1½ cups (375 ml) wild arugula, washed, dried and roughly torn, to serve

First make the sauce. Pour the tomatoes into a small saucepan, then half-fill the can with water and pour this into the pan. Stir in the shallot, garlic and herb sprigs or leaves and add salt and pepper to taste. (Mom always added a pinch of sugar to enhance the flavor of the tomatoes.) Bring to a boil and simmer gently for at least an hour, until thickened and dark red.

As the sauce simmers, boil the potatoes for 10 to 15 minutes, until tender, then drain and mash them well. Try to get them as smooth as possible because lumps will be noticeable in the gnocchi. Sprinkle on the basil, flour and plenty of salt and pepper. Using a wooden spoon or your hands, bring together to make a firm dough. Knead the dough gently for a couple of minutes then roll out into sausages about ½ inch (1 cm) thick. Cut the sausages into pieces 1 inch (2.5 cm) long.

Put a large pot of water on the heat and bring to a boil then turn down to a simmer. Add the gnocchi to the simmering water and cook for 1 to 2 minutes, until they rise to the surface. Scoop them out as they rise, using a slotted spoon. Toss with the tomato sauce, fold in the arugula leaves and serve.

VICKI'S PEPPERS WITH PESTO SAUCE

Vicki works with me on the herb farm and, like many who work here, she is a true foodie who loves fresh ingredients. This pesto sauce not only goes really well with the peppers, it is also a great way of preserving the flavor of the basil leaves for a few days. Any leftover pesto can be mixed with cooked pasta or added to a tomato salad. This is delicious served with a fresh salad, plain boiled rice or poached salmon.

Serves 4

For the pesto sauce
1 tbsp (15 ml) pine nuts

Start by making the pesto sauce. Blend the pine nuts, basil leaves, garlic and Parmesan in a blender until smooth. Add the oil slowly and continue to blend the mixture until you have a thick paste. Season with salt to taste. Pour the sauce into a sealed plastic

¼ cup (60 ml) chopped basil leaves (sweet, Greek or lettuce)
2 cloves garlic, sliced
½ cup (125 ml) grated Parmesan
7 tbsp (105 ml) sunflower oil
Salt

4 red bell peppers, halved
Olive oil, for greasing and drizzling
¼ cup (60 ml) cream cheese
1 medium-sized red chile, finely chopped and seeded
1 tbsp (15 ml) chopped sweet marjoram
Salt and freshly ground black pepper

container and store in the fridge until required. It will keep for up to 1 week as long as the oil does not dry out; if it is looking dry, top up with more oil.

Preheat the oven to 400°F (200°C). Place the pepper halves in a lightly oiled ovenproof dish. To each pepper half add 1 tbsp (15 ml) cream cheese and a sprinkling of chopped chile, followed by 1 tbsp (15 ml) of the pesto sauce. Sprinkle the sweet marjoram over the peppers, followed by a drizzle of olive oil, and season with salt and pepper. Place the dish in the center of the oven for 20 to 25 minutes.

BASIL MAYO

This mayonnaise goes well with cold fish or chicken and is fabulous with boiled eggs. I have to admit that I use a food processor to make it, as I find it quicker and more reliable. My mother was transfixed when I demonstrated how easy it was compared to how long it took her to make it by hand. She did, however, consider it cheating and not proper cooking!

Warning There can be an increased risk of salmonella poisoning when eating raw or lightly cooked eggs. Pregnant women, the elderly and young children should take particular care, and such dishes are not recommended.

Makes 1¼ cups (300 ml)

2 medium egg yolks
1 tbsp (15 ml) lemon juice
1 tsp (5 ml) Dijon mustard
Salt and freshly ground black pepper
1¼ cups (300 ml) light olive oil or vegetable oil, or a mixture of the two
2–4 tbsp (30–60 ml) finely chopped basil leaves (lemon basil is especially good here)

Place the egg yolks, 2 tsp (10 ml) of the lemon juice, the mustard and a pinch of salt into the bowl of a food processor or blender and process until the mixture just begins to thicken.

Pour the olive oil into a measuring cup and, with the motor running, gradually add it to the egg-yolk mixture in a thin, steady stream, occasionally stopping to scrape down the sides of the bowl, until the mixture is thick, creamy and pale. You need to add the oil slowly, but not too slowly or the mixture might thicken too quickly. (If this happens, add about 2 tsp (10 ml) hot water to thin down the mayonnaise before adding the remaining oil.)

Add the remaining lemon juice, stir in the basil, taste and adjust the seasoning if necessary. Transfer to a small airtight container. (A good tip is to place a piece of plastic wrap directly on the surface of the mayonnaise, to prevent a skin forming, before covering with a tightly fitting lid.) Place in the fridge and use as required.

This will keep in the fridge for up to 3 days.

SWEET BASIL AND LEMON SORBET

A combination of basil leaves – lettuce, Greek and sweet – with the sharpness of lemon is wonderful. This is a simple summer dessert that always finds favor with my family and friends.

Serves 4

2/3 cup (150 ml) water
3/4 cup (175 ml) fruit (superfine) sugar
Zest of 2 lemons
1 large bunch basil leaves (whichever type you wish), reserving some to serve
2/3 cup (150 ml) lemon juice

Place the water, sugar and lemon zest in a small saucepan, bring to a boil and simmer for 4 minutes. Remove from the heat and allow to cool for a while.

Remove the basil leaves from the stems (discarding the stems) and purée the leaves with a mortar and pestle or blender. Add the lemon juice and basil purée to the lemon-zest syrup, stir well, then allow to cool for 30 minutes to allow the flavors to infuse. If you wish to get fancy, strain the infusion through a sieve or, if, like me, you love the leaves, simply pour it straight into a plastic tub or earthenware freezer-proof dish and place it in the freezer.

Generally sorbet takes 2 hours to set. To keep it from getting rock hard, remove the container from the freezer after 30 minutes, beat the sorbet with a fork and return it to the freezer. Repeat this three more times. You will find that this will make the sorbet crystallize rather than set like a rock made of ice.

Serve decorated with some fresh basil leaves.

BASIL PANNACOTTA

When Jamie Oliver first started training the students at his restaurant Fifteen, I was most impressed by one of them who, after hearing my talk on herbs and how in India basil is infused in milk and given to children as a bedtime drink, produced a pannacotta infused with basil. It was delicious, and this is my version of what I tasted that day. Serve it with fresh fruit such as figs, red currants, peaches or nectarines.

Serves 4

2 big bunches basil (purple, cinnamon, Thai or lemon – whichever you wish)
1/3 cup (70 ml) milk
2 vanilla pods, scored and seeds removed
Finely grated zest of 1 lemon
1½ cups (375 ml) whipping (35%) cream
3/4 tsp (3 ml) powdered gelatin, soaked in water
Powdered (confectioners') sugar

Remove the basil leaves from their stems and chop very finely, leaving a few whole to decorate.

Put the milk, vanilla pods and seeds, lemon zest and half the cream into a small saucepan, bring gently to a boil and simmer for 10 minutes, or until reduced by a third. Remove from the heat and pour into a bowl. Remove the vanilla pods and stir in the finely chopped basil leaves and the soaked gelatin until dissolved.

Allow to cool a little, then place the bowl in the fridge, stirring occasionally until the mixture coats the back of a spoon. Remove from the fridge and either strain the mixture through a fine sieve to remove the basil or leave them in if, like me, you like the direct flavor of the leaves.

Whip the remaining cream with the powdered sugar, then mix

together the two cream mixtures. Divide among 4 individual serving molds – I usually use small glasses. Cover and chill for at least 1 hour in the fridge.

When ready to serve, dunk the bottom and sides of the molds into hot water and then tip the pannacotta out onto a serving plate. Decorate with a few basil leaves to serve.

BASIL COOKIES

Baking cookies has been part of my childhood and my children's. Hours have been spent around the kitchen table creating many different shapes and recipes. This is a reliable and tasty cookie that can be served with fruit fools, sorbets or simply on its own.

Makes 15–20

Preheat the oven to 350°F (180°C).

7 tbsp (100 ml) butter
¼ cup (60 ml) sugar
2/3 cup (150 ml) ground almonds
1 cup (250 ml) all-purpose flour
1 large tbsp (18 ml) chopped basil leaves (sweet, lemon, cinnamon or purple – whichever you wish)

Cream together the butter and the sugar, add the ground almonds, mix well, then add the flour. Knead together on a lightly floured board to form a dough. Roll the dough in the chopped basil leaves until the leaves are amalgamated into the dough, then roll it into a 2-inch (5 cm) diameter sausage. Cut the roll into slices 1½ inches (1 cm) thick.

Place the slices on a baking sheet that is well greased or lined with nonstick baking parchment.

Bake for 10 to 15 minutes until lightly golden. Remove at once and cool the cookies on a wire rack.

Excess basil

Basil sauce

This sauce goes well with cheeses, tomatoes, lettuce and cold meats and fish. The lemon basil sauce version is particularly good with cold salmon or trout.

1 bunch basil (sweet, lemon, purple or Greek – whichever you wish)
Fruit (superfine) sugar (enough to cover the chopped leaves)
White wine vinegar

Remove the basil leaves from the stalks, then chop the leaves very finely. Add the sugar and keep chopping so that the oils and flavors of the basil are amalgamated into the sugar.

Once you are happy that it is all mixed together, transfer the chopped basil and sugar to a small bowl. Stir in just enough white wine vinegar to make the sauce runny but not so much that you have a large amount of vinegar. Check the sweetness and add extra sugar if required.

Basil oil

This is a delicious way of using up lots of basil leaves. However, when making oils using fresh produce, you have to be extremely careful. Although oil by itself does not pose a risk for botulism, the addition of fresh herbs, in particular garlic, to oils can make this product potentially unsafe. Lemon juice, when added to the oil and herbs, will act as a natural preservative that will help to prolong the life of the infused oil.

This basil oil is great not only on salads but also with hard-boiled eggs, tomatoes, fish and cold chicken.

Makes 1 cup (250 ml)

3 good handfuls of basil leaves
1 cup (250 ml) light olive oil
2 tsp (10 ml) lemon juice

Wash and dry the leaves on paper towels. Finely chop the leaves (this can be done in a food processor), add the oil and the lemon juice and mix well. Pour into a container with a sealing lid and place in the fridge. Use within 5 days; shake well before use, as the lemon juice will separate.

Alternatively, after 2 days strain the oil through an unbleached paper coffee filter, pour into a clean, dry container with a sealing lid and keep in the fridge. Use within 3 days; shake well before use.

Warning Do not put fresh leaves in the bottle to make it look pretty. When the oil level drops and the leaves become exposed to the air, they will turn moldy and this will contaminate the oil and can cause salmonella. If you wish to use leaves to decorate the oil, make sure that they are properly dried before adding.

BAY

(also known as Sweet Laurel, Sweet Bay)
Laurus nobilis

This magnificent evergreen tree has always been part of my life, for my mother had a very large bay tree growing in the garden at both the houses where I spent my childhood, and I also planted one in my first house, which grew so large it had to be moved. Even today I can picture my mother wearing an apron, as one did in the 1950s, picking handfuls of bay leaves, which she used when making baked egg custards in her trusty coal-fired Rayburn stove.

Description

This is one of the few culinary herbs from the Mediterranean that is a slow-growing, long-living evergreen tree. In the right conditions it will grow to 25 feet (8 m) high and reach 10 feet (3 m) across. It has small, waxy pale yellow flowers in spring, followed by oval green berries that turn black when ripe. These berries appear only on the female tree, so if you wish to pick berries you will need a male tree planted nearby, so that the flowers on the female tree will be pollinated and thus produce berries.

The oval dark green leaves are shiny on the upper surface and matt on the underside; when held up to the light, they are translucent, showing all the veins. About 80 years ago a number of false bays were planted in the UK; it is also a laurel but does not have the flavor of the true, sweet culinary bay. The easiest way to see the difference between the two trees is to hold up a leaf to the light; if you cannot see through the leaf and it does not have any scent when you break it in half, it is false bay. If, on the other hand, you can see through the leaf and see the veins and the leaf smells wonderfully aromatic when broken, it is the true sweet bay.

So, bearing in mind its eventual height and spread, this herb needs to be positioned with care. Alternatively, it will flourish in a container, where you can more easily control its growth and give it added protection in cold weather. In hot, not humid, climates, plant it in well-drained soil in partial shade. In cool climates, plant it in full sun in well-drained soil, and in cold climates, plant it in a container and protect it when temperatures fall below 14°F (-10°C).

History in cooking

This herb has been used mainly as flavoring for many thousands of years. The Bedouins of North Africa traditionally use the leaves to flavor their coffee. Historically the leaves were not only used fresh, usually being added to a long-cooking pot over the fire, but also dried, then ground over fresh vegetables as we would grind salt and pepper.

Harvesting and uses

Leaves

The evergreen leaves can be picked year round and have a wonderful warm, spicy scent and flavor with a hint of nutmeg and citrus. They add depth to all forms of food. To get the best from them, add fresh leaves at the beginning of cooking so that their flavor can slowly permeate the food.

Seeds

Harvest seeds in the late autumn once they are fully ripe and slightly soft to the touch. In Mediterranean regions a cooking oil is extracted from the seeds.

Properties

When used in cooking, bay leaves promote the digestion and absorption of food; in particular they assist in the breakdown of heavy food such as meat. They also stimulate the digestive tract, help to settle the stomach and are said to relieve flatulence!

Other varieties

Golden Bay
Laurus nobilis 'Aurea'
This is a golden-leaved variety of the standard bay tree, with a milder flavor.

Willow Leaf Bay
Laurus nobilis f. *angustifolia*
This bay has attractive narrow, oval dark green leaves and is smaller in height, reaching 23 ft (7 m). It can be used in the same way as the standard bay.

Indian Bay, Tej Patta, Malabathron
Cinnamomum tamala
The leaves of this evergreen bay are similar to those of its European cousin; they are dark green and oval with three main veins running the length of the leaf. Unlike the European variety, which can be picked young, these leaves are not ready for harvesting until the trees are 10 years old. They can then be picked for the next 90 years, and are renowned in northern Indian cooking.

BAY AND GARLIC–CRUSTED PORK

This is a very old recipe that my mom used to cook on Sundays. It was my job to chop the bay leaves and garlic and then pulverize them with salt in a mortar and pestle. Pulverizing the leaves releases their flavor into the salt, which is why this recipe tastes so good. Serve with roast vegetables or mustard mashed potatoes and purple sprouting broccoli.

Serves 6

8 cloves garlic, peeled and sliced
8 bay leaves
Coarse sea salt and freshly ground black pepper
4 medium onions, peeled (root ends left intact), each cut into 8 wedges
3 tbsp (45 ml) olive oil
1 loin of pork (enough for 6 – ask your butcher to bone and roll it, as this makes it much easier to carve)

Preheat the oven to 325°F (170°C).

Using a sharp knife, finely chop together the garlic and bay leaves. Put them in a mortar and pestle with 2 tsp (10 ml) of coarse salt. Crush together with the pestle until it forms a sort of paste.

In a large roasting pan, toss the onion wedges with 2 tbsp (25 ml) of the olive oil and season with salt and pepper. Push the onions to the edges of the pan and place the pork in the center, fatty side up. Rub the top with the remaining oil, then rub in the bay and garlic mixture, coating the skin evenly.

Roast until cooked, approximately 3 hours, then transfer the meat and onions to a serving platter. Let the meat rest, loosely covered with foil, for about 10 minutes before carving.

BOUQUET GARNI

A quote from one of my grandmother's cookbooks, *Food for Pleasure* (published in 1950 by Rupert Hart-Davis), reads: "A bouquet garni is a bunch of herbs constantly required in cooking." As far as she was concerned, this was the right way to use herbs.

A bouquet garni is a small bundle of fresh herbs that is used to flavor slowly cooked dishes. The herbs are tied together tightly with a long piece of string so that they can easily be removed from the casserole or stew at the end of the cooking time. Alternatively, you can enclose the herbs in a cheesecloth bag, also attached to a long piece of string.

Different combinations of herbs will enhance different foods, and here are a few of the best bouquets garnis:

A standard bouquet garni for a meat or chicken casserole
1 bunch parsley, including the stems
3 thyme sprigs
1 clove garlic, peeled
2–3 bay leaves

Other variations using the amounts of herbs to suit your palate and dish:

Bouquets garnis for meat
Oregano, thyme, bay and lovage
Thyme, sage, parsley and bay

Bouquets garnis for poultry
Bay, lemon thyme, lemon balm and lemon grass (the grass ends)
Rosemary, summer savory, hyssop and bay

Bouquet garni for game
Myrtle, bay, orange-scented thyme and parsley

Bouquet garni for fish
Green onions (the stems), French parsley, bay and tarragon

WHITE CHOCOLATE AND BAY MOUSSE

Nigel Slater rates among my top 10 culinary experts; he uses herbs lightly, respecting their flavor and texture. We have, over the years, had many a discussion about culinary herbs – their merits and their garden prowess – and I have even been known to carry a crate of herbs up to London on the train especially for his garden. This is one of his recipes, which is sublime, to which I have added bay leaves, as these complement the cardamom pods and add another dimension to the infused milk.

As a chocoholic I must, like Nigel, recommend that you use good chocolate to make this recipe, as it honestly will not work with less. Use Lindt vanilla or, even better, Valrhona vanilla, which is the Rolls-Royce of a chocolate.

Warning There can be an increased risk of salmonella poisoning when eating raw or lightly cooked eggs. Pregnant women, the elderly and young children should take particular care, and such dishes are not recommended.

Serves 6–8

½ cup (125 ml) milk
3 bay leaves
8 plump cardamom pods
8 oz (250 g) white chocolate
1 cup (250 ml) whipping (35%) cream
3 egg whites
Some top-notch unsweetened cocoa powder, to dust

Place the milk and bay leaves in a small saucepan. Break the cardamom pods open and extract the seeds, crush them lightly and add to the milk and bay. Very gently warm the milk until it's just below boiling point. Remove from the heat.

Break the chocolate into small pieces and melt them in a bowl set over a pot of gently simmering, not boiling, water. Make sure that the bottom of the bowl does not touch the surface of the water; otherwise your chocolate will dry out and become lumpy. As soon as the chocolate starts to melt, turn off the heat – the residual heat will melt the rest.

In a bowl, whip the cream until it forms soft peaks (i.e., not too firm). In another bowl, beat the egg whites until stiff and forming peaks.

When the chocolate is completely melted, remove the bowl from the pan. Pour the warm milk over the chocolate, passing it through a sieve to catch the bay leaves and cardamom seeds. Stir until the mixture becomes smooth. Scoop the mixture onto the beaten egg whites, gently fold in using a large metal spoon, then fold this mixture into the whipped cream.

Spoon into small ramekins or espresso coffee cups and refrigerate for 3 to 4 hours until set. Dust with cocoa powder to serve.

RICE DESSERT WITH BAY LEAF

This simple, heart-warming dessert is just perfect on a cold winter's day, especially when served at a lunch with friends that goes on for hours. When infused with the bay leaf, the dessert is spicy and warm – the herb totally complements this dish.

This is best made using whole milk, but if you are lucky enough to live in the country you could use raw (unpasteurized) milk. As my son, when young, would say, it has not been "past your eyes." However, I should add a warning, as raw (unpasteurized) milk comes straight from the cow, without being pasteurized. Pasteurization is a process of heat treatment that kills harmful food-poisoning bacteria, so if you do use unpasteurized milk it could be harmful to vulnerable people such as children, people who are unwell, pregnant women and the elderly. If you use unpasteurized milk or cream, be especially careful to keep it properly refrigerated, as it has a very short shelf life.

When I was a child, Mom served the rice dessert with a dollop of homemade jam. If she wasn't looking, my brother and I would make swirling patterns with the jam. Serve with jam, whipped cream or stewed plums, or simply on its own.

Serves 6

2 tbsp (30 ml) short-grain rice
2 tbsp (30 ml) butter, plus extra for greasing
2 tsp (10 ml) granulated sugar
2½ cups (600 ml) whole milk
2 bay leaves
Nutmeg

Preheat the oven to 400°F (200°C).

Place the rice in a sieve and rinse it under cold running water. Grease an ovenproof dish with a little butter and add the rice, then the sugar and the milk. Stir well and add the bay leaves, tucking them under the surface of the milk. Grate the nutmeg over and, finally, scatter small slices of butter over the surface of the dessert.

Place the dish on a baking sheet and bake for 20 to 30 minutes, then reduce the temperature to 300°F (150°C) for a further 1 hour or until the milk has been absorbed into the rice, the texture is soft and creamy and you have a wonderful golden skin.

Excess bay

As this is an evergreen tree that can be picked all year round, it is unlikely that you will have an abundance of leaves that you urgently need to preserve. However, if a friend gives you a branch and you wish to preserve the leaves for future use, I recommend drying a few. Alternatively, infuse them into salt, oil or vinegar. When using dried leaves in cooking, use half the amount of fresh ones mentioned in the recipe.

Drying bay leaves

Remove the leaves from their branches. Spread them out, with space between each leaf, onto some cheesecloth that has been stretched over a simple wooden frame. Place the rack of leaves in a dark room that is warm, dry and well ventilated. Turn the leaves over every other day until fully dry. When the leaves are dry and crisp enough to crumble, they are ready for storage. Put them in a dark glass jar with a screw top.

Bay salt

This salt is simple to make, delicious to use and makes a great Christmas present.

Makes 1 cup (250 ml) salt

8 oz (250 g) noniodized salt, such as sea salt
6 bay leaves

With a mortar and pestle, pound the salt with the leaves so it picks up the flavor of the bay. Bottle the salt with the crushed bay leaves and keep in a dark cupboard.

The flavored salt can be used immediately and is best used within 3 months.

Bay oil

This is an unusual oil but is certainly worth making if you have a glut of leaves, as the flavor is beautiful and the oil can be used with many dishes, from mayonnaise to marinades.

For more information about preserving and the risks of using herbs in oils, see page 36.

3 good handfuls of bay leaves
1 cup (250 ml) mild olive oil
2 tsp (10 ml) lemon juice

Wash the leaves and dry on paper towels. Finely chop the leaves (this can be done in a food processor), add the oil and the lemon juice and mix well. Pour into a container with a sealing lid and place in the fridge. Use within 5 days; shake well before use, as the lemon juice will separate.

Alternatively, after 2 days strain the oil through an unbleached coffee filter, pour into a clean, dry container with a sealing lid and keep in the fridge. Use within 3 days; shake well before use.

BERGAMOT

(also known as Oswego Tea, Bee Balm, Blue Balm, High Balm, Low Balm, Mountain Balm, Mountain Mint or Wild Bergamot)
Monarda fistulosa

I have a soft spot for this herb, which has, in summer, a magnificent flamboyant flower that looks like a hat that could be worn to a society wedding or the Chelsea Flower Show. It is a native of North America, where it was introduced to the settlers by the Oswego Indians. So that there is no confusion, this herb bears no resemblance or similarity to the small fruit that is also called bergamot, *Citrus bergamia*, which is predominantly found in Italy. It is from that fruit that the bergamot essential oil is extracted.

Description

Bergamot is a hardy perennial herb that dies down in winter, reappearing in the spring. When in flower it will reach 4 feet (1.2 m) high and will spread, in light soils, 1½ feet (45 cm). The bergamot flowers appear from summer until early autumn, and they are a lovely lilac with mauve bracts. The leaves are highly aromatic, toothed and slightly hairy.

Bergamot grows well in moist, nutrient-rich soil, preferably in a semi-shady spot, especially in deciduous woodland. It will tolerate full sun, though, if the soil retains moisture. Like many other perennials, bergamot should be dug up and divided every three years, discarding the dead center.

History in cooking

It is said that in the 18th century bergamot became known as "Oswego Tea" when a Quaker botanist sampled a tea made from the leaves at Fort Oswego, New York, and gave it this name. It became such a popular tea during the colonial period that in the mid-18th century the settlers started sending bergamot seeds back to England. While visiting my daughter in the United States I bought a number of old medicinal herb books that show that the early North American settlers learned of the medicinal properties of bergamot from the Native Americans. They used it to treat many ailments, including making a tea from the leaves to help respiratory difficulties.

Harvesting and uses

Leaves

Pick the leaves from late spring until early autumn before the plant flowers, because they become bitter as they age. They have a warm, minty, spicy flavor. Use the leaves with cheese, pork and vegetables such as cauliflower. Their spicy flavor also enhances fish dishes.

Flowers

These can be picked throughout the summer until early autumn. Remove the flowerets individually from the flower head and scatter over salads, both sweet and savory.

Properties Bergamot is a member of the mint family, and like mint it is very beneficial as a digestive. A tea made from the leaves is said to help insomnia, nausea and flatulence.

Other varieties Lemon Bergamot
Monarda citriodora
This bergamot is an annual, and it has the most superb, intensely lemon-scented leaves that are great for use in desserts and savory dishes and for making a delicious cup of tea. The flowers are a beautiful mauve surrounded by pale mauve bracts.

Bee Balm, Red Bergamot
Monarda didyma
The leaves of this variety can be used with pork, fish and salad dishes. They also make a good cup of tea. It has a "wow" factor – its red flower with dark red bracts. These look great when scattered over a green salad.

BERGAMOT AND COUSCOUS SALAD

A delicious fast salad. My mother spent hours steaming couscous to make it light and fluffy; sadly, she did not live to see the couscous that I can now buy in the supermarket, which takes just minutes to prepare and makes a wonderful simple meal. The flavor of the bergamot leaves and flowers makes this salad taste good and look good.

Serves 4–6

½ cup (125 ml) instant couscous
¾ cup + 2 tbsp (200 ml) boiling water
2 tbsp (30 ml) unsalted butter
2 bunches green onions, chopped
½ lb (225 g) tomatoes, peeled, chopped and drained
1 tsp (5 ml) chopped bergamot leaves
2 tsp (10 ml) bergamot flowers (petals removed from the green calyx)
4 tbsp (60 ml) olive oil
3 tbsp (45 ml) lemon juice
Salt and freshly ground black pepper

Put the couscous in a bowl and pour on the boiling water – read the package for specific instructions, as some brands need more water, some less. Add the butter, stir, then cover and leave to stand for 5 minutes.

Fluff up the couscous with a fork and pour into a serving bowl. Allow to cool before adding the chopped green onions, tomatoes and bergamot leaves and petals. Stir well, then add the oil and lemon juice and mix well. Season to taste with salt and pepper.

SALMON STEAKS WITH BERGAMOT

This is a lovely late spring dish, when the bergamot leaves are at their most succulent. The combination of flavors of the salmon and the bergamot leaf is subtle and complementary. Serve with new potatoes and a crisp green salad.

Serves 4

4 salmon steaks (or cod or halibut)
3 tbsp (45 ml) unsalted butter
1 tbsp (15 ml) olive oil
1 tbsp (15 ml) chopped bergamot leaves, plus whole ones to garnish
2 tsp (10 ml) all-purpose flour
⅔ cup (150 ml) white wine

Rinse the salmon steaks and pat dry with paper towels. Melt the butter with the olive oil in a large frying pan. Add the salmon steaks and the chopped bergamot leaves. Cook the fish over moderate heat for 3 minutes on each side, until lightly browned. When the steaks are cooked, remove them from the pan and put them in a warmed serving dish.

Add the flour to the juices left in the pan, stir well for 1 minute, then add the white wine, stirring to prevent any lumps developing. Bring to a boil and cook for 2 minutes.

Pour the sauce over the salmon steaks and add some extra leaves to garnish.

PORK TENDERLOIN WITH BERGAMOT SAUCE

Pork combines well with the minty, aromatic, spicy flavor of the bergamot sauce to make this a special dinner. Serve with mashed potatoes and fresh green broccoli.

Serves 4–6

2 pork tenderloins
(approx. 5 oz/150 g each)
⅓ cup (75 ml) butter, divided
Olive oil

For the bergamot sauce
2 shallots, very finely chopped
7 tbsp (100 ml) all-purpose flour
1 cup (250 ml) hot vegetable
or chicken stock
2 tbsp (30 ml) bergamot leaves,
finely chopped, divided
Salt and freshly ground
black pepper
1 tbsp (15 ml) crème fraîche

Preheat the oven to 400°F (200°C).

Pat the tenderloins dry with paper towels and cut into ¾-inch (5 cm) thick slices.

Melt half the butter with a splash of oil in a frying pan over medium heat. Gently fry the pork slices, turning once halfway through cooking, for about 5 to 7 minutes, until cooked. Arrange the slices in a warmed serving dish.

Prepare the sauce by sweating the shallots in the remaining butter until soft. Stir in the flour and cook for about 1 minute, stirring all the time. Whisk in the stock and simmer until it thickens, stirring occasionally to prevent it sticking. Add 1½ tbsp (22 ml) of the chopped bergamot leaves. Simmer for several minutes, then season with salt and pepper to taste.

Remove from the heat, stir in the crème fraîche and pour over the arranged pork slices. Garnish with the remaining chopped bergamot leaves.

BERGAMOT AND GOOSEBERRY JELLY

This jelly emphasizes the warm, spicy mint flavor of the bergamot when combined with the sharp flavor of the gooseberries. It is a good accompaniment for cold or hot pork, roast lamb and Cheddar.

Makes approx. 2 x 1 pint (350 g)
jars

2 lb (1 kg) gooseberries,
topped and tailed
1 bunch bergamot leaves
4 cups (900 ml) cold water
Approx. 1 lb (450 g) sugar
2 tbsp (30 ml) lemon juice
2 tbsp (30 ml) white wine vinegar
4 tbsp (60 ml) chopped bergamot
leaves

Wash and sort the gooseberries and add the good ones to a large saucepan with the whole bergamot leaves and the water. Bring to a boil and simmer until the fruit is soft and pulpy. Pour into a jelly bag and leave to drain overnight.

Next day, measure the juice and add 1 lb (450 g) sugar for every 2½ cups (600 ml) of liquid. Pour the juice and sugar into a heavy saucepan, bring back to a boil and boil steadily until the setting point is reached, about 20 to 30 minutes (see page 21). Skim off the surface scum and stir in the lemon juice and vinegar and the chopped bergamot leaves.

Pour into warm sterilized jars (see page 12) and seal when cool. This will keep in unopened jars for 1 year. Once opened, store in the fridge and use within 1 month.

Excess bergamot

Bergamot flower ice cubes

Bergamot flowers are ideal for freezing in ice cubes. Pick the flowers when they are fully open. These cubes look lovely not only in drinks but also added to fruit salads or in an ice bucket on special occasions.

Bergamot flowers
Cooled boiled water

To keep the ice cubes clear, use boiled water that has been left to cool. Fill the ice-cube tray with the water, then add a single flower to each section. If you find the flowers difficult to handle, use a pair of tweezers to place them in the water. Leave to set in the freezer for 12 hours.

Once frozen these ice cubes can be bagged, but they will stick together, so I advise keeping them in the trays. Use within 3 months.

Bergamot sauce

This sauce goes well with cold or hot lamb and cold pork.

1 small bunch bergamot leaves
Fruit (superfine) sugar (enough to cover the leaves when chopped)
White wine vinegar

Remove the leaves from the stalks and chop them very finely. Add the sugar and keep chopping – this way the oils and flavors of the bergamot are amalgamated into the sugar.

Once you are happy that it is all mixed together, transfer the bergamot and sugar to a small bowl. Stir in the white wine vinegar – enough to just make it runny and not so much that you have lots of vinegar. Check the sweetness and add extra sugar if required.

This will keep in the fridge in a sealed jar with a nonmetallic lid for 7 days.

Bergamot vinegar

Bergamot leaves
White wine vinegar

Fill a wide-mouthed bottle with bergamot leaves and pour white wine vinegar over them to fill the bottle completely. Screw on the lid and stand in a dark place for 2 to 3 weeks.

Strain through unbleached paper coffee filters into sterilized bottles (see page 12). Label and store – it will keep in a dark cupboard for a couple of years.

BORAGE

(also known as Burrage, Common Bugloss,
Star Flower, Bee-bread)
Borago officinalis

I have positive and happy memories of this herb, from making necklaces by stringing flowers together in my teens to using the flower heads in ice cubes to fill an ice bucket for a special occasion in my twenties, to the present day, when harvesting my slender green beans. Besides having a beautiful flower, this is the one herb that helps with pollination of vegetables, as all forms of bees love it – hence one of its common names: "bee-bread." Personally I think that its culinary delights are overlooked. The leaves are covered in tiny hairs, which some people can find annoying, as they can irritate the skin, but they do no harm. So it is important when using leaves for salads that you choose young, succulent leaves, which you will find taste like cool cucumber and whose tiny hairs, which are so annoying when mature, simply dissolve on the tongue.

Description

Borage is an attractive herb with pretty blue flowers that looks lovely in the garden or in the vegetable patch. Each plant lasts one year, and once it has flowered it will happily disperse its seeds around the garden. Luckily the seedlings are easily removed if you find you have a profusion of them, and they also taste delicious added to salads.

Please do not, like a few friends of mine, confuse this herb with alkanet, *Anchusa officinalis*, which looks similar and belongs to the same family. Alkanet is a perennial so it will appear in the same spot in the garden every year. The difference between the two is recognizable once you know: the leaves of alkanet are long, lance-shaped and hairy; borage leaves are oval, medium-sized and hairy. The flowers on both are blue, but borage has black stamens that look rather like a bird's beak and the flower hangs down. Alkanet flowers look at you and are smaller than borage flowers, with a white center – more like their cousins, forget-me-nots.

Sow borage seed from spring until midsummer directly into the garden soil or into a large container, as it has a long tap root that dislikes being disturbed once it gets growing. It prefers a well-drained, light soil; however, it thrives in my very heavy clay soil when in a sunny position.

History in cooking

Records of the use of borage date back to the ancient Romans and Greeks; it has been used medicinally as a tea to reduce high temperatures and as a remedy for colds and flu. Interestingly, in Roman times they considered borage a potherb/vegetable and added it to their vegetable stews.

Harvesting and uses

Leaves

The young leaves of this herb are by far the best for using in the kitchen. As this is a bit of a thug of an herb, there are always new shoots and new leaves appearing from spring until the first hard frosts. Always pick the leaves before the flowers form. When eaten fresh, the leaves have a cool cucumber flavor and are excellent in salads or with cream cheese, fish or vegetables. When cooked, they have a light, refreshing flavor that makes a lovely summer soup.

Flowers

Pick the flowers from late spring right through the summer until the first frosts. Ideal for adding to fruit and savory salads, rice dishes, desserts of all sorts and ice cubes.

Properties

The leaves and flowers are rich in potassium and calcium and therefore are a good blood purifier and tonic. Because it is a tonic plant for the adrenal glands, borage provides invaluable support for a stressful lifestyle.

Other varieties

White-Flowering Borage
Borago officinalis 'Alba'
This can be used in exactly the same way as the blue-flowering borage.

BORAGE SOUP

This is a versatile soup, as it can be served both hot and cold, which makes it a perfect British summer dish – when the weather can also be very hot or cold.

Serves 4

¼ cup (60 ml) unsalted butter
¼ cup (60 ml) long-grain rice
3 cups (750 ml) hot homemade (see page 13) or good bought chicken stock or vegetable stock
½ lb (225 g) borage stems with young leaves and a few flowers to garnish
Salt and freshly ground black pepper
¾ cup (175 ml) crème fraîche or whipping (35%) cream

Melt the butter in a large saucepan, add the rice and cook over low heat for a few minutes, stirring all the time. Add the stock, cover and simmer for 15 minutes.

Remove the flowers from the borage stems and set aside for later. Remove the borage leaves from the stems, wash and add to the stock and rice. Simmer for a further few minutes, until the rice is cooked.

Remove from the heat, check the seasoning and, using a hand blender or food processor, blend the soup. Serve hot with a swirl of crème fraîche or whipping cream, or pour it into a bowl and allow to cool before placing in the fridge.

When serving it cold, stir the soup well before serving and spoon into individual bowls. Add a swirl of crème fraîche or whipping (35%) cream and garnish with a few bright blue borage flowers.

BORAGE, PEAR AND RASPBERRY SALAD

A true summer salad bursting with color. The young borage leaves with their cool cucumber flavor complement the pear and raspberries.

Serves 2

10 young borage leaves, finely sliced (don't worry, the hairs dissolve on the tongue)
1 handful wild arugula leaves, coarsely chopped
4 tbsp (60 ml) raspberries
3 pears (Anjou or Comice), peeled, cored and sliced
Lemon juice (optional)
3 tbsp (45 ml) olive oil
1 tbsp (15 ml) balsamic vinegar
Borage flowers

In a serving bowl, mix together the borage leaves and wild arugula. Add the raspberries, then the sliced pears. If you want to make this in advance, slice the pears and squeeze some lemon juice over them to prevent them turning brown.

Make a vinaigrette with the olive oil and vinegar, pour over the salad and toss. Scatter the borage flowers overtop and serve.

BORAGE ICE CUBES

Borage flowers
Cooled boiled water

Add color to your drinks and fruit salads with these pretty cubes. As with bergamot, pick the borage flowers when they are fully open.

To keep the ice cubes clear, use boiled water that has been left to cool. Fill the ice-cube tray with the water, then add a single flower to each section. If you find the flowers difficult to handle with your fingers, use a pair of tweezers to place the flowers. Leave to set in the freezer for 12 hours.

These will keep in a freezer for up to 3 months before becoming cloudy.

BORAGE FLOWER ICE BOWL

Stems of borage flowers and leaves
Cooled boiled water

Slightly fiddly to make but spectacular to look at, this is worth the effort for a special occasion or when you want to show off. Perfect for serving fruit such as strawberries or slices of nectarines, peaches and melons.

Remove the flowers from their stems.
Take two clear glass mixing bowls that fit inside one another. Half-fill the larger bowl with cool boiled water and sit the smaller bowl inside. Position the smaller bowl about ¾ inch (2 cm) above the bottom of the larger bowl by weighing it down with gravel, a stone or a weight, then tape it centrally into place.

Arrange the flowers and leaves by tucking them into the water between the two bowls. When you are happy with their position, top up the bigger bowl with more cooled boiled water. Place the bowls in the freezer for at least 24 hours. When you want to use it, take the bowls from the freezer, remove the tape and gravel and leave the ice bowl to melt slightly. This makes it easier to remove the glass bowls.

Excess borage

Borage flowers can be prolific, and one of the best things you can do with this abundance is to crystallize them. They can then be used in a multitude of ways, including decorating desserts and cakes and placing on homemade chocolates.

Crystallized borage flowers

When I wrote my book *Cooking with Flowers,* I discovered that there are a number of methods for crystallizing flowers, the most common being to dip them in beaten egg white with sugar – with or without alcohol. However, the technique I prefer uses gum arabic and rose water, as this preserves the flowers for a few months when kept in an airtight container. This method does take time, so be patient.

Rose water for cooking can be found in gourmet supermarkets and Middle Eastern shops, or online from various suppliers. Gum arabic can be found at some pharmacies and in shops selling cake-making and icing accessories.

1 tbsp (15 ml) rose water
1 tsp (5 ml) gum arabic
Borage flowers
Powdered (confectioners') sugar or fruit (superfine) sugar

When crystallizing flowers it is essential to be well prepared, because the fresher they are when you are doing it, the better the end result. So prepare the gum arabic solution first by pouring the rose water into a small jar with a close-fitting lid and a wide-enough neck to be able to pop the flowers in and retrieve them. Add the powdered gum arabic. Replace the top and shake the bottle until the powder has dissolved, about 1 to 2 minutes. Do not be tempted to put the powder into the jar before the rose water, because it becomes incredibly difficult to make the powder dissolve fully.

Pick the borage flowers in the late morning, choosing perfect specimens. Remove them from the stems, making sure you have no green parts. Dip each one in water to remove any insects or dust, then very gently dry them on some paper towels.

Preheat the oven to 225°F (110°C).

Immerse the flowers completely in the gum arabic solution by dropping them one at a time into the jar. Retrieve them from the jar using a fine artist's paintbrush and put them on a sheet of waxed paper that has been covered with sugar. Sprinkle more sugar over the top and use another fine paintbrush to remove any sugar that has formed lumps in the heart of each flower.

Place the now well-sugared flowers on a sheet of parchment paper on a wire rack and dry in the oven with the door ajar. This will take approximately 2 to 3 hours. When the flowers are hard to the touch, remove from the oven. Store them in layers between waxed paper in airtight jars or rigid containers. Stored this way they will keep for up to 6 months.

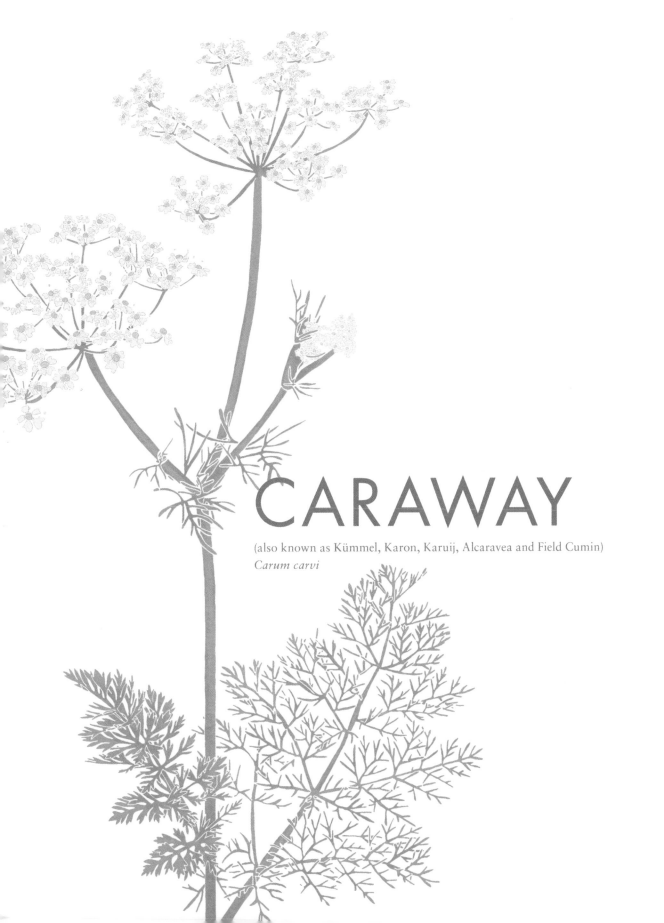

CARAWAY

(also known as Kümmel, Karon, Karuij, Alcaravea and Field Cumin)
Carum carvi

My grandmother and mother both used the seeds of this herb profusely in vegetable dishes and in cakes and cookies. One childhood recipe that I remember well is baked potatoes covered in seeds and cheese.

Caraway is used in many countries from India to Europe, Australia and North America. In the UK it is one of our native herbs but has recently become endangered in the wild because of changes in agricultural practices. Where it grows wild it is known as field cumin.

Description

Caraway is an attractive biennial that produces leaves in the first year, and in the second year, attractive small clusters of tiny white flowers with a hint of pink throughout the early summer. The leaves are similar to its cousin the carrot – light green and feathery, with a delicate parsley-like flavor. The root is comparable to parsnip, but it is much smaller and has a mild anise flavor.

Caraway is easily grown from seed sown directly into the garden or into a large, deep pot placed in a sunny position. This is preferable to sowing in shallow seed trays, as it has a long tap root that hates being transplanted. Being a biennial, it will bolt and run to seed if it feels that it is going to die.

Either sow in early autumn when the seed is fresh, which is also when you get the best germination, or in the spring after all threat of frost has passed. In the garden, sow directly into a well-prepared site in well-drained soil in a sunny position. If you are growing caraway for a root crop, sow in rows, then thin to 8 inches (20 cm) apart and keep free of weeds. Caraway perpetuates itself in the garden by self-sown seeds, which will, with a little control, maintain rotation of crop.

History in cooking

This is a very ancient herb that has survived relatively unchanged for thousands of years. Records show that it was used in the Stone Age, and it has also been found in Egyptian tombs and at the ancient caravan stops along the Silk Road. In Elizabethan feasts it became a traditional way to finish the banquet; it is mentioned by Shakespeare in *Henry IV*, when Falstaff is offered a Pippin apple and a dish of caraways. It has been, and still is, popular in Europe, and when Queen Victoria married Prince Albert, the UK renewed its interest in his favorite seed.

Harvesting and uses

Leaves
Gather fresh young leaves in the late spring and early summer of the first season for use in salads. They are not worth drying or freezing.

Flowers
Pick in the second summer to use in salads – both savory and sweet.

Seeds
Harvest in the second autumn. Use with vegetables and meats and in cakes and breads. In Europe, caraway seed is inextricably linked with cooked cabbage, especially sauerkraut.

Roots
Dig up roots in the second autumn for use as a food crop. They can be used as you would other root vegetables such as parsnip, but caraway root has a much stronger flavor. Either steam, boil or roast.

Properties The seeds of this herb are rich in mineral salts and proteins and are extremely beneficial for the digestive system, as they ease stomach cramps and nausea. When chewed at the end of a rich meal, they relieve indigestion and help to clear the breath of garlic.

Other varieties None.

TUNISIAN SALAD WITH CARAWAY SEED AND MINT

Serves 2 as a main course,
4 as a starter

1 lb (450 g) eggplant
4 tbsp (60 ml) olive oil, divided
2 cloves garlic, unpeeled
1½ lbs (700 g) green or red bell
peppers,
halved and seeded
Coarse sea salt and freshly
ground black pepper
1½ tbsp (22 ml) roughly chopped
canned or marinated
fresh anchovies
1 tsp (5 ml) caraway seeds
3 large green chile peppers, seeded
and finely chopped
2 tbsp (30 ml) lemon juice
1 tbsp (15 ml) small capers
2 tbsp (30 ml) chopped mint (use
spearmint, not peppermint)

A warm aromatic salad that is great to serve either as a starter with a little toasted pita bread or as a main course. Caraway seed and mint is a classic Middle Eastern combination; anise and mint are both good for the digestion.

Preheat the oven to 400°F (200°C).

Wash and dry the eggplant, rub 1 tbsp (15 ml) of the oil over the skin and place it, whole, in a roasting pan. Cook in the oven for 20 minutes. Add the garlic cloves, bell peppers and 2 tbsp (30 ml) of the oil to the eggplant in the roasting pan. Season with salt and pepper and cook for a further 30 minutes.

Remove the roasting pan from the oven and cool, then skin and roughly chop the bell peppers, garlic and eggplant. Return all the vegetables to the roasting pan, then add the anchovies, caraway seeds, chopped chile peppers, lemon juice, capers and the remaining oil. Season, then mix well and cook, uncovered, for 10 to 15 minutes, until the liquid has evaporated. Place in a serving dish, sprinkle with chopped mint and serve at room temperature.

This salad can be kept for a few days in the fridge. Before serving, remove it from the fridge and leave at room temperature for a minimum of 40 minutes to allow the flavors to develop.

CARAWAY ROAST POTATOES

Serves 4

16 small potatoes
(red or Yukon Gold)
2 tbsp (30 ml) olive oil
1 tbsp (15 ml) caraway seeds
1 tbsp (15 ml) sea salt
Freshly ground black pepper

This early autumn dish epitomizes how using herbs can simply transform a dish. The aroma of the caraway seeds as they roast will enhance the potatoes and bring everyone to the table. Serve with crispy bacon slices and sour cream or crème fraîche.

Preheat the oven to 400°F (200°C).

Wash and dry the potatoes, then pierce the skins a couple of times to enable the steam to escape during cooking. Toss the potatoes in olive oil in a roasting pan, making sure they are well covered, then sprinkle with the caraway seeds, sea salt and pepper.

Place the pan in the oven and roast for 35 to 45 minutes, until cooked and golden brown.

RED CABBAGE, APPLE AND CARAWAY FLAMANDE

The scent of this cooking conjures up images of my mother in her kitchen with her sleeves rolled up, her inimitable apron fastened on and her tiny hands bedecked in rings. This is such a useful dish; it goes well with sausages and all meats, cold or hot, as well as cheese – especially a true farmhouse Cheddar.

Serves 4

1 medium red cabbage, outer leaves removed, cut into quarters and shredded
3 tbsp (45 ml) unsalted butter, plus extra for greasing
4 crisp eating apples, peeled, quartered and cored
1 tbsp (15 ml) fruit (superfine) sugar
2–3 tbsp (30–45 ml) red wine vinegar
Salt, freshly ground black pepper and nutmeg
2 tsp (10 ml) caraway seeds
1 bay leaf

Preheat the oven to 300°F (150°C).

Put the shredded cabbage in a buttered casserole in layers with the quartered apples, sprinkling the layers with the sugar, vinegar, salt, pepper, nutmeg and caraway seeds. Add the bay leaf to the first layer.

Dot the top surface with butter. Cook, covered, for 3 to 3½ hours.

SPICED CARAWAY PEARS IN WINE

I make this in the autumn when the pears are in season. Many fruits are enhanced by caraway, and pears are no exception. This is a dessert for special friends.

Serves 6

2 tsp (10 ml) caraway seeds
3 cups (750 ml) red wine
1 cinnamon stick, 1½–2½ inches (4–6 cm) long
3 cloves
¼ tsp (1 ml) freshly grated nutmeg
Zest and juice of 1 orange
2 tbsp (30 ml) red currant jelly
1 cup (250 ml) brown sugar
6 firm pears
Whipping (35%) cream, to serve

Preheat the oven to 300°F (150°C).

Using a deep ovenproof or flameproof casserole dish with a lid, fry the caraway seeds over medium heat until they start to release their aroma. Then add the wine, cinnamon, cloves, nutmeg, orange zest and juice, red currant jelly (this was my mom's hidden ingredient) and sugar. Slowly, stirring all the time, bring to the simmering point and cook until all the sugar has dissolved.

Peel the pears, leaving the stalks intact, and add to the simmering liquid. Cover with a lid and then put in the oven for 1½ to 2 hours, depending on the ripeness and size of the pears. Leave to cool. Once cold, place in the fridge for at least 24 hours to marinate.

To serve, remove the pears from the marinating liquid. Place in a heatproof serving dish with their stalks up. Put the casserole dish back on the stove, bring to a boil and reduce the liquid until it becomes syrupy.

Serve the pears with the hot liquid strained over and a dollop of whipped cream.

CARAWAY SEED CAKE

Caraway seeds feature in many old recipes, especially in baking, where the anise flavor of the seeds can be tasted clearly. Here is a traditional recipe that I have brought up to date using modern ingredients.

This cake used to be served for tea; it makes a good weekend cake, ideal after a long walk – or even for taking on the walk.

Serves 8

⅔ cup (150 ml) soft butter, plus extra for greasing
2¼ cups (550 ml) all-purpose flour
½ tsp (2 ml) baking powder
¾ cup (175 ml) fruit (superfine) sugar
3 large eggs
2 tbsp (30 ml) milk
1 tsp (5 ml) vanilla extract
1 tbsp (15 ml) caraway seeds

Preheat the oven to 350°F (180°C). Butter an 8-inch (20 cm) diameter round cake pan or a 2-pound (1 kg) loaf pan and line with waxed or parchment paper.

Sieve together the flour and baking powder into a large bowl. In another large bowl, cream together the butter and sugar until light and fluffy, then beat in the eggs, one at a time, adding 1 tsp (5 ml) of the flour mixture with each egg to prevent the mixture curdling. When the eggs are well incorporated, gently stir in the rest of the flour mixture. Stir in the milk, mixed with the vanilla extract, and the caraway seeds, mixing lightly.

Spoon the mixture into the prepared pan and bake for 50 minutes or until a skewer inserted into the center of the cake comes out clean. Leave to cool in the pan for 10 minutes, then turn out onto a wire rack to cool completely.

Serve in wedges or slices, spread with plenty of butter. This cake will keep in an airtight container for up to 3 days.

Excess caraway

The seeds of caraway are worth collecting, as you can use them in the winter months to spice up many dishes.

Harvesting caraway seeds

It is important to recognize when the seeds are ripe for harvesting. If you are unsure, gently tap the plant; if the seeds fall, it is time.

Harvest the seeds on a dry, sunny day and always collect seeds after midday so that any morning dew will have dried away. It is worth taking a paper bag or a seed tray lined with newspaper to the plant; then you can collect as many seeds as possible and prevent them spreading around the garden. Also take a plant label to identify the seeds at once in case you're harvesting other things.

Once you have collected enough seeds, clean them by removing them from the stems. Discard the stems and spread the seeds out thinly on some cheesecloth or paper towels, place in a dry, airy room and leave for a few days until the seeds are totally dry. Check the seeds before storing, though, as there is no point in keeping damaged or half-eaten seeds. Store the seeds in a dark glass jar, cardboard box or paper envelope that is labeled. They will keep this way for 1 year.

CATNIP

(also known as Catnep, Catmint)
Nepeta cataria

Catnip, or catmint, is well known for being a cat's aphrodisiac and less well known for being a culinary delight. I first discovered catnip being used in a kitchen in Italy, where it was cooked with wild mushrooms – simply delicious. Since then I have added catnip to many dishes because the minty, spicy, peppery flavor of the leaf goes so well with vegetables, chicken and pasta.

Description

Catnip in flower is beautiful; it produces lots of clusters of pale pinkish white tubular flowers in summer that, as they open, become a haven for bees and butterflies. This herb is a hardy perennial and will die back into the ground in winter, reappearing in the following spring. The oval gray-green leaves are very pungent when crushed, like mint with a hint of musk.

Catnip can be raised from seed in spring or cuttings in early summer or by dividing established plants in the autumn. Plant in well-drained soil in full sun or light shade. This plant dislikes sitting in a heavy, wet soil; in winter it can be known to "rot off" if it becomes excessively wet.

History in cooking

Catnip tea has been well known in Europe since Roman times as a refreshing tea that can be drunk to settle the stomach. In the Middle Ages the leaves were used to flavor meat and the young shoots were used in salads.

Harvesting and uses

Leaves

These have an aromatic mint, spice and pepper flavor and are quite strong, so go slow the first time you use this herb in the kitchen. Use freshly picked young shoots in early spring in salads, with vegetables and fungi, or rubbed on meat – this is particularly good with lamb. Mature leaves in summer and into autumn have a bitter mint flavor that can be used with fungi and in casseroles, stews, soups and sauces. The leaves freeze well and can also be preserved in butter, oil or vinegar. They make a good savory jelly that goes well with meat dishes – again, especially lamb.

Flowers

Pick from early summer until autumn. The whole flower is edible. When preparing the flowers for use in a recipe, remove any green bits; otherwise the flavor of the flower will be impaired (the leaves have a more powerful flavor). The flowers combine well with pasta, rice and vegetables of all sorts, adding an extra bite. Always add at the end of cooking.

Properties   Catnip, especially *Nepeta cataria*, contains citronella, a lemon-scented volatile oil that has antiviral properties. It also contains thymol, a substance found in thyme, which is an antiseptic that helps kill any minor bugs that might be in the food prior to cooking. It also helps balance fatty foods, making them easier to digest. There is a bitter flavor to the leaf that, as with all other bitter herbs, stimulates digestion and so is good for your liver and kidneys.

Other varieties   Lemon Catnip
Nepeta cataria 'Citriodora'
This variety has gray-green leaves that have a mint, thyme and lemon flavor with a slight bitter tang. Good with fish and chicken and for making salad dressings. It has creamy pink flowers.

Italian Catnip, Nepetella
Nepeta nepetella
Italian catnip has oblong, narrow gray-green leaves with spikes of very pale mauve flowers with a hint of blue in summer. It is this variety that I eat with wild mushrooms. It has an amazing flavor that is aromatic and minty with a slight bitter note.

CATNIP POT-ROASTED CHICKEN

Catnip combined with poultry, and in particular chicken, makes a great flavor combination. I love recipes where I put all the ingredients together in a dish with a tight-fitting lid, shove it in the oven and walk away, returning a few hours later to find the kitchen full of enticing aromas. This is one such dish. Accompany it with mashed potatoes or a lovely crisp green salad with a lemon catnip dressing, if you like. Make the dressing by combining 3 tbsp (45 ml) olive oil, 1 tbsp (15 ml) balsamic vinegar and 1 tbsp (15 ml) chopped lemon catnip leaves.

Serves 4–6

3 large sprigs (1 handful) catnip, leaves removed from the stem
Sea salt and freshly ground black pepper
2½ lb (1.2 kg) chicken
1 rosemary sprig
4 red onions, quartered
2 large Granny Smith apples, cored and cut into large cubes
Olive oil
2½ cups (600 ml) cider

Preheat the oven to 375°F (190°C).

Finely chop the catnip leaves with 1 tsp (5 ml) sea salt. Rub the salt and catnip mix inside the chicken cavity and all over the outside. Put the rosemary sprig in the middle of the chicken.

Place the onions and apples in a casserole dish and add 2 tbsp (30 ml) of olive oil. Sprinkle with a little salt and pepper and toss well so everything is covered with oil. Put the chicken on top, rub the skin with a little oil and pour the cider over. Cover the casserole and put in the center of the oven. Cook for 1 hour and 35 minutes. At the end of the cooking time, either check the chicken with a meat thermometer or check the legs and thighs; the meat should be just falling off the bone.

Remove the chicken from the dish. Strain the juice from the onions and now-collapsed apple into a bowl. Blend the onion and apple to a smooth purée and add some of the reserved juice to make a thin sauce. Carve the chicken into portions and serve with the sauce poured over.

MUSHROOM, CATNIP AND POTATO PIE

This is a useful dish, as it can be a light lunch, a light supper or a side dish with cold meats. It really shows off how well catnip goes with mushrooms, as it complements and enhances their flavor without dominating. The mashed potato topping has eggs added to it – this was my mother's trick; without doubt it makes the best mash you have ever eaten. Serve with a crisp green salad or some fresh cooked spinach.

Serves 4

3½ tbsp (50 ml) unsalted butter, plus extra for greasing
¾ lb (350 g) brown mushrooms (even better if they are fresh field mushrooms)
2 cloves garlic, peeled and sliced very finely
1 tbsp (15 ml) chopped catnip leaves
1 tbsp (15 ml) chopped flat-leaf parsley
Salt and freshly ground black pepper
7 oz (200 g) Gruyère, cut into small pieces

Preheat the oven to 375°F (190°C) and lightly butter an ovenproof dish.

First make the mashed potatoes. Wash the potatoes but do not peel. Place in a large saucepan of cold, salted water and bring to a boil. Cook until tender. Remove from the heat, drain and remove the skins, which should just slip off. Mash with the butter and hot milk and stir in the beaten eggs and ⅔ of the grated Parmesan.

While the potatoes are cooking, wash the mushrooms and cut into thick slices if large or quarters if small. Fry them with the butter and garlic until golden and sweet. Stir in the catnip, cook for 1 minute, then add the parsley, salt and pepper.

Smooth half of the mashed potatoes over the bottom of the dish, scatter with the Gruyère, then add the cooked mushrooms and all their cooking juices. Top with the remaining mashed potato, smooth it out and sprinkle with the remaining Parmesan.

Bake in the oven for 30 minutes, until the crust is golden brown.

For the mashed potato
3 lb (1.5 kg) potatoes for mashing (such as Yukon Gold)
3½ tbsp (50 ml) unsalted butter
⅓ cup + 2 tbsp (100 ml) hot milk
2 eggs, beaten
2½ oz (75 g) Parmesan, freshly grated, divided

CATNIP-INFUSED VEGETARIAN GOULASH

The dry, aromatic, minty flavor of the catnip enhances this vegetarian goulash. Serve with fresh pasta or egg noodles.

Serves 4

2 tbsp (30 ml) olive oil
2 medium onions, sliced
2 tsp (10 ml) whole wheat flour
1 tsp (5 ml) paprika, divided
½ lb (250 g) skinned tomatoes or
14-oz (398 ml) can of Italian
tomatoes
1 tsp (5 ml) tomato paste
Pinch of soft brown sugar
1 cup + 2½ tbsp (275 ml) hot water
1 tbsp (15 ml) catnip leaves,
removed from the stem and finely
chopped, divided
1 cup (250 ml) cauliflower florets
½ lb (225 g) new or small carrots,
cut into chunks
½ lb (225 g) new or small potatoes,
cut in half
½ red bell pepper,
seeded and chopped
Salt and freshly ground
black pepper
2/3 cup (150 ml) sour cream or
Greek yogurt

Preheat the oven to 325°F (170°C).

Heat the oil in a flameproof casserole, add the onions and fry gently until soft and clear, then stir in the flour and ¾ tsp (4 ml) paprika.

Roughly chop the tomatoes and add to the casserole. Mix the tomato paste and sugar with the hot water and add to the casserole with ¾ tbsp (11 ml) catnip leaves. Bring to a boil, stirring all the time. Add all the vegetables and the seasoning. Cover and bake in the oven for 30 to 40 minutes.

Remove from the oven and stir in the sour cream or yogurt, plus the remaining paprika. Serve decorated with the remaining catnip leaves.

TAGLIATELLE AND NEPETELLA SAUCE

Both nepetella (Italian catnip) and catnip have a dry mint flavor that goes so well with tomatoes and the sharpness of capers. The combination reminds me of hot summer days in the Mediterranean.

Serves 4

Olive oil
1 clove garlic, finely chopped
2 tbsp (30 ml) nepetella or 1 tbsp (15 ml) catnip leaves, finely chopped
1 tbsp (15 ml) parsley, finely chopped
2½ tbsp (50 g) fresh or preserved capers (rinse preserved ones and drain these well), coarsely chopped
½ lb (250 g) peeled tomatoes or 14-oz (398 ml) can of Italian tomatoes, chopped
Pinch of soft brown sugar
14 oz (400 g) fresh or dried tagliatelle
Salt and freshly ground black pepper
Freshly grated Parmesan

Heat some oil in a large frying pan, add the garlic and soften. Add the nepetella or catnip, parsley and capers. Turn the heat down low. Add the tomatoes and sugar. Cook gently for 5 to 10 minutes.

While the sauce is cooking, bring a large pot of water to a boil and add the tagliatelle. If the pasta is fresh, cook for a few minutes until al dente; if dried, cook according to the package instructions.

Once the sauce is cooked, remove from the heat and season with salt and pepper to taste.

When the tagliatelle is cooked, drain, add to the sauce and stir well. Serve at once with the Parmesan.

Excess catnip

Catnip butter

This can be used to fry mushrooms, for serving with lamb cutlets or even as a base for a fruit crumble. It is important to use unsalted butter in this recipe because it is mild in taste; the added herbs will provide the flavor.

Makes ½ cup (125 ml) butter

Handful of catnip leaves, removed from their stems
½ cup (125 ml) unsalted butter

Gently chop the catnip leaves to release the oils, then mix the leaves with the butter. (The simplest and easiest way of blending the herb and butter together is to use a fork.)

When it has been thoroughly mixed, pack the herb butter into a roll of waxed paper and place in the fridge for up to 24 hours before use. The longer you leave it, the better the flavor.

This butter can be frozen; put it into a plastic container and label it. It will keep for up to 3 months.

CELERY LEAF

(also known as Wild Celery, Smallage, Ajmud, Persil)

Apium graveolens

Having been growing herbs professionally for more than 25 years, I still find it magical when I discover something new about an herb I thought I knew a lot about. Celery leaf is one such herb, for not only is it the origin of commercially cultivated celery but it can also be found growing wild throughout Europe and North Africa. So I was fascinated to find out that a descendant of this wild form is considered an important minor spice in India, where the seed is used in several tomato-based Indian curries.

Description

The main difference between the cultivated celery you buy in the store and the herb is that the mature stems of the wild form are bitter and inedible, unlike those of the cultivated varieties.
This hardy herb lasts two years and will reach a height of 3 feet (1 m) when in flower during the second year. Clusters of tiny green-white flowers appear early in the second summer, followed by ridged gray-brown seeds. The bright, aromatic mid-green leaves are similar to those of its cousin French parsley, with which, when young, it is often confused.

If you are growing wild celery just for leaf, not for seed, sow it annually in the late spring in a prepared site in the garden when all threat of frost has passed. Celery leaf likes a good deep soil that does not dry out in summer, and it is a hungry plant, so always feed the chosen site with well-rotted manure in the previous autumn.

History in cooking

Historically celery leaf has been used for thousands of years; records show that the seeds were found in Tutankhamen's tomb (1327 BC). Also it is known that the ancient Greeks used it, as did the ancient Egyptians. The salad stem celery (*Apium graveolens* var. *dulce*) was originally bred in the 17th century from the wild form.

Harvesting and uses

Leaves
The young shoots can be picked throughout the growing season and are delicious in salads or added to mashed potatoes. They are also great added to soups or sweated down with onions. In my opinion, the tough mature leaves are inedible and bitter.

Flowers
These have a light celery flavor, great in tomato salads. Pick them in the second year in early summer.

Seeds
Harvest these in the second season in late summer and early

autumn, when they are fully ripe and start falling from the seed head. These are very useful; grind them in a mortar and pestle or add them whole to stews, casseroles and soups. They are also lovely added to dough for flavorsome bread. In India celery seed is an important minor spice.

Stems

The stems are best cut in the first season, before they produce flowers in the second spring.

Roots

As a cousin of the carrot, this herb produces good-sized tap roots and was traditionally grown as a root crop. Harvest the roots in the second year of growth.

Properties

Because of the deep tap root, the leaves are very beneficial, being high in calcium, iron, carotene and vitamins B_1, B_2, C and K. The seeds are also beneficial. However, a slight but noteworthy word of caution: some people are allergic to the seeds, and they have been known to cause an anaphylactic reaction similar to that in a peanut allergy.

Other varieties

None.

CELERY LEAF AND MASHED PARSNIP PATTIES

My aunt, many years ago, introduced me to mashed parsnips. This dish is not only delicious in its own right, but when combined with celery leaf, with its unique flavor, it makes a lovely light supper or lunch.

Serves 2–4

1½ lb (750 g) large parsnips, peeled and cut into large chunks (discard any woody cores)
1 small onion, finely chopped
1 clove garlic, crushed
½ cup (125 ml) ricotta or cottage cheese
2 tbsp (30 ml) celery leaf, finely chopped
2 eggs, separated
Salt and freshly ground pepper and nutmeg
Butter, for greasing
Grated Cheddar, or any hard cheese

Preheat the oven to 400°F (200°C).

Boil the parsnips in a large saucepan of slightly salted water until tender. Drain and mash with the onion, garlic and ricotta and add the finely chopped celery leaf. Beat in the egg yolks and season well with salt, pepper and nutmeg.

Whisk the egg whites until stiff, then fold into the parsnip mixture. Place about 6 to 8 spoonfuls of the mixture in a greased baking dish (depending on its size), sprinkle each one with grated cheese and bake for 30 to 35 minutes, until nicely browned. Serve immediately.

CELERIAC AND CELERY LEAF SALAD

Celeriac, celery stems and celery leaf together make a light and refreshing dish. Topping it off with pomegranate seeds not only makes it look a picture but adds further texture and flavor and creates a mouthwatering salad. This is lovely served with cold meats or soft cheeses and some crusty homemade bread.

Serves 4–6

1 medium-sized celeriac, washed, peeled and finely sliced
1 large handful young celery leaf stems, leaves removed, stems washed and finely sliced (do not use the large stems that have flowers on, as these will be very bitter)
2 tbsp (30 ml) celery leaf, finely chopped
2 tbsp (30 ml) ripe pomegranate seeds, divided
3 tbsp (45 ml) olive oil
1 tbsp (15 ml) lemon juice
Salt and freshly ground pepper

Mix together the sliced celeriac and the celery stems with the celery leaf and 1 tbsp (15 ml) pomegranate seeds. Combine the olive oil and lemon juice to make a salad dressing and season to taste. Dress the salad and toss well, then add the final 1 tbsp (15 ml) pomegranate seeds and serve.

CELERY SEED CHEESE STRAWS

These straws are always eaten with gusto. I remember making them with my mother, then in turn making them with my own children. Some people can be allergic to the seeds, so do check before serving this dish to others, as celery seed has been known to cause an anaphylactic reaction similar to that in a peanut allergy. Serve the straws on their own or with salads, or use with dips.

Makes approx. 24

7 tbsp (105 ml) unsalted butter, plus
extra for greasing
1 cup (250 ml) all-purpose flour,
plus extra for dusting
5 oz (150 g) mature Cheddar, finely
grated
1 tsp (5 ml) celery seed
Freshly ground black pepper
1 egg yolk

Preheat the oven to 425°F (220°C). Lightly grease a large baking sheet with butter and cover it with a piece of baking parchment.

Sift the flour into a large bowl, add the grated cheese, celery seed and pepper and mix well. Cut the butter into small cubes, add them to the flour and rub them into the mixture using your fingertips. Once the mixture has become very fine crumbs, add the egg yolk, stirring it in using a narrow spatula or butter knife (rather than a spoon) to keep the mixture lighter.

Gather the now-forming pastry into a ball. Dust the work surface with flour and gently roll out the dough into a square approximately ¼ inch (5 mm) thick. With a sharp knife, cut the square into strips and then each strip into roughly 3-inch (7–8 cm) lengths. Carefully lift them onto the baking sheet, leaving a small space between each one.

Place them in the oven for about 6 minutes. After this time, check them – they should be a pale golden color. If they are not, leave them to cook a few minutes longer.

Remove the baking sheet from the oven and allow the straws to cool and firm up, then transfer the baking parchment with the straws on it to a wire rack to cool completely.

Excess celery seed

Celery seed salt

This is a useful way to store an abundance of seeds. Make sure that the seeds are totally dry before you start and that they are cleaned – no stems or damaged seeds. This salt can be used as a seasoning and is often used to enhance the flavor of a Bloody Mary cocktail.

2 tbsp (30 ml) celery seed
5 tbsp (75 ml) sea salt

Combine the celery seed with the sea salt in a food processor, or pound small amounts at a time in a mortar and pestle.

Store in a jar with a tightly fitting lid in a dark cupboard for up to 6 months.

CHERVIL

(also known as Kerbel, Kervel, Cerfoglio)
Anthriscus cerefolium

This, in my opinion, is an underrated herb, as its delicate anise flavor can permeate food very subtly. It is also a robust herb to grow, surviving cold winters to give fresh leaves as soon as the weather picks up. My mother always had it in her garden, and even when she moved into an apartment she had it in pots outside her kitchen door. It was one of her must-have herbs when making Salsa Verde (see page 233), which she served with new potatoes or poached white fish.

Description

Chervil is an attractive hardy herb that lasts two years; however, many who are growing it for leaf production will resow it each year. It will reach a height of 2 feet (60 cm) when in flower in the second year. The tiny white flowers, which have a hint of pink, grow in clusters from spring until early summer. The light green fern-like leaves have a slight anise flavor. In the early autumn or spring, when night temperatures drop, the leaves can develop a purple tinge that does not impair the flavor.

This is an easy herb to grow, as it is raised from seed that germinates rapidly in the warmth of spring as the air and soil temperatures rise. The seed must be fresh, as it loses it viability after one year. Young plants are ready for cutting about six to eight weeks after sowing, thereafter continuously providing leaves as long as the flowering stems are removed. Plant in the garden in a light soil that retains moisture in the summer but is not waterlogged in winter. A semi-shaded position is best because chervil will bolt if the soil dries out or gets too hot. For this reason some gardeners sow it between rows of other garden herbs or vegetables, or under plants that drop their leaves in autumn, to ensure the chervil has some shade during the summer months.

History in cooking

This herb has been used for thousands of years throughout Europe and North Africa, and it is said to be a native of Siberia. It was almost certainly brought to the UK by the Romans in their wagon trains. It is considered to be one of the Lenten herbs (a herb traditionally eaten in quantities during the Christian period of Lent, especially on Maundy Thursday) and is thought to have blood-cleansing and restorative properties.

John Gerard, the Elizabethan physician who was superintendent of Lord Burleigh's gardens, wrote in his book *Gerard's Herbal* of 1636: "The leaves of sweet chervil are exceeding good, wholesome and pleasant among other salad herbs, giving the taste of Anise seed unto the rest."

Harvesting and uses

Leaves

Leaves can be picked six to eight weeks after spring sowing. They are then available all year until the first hard frosts. They are not damaged by frosts, but they do become limp and unusable until the temperature picks up.

It is best to use the leaves fresh as they are not easy to dry, and when frozen, then thawed, they are a bit mushy. However, this mush can happily be used in soups and sauces when you do not need the perkiness of fresh leaves. The leaves are good in salads, soups and sauces and in vegetable, chicken, white fish and egg dishes. Always add freshly chopped chervil leaves toward the end of cooking to preserve their flavor.

Stems

Packed with flavor, the stems can be used from spring onward, and unlike the leaves they can be used all through cooking. They are particularly good for flavoring sauces, stocks and soups.

Properties

Eaten raw, the leaves add additional vitamin C, carotene, iron and magnesium. They are also a good appetizer and carminative. A tea can be made from the leaves to stimulate digestion and alleviate circulation disorders, liver complaints and chronic catarrh.

Other varieties

None.

ASPARAGUS AND CHERVIL SOUP

This was one of my mother's standbys – she was immensely proud of her asparagus bed, which had a ceremonious cut each year. The combination of asparagus and chervil is excellent, as the light anise of the chervil acts as a digestive with the asparagus.

Serves 4–6

3 tbsp (45 ml) olive oil
2 leeks, washed well and finely sliced
2 baking potatoes, peeled and finely chopped
1½ qt (1.5 L) homemade (see page 13) or good bought chicken stock
2 lb (1 kg) asparagus, washed and trimmed, tough ends removed
Generous handful of chervil
1¾ cups (425 ml) whipping (35%) cream
Salt and freshly ground black pepper

Heat the oil in a large pan and fry the leeks over moderate to low heat until very soft. Add the potatoes and stir so they absorb the oil. Add the stock, increase the heat slightly to bring to a boil, then cook for 10 minutes.

Slice the asparagus stems and tips into ¾-inch (2 cm) pieces and add to the potatoes. Boil for a further 7 minutes or until tender. Strip the chervil leaves from their stems and add the stems to the soup. Cook for a few minutes, remove the soup from the heat, then liquify in a blender or food processor.

Finely chop most of the chervil leaves, reserving some whole ones to serve. Stir the chopped leaves into the soup with the cream.

Season to taste and thin with water if wished. Garnish with chervil leaves and serve hot or cold.

CAMEMBERT IN ASPIC

According to my grandmother, she had this wonderful dish when lunching with Lady Jekyll and she never forgot it – nor has anyone who has eaten it since.

My grandmother's version was very heavy going and took hours to prepare, so here is my adaptation. The light anise flavor of the chervil goes so well with the stronger tastes of cheese and consommé and balances out the flavors well. Delicious served with dry toast or oat crackers for a light lunch.

Serves 4–6

1¾ cups (415 ml) beef consommé
1 bunch chervil, finely chopped (including the stems), reserving some to garnish
1 ripe Camembert or Brie (approximately ½ lb/250 g)

Very gently warm the consommé and the chervil, but do not boil. Remove the outer white rind of the Camembert or Brie. Choose a serving bowl just a bit bigger than the cheese and pour in some of the warmed consommé. Add the cheese, pour on the remaining consommé and place in the fridge, covered with plastic wrap, until set (about 2 to 3 hours).

Garnish with some fresh chervil.

MARINATED TROUT WITH CHERVIL AND PEPPERCORN DRESSING

Chervil's light flavor enhances that of many fish, and when combined with dill the flavors complement each other. This dish makes a lovely summer meal, either for a light supper or lunch, or even a first course served with brown bread or new potatoes, depending on your appetite.

Serves 4

1 lb (500 g) rainbow trout fillets
6–8 tbsp (90–120 ml) olive oil
Juice of 1 lemon, divided
1 bunch dill leaves, finely chopped, reserving some whole ones to serve
1 tbsp (15 ml) coarse sea salt
Freshly ground black pepper
Chervil leaves, to serve

For the chervil and peppercorn dressing
4 tbsp (60 ml) crème fraîche
1 tbsp (15 ml) table (18%) or half-and-half (10%) cream
2 tbsp (30 ml) chervil leaves, finely chopped
1 tsp (5 ml) green peppercorns, soaked for 1 minute in boiling water, then drained

Wash the trout fillets and pat them dry with paper towels. Place them in a shallow china dish, pour on the olive oil and 2 tbsp (30 ml) lemon juice, scatter the dill over, then sprinkle with sea salt and a small amount of black pepper. Cover with plastic wrap or foil and leave in a cool place, not the fridge, for at least 12 hours, turning the fillets occasionally.

When you wish to serve, whip together the crème fraîche and cream and fold in the chopped chervil and drained green peppercorns.

Remove the trout from the marinade, scraping off the salt and pepper (do not worry about the dill). Using a very sharp knife, slice the fillets into paper-thin slices and arrange on 4 plates, each with a spoonful of the chervil and peppercorn dressing. Sprinkle the fish with the remaining lemon juice, scatter over some fresh chervil and dill leaves and serve with any remaining dressing.

Excess chervil

Chervil sauce

This is a lovely, delicate fresh sauce that shows off the full potential of chervil. It is good with poached chicken, chicken salad, white fish and hard- or soft-boiled eggs.

Makes approx. 2 cups (450 ml)

12 chervil sprigs
⅔ cup (150 ml) table (18%) or half-and-half (10%) cream
2 tbsp (30 ml) unsalted butter
1 tbsp (15 ml) all-purpose flour
1¼ cups (300 ml) hot chicken stock (homemade if possible; see page 13)
Salt and freshly ground black pepper

Remove the chervil leaves from the stalks and reserve 2 tbsp (30 ml) leaves for use later. Put the stalks and any remaining leaves into a small saucepan with the cream and slowly bring to just below boiling point, stirring all the time. Remove from the heat, cover, and allow to cool and infuse for at least 20 minutes.

Melt the butter in a medium saucepan, stir in the flour and cook for 1 minute. Add the hot chicken stock, stirring well until blended. Strain the infused cream into the pan and cook gently for a few minutes. Add salt and pepper to taste. Chop the reserved chervil leaves, stir into the sauce and serve.

CHICORY

(also known as Blue Endive, Bunks, Strip for Strip, Blue Sailors,
Succory, Wild Chicory, Wild Succory)
Cichorium intybus

This herb holds so many memories for me. As a child I disliked it; Mum and grandmother often used to cook the blanched roots, and to a child's palate they were very bitter. When my children were young, we took a canal trip through France on the Canal du Midi, and there are two things I especially remember from this trip: the first was Hannah and Alistair going to buy fresh bread every morning, proudly practicing their French, and the second was seeing chicory in full flower growing wild along the canal banks in the bright sunshine.

Description

Chicory is stunning when in flower; the flowers in midsummer are a clear blue, so it is worth growing a few plants for the flowers alone. Chicory will reach a height of 3 feet (1 m) when in bloom, so plant it at the back of a border or against a fence so that it does not blow over. It is a hardy perennial that will die back into the ground in winter, reappearing the following spring. The leaves are mid-green, hairy underneath and coarsely toothed.

It can be easily grown from seed sown in the spring or late summer, using fresh seed, or by division of the roots in the following spring (make sure you get a growing bud with each piece of root). It prefers a sunny site in a light, preferably alkaline soil. If you are planning to harvest the roots, prepare the site well prior to seed sowing by digging deeply and applying loads of well-rotted compost and/or manure.

History in cooking

The use of chicory can be traced back to the ancient Egyptians, who, like the Arabians, used to blanch the leaves as a salad, a custom continued to this day. Careful English wives grew chicory among their herbs, as it was good for purging and for the bladder. Since the 17th century, dried, roasted and ground roots have been used as a coffee substitute. In fact, Dickens in his *Household Words* described the extensive cultivation of chicory in England for just this purpose.

Harvesting and uses

Leaves

Gather leaves from early spring until early autumn and use them fresh, as they do not dry or freeze well. Young leaves can be added to summer salads to give a light bitter flavor. Forced leaves can be used as a winter salad, as they have a strong bitter flavor.

Flowers

Collect flowers in early summer until early autumn and use them in salads.

Roots

Dig up the roots from the second year onward in late autumn and shorten to 8 inches (20 cm). Remove all the side shoots and leaves and stack the roots in dry sand in the dark. Roasted chicory roots are still widely used as an excellent substitute or adulterant for coffee. Young roots can be harvested early in the second autumn, boiled like carrots and served with a white sauce, which makes a good contrast to the bitterness of the root.

The chicory roots can also be blanched, and the result is known as a Belgian endive. Traditionally the blanching was done in mid-autumn. A few roots were dug up from the garden and the tops were cut off to just above the crown, then the roots were planted close together in a box of loamy soil. They were kept in total darkness, and after four to six weeks the roots produced tight blanched new top growth. If you want to try this at home, bear in mind a couple of practical points: do not allow any light in during the forcing period or the Belgian endives will become bitter, and always delay the picking of the forced Belgian endive until you need it, because after just 1 hour of being in the light it will become limp.

Properties

We need to rediscover an appreciation of bitter foods like chicory, as they benefit the endocrine and digestive system. There is an old saying, "Bitter to the tongue is sweet to the tum." Fresh leaves contain vitamins A, B and C.

Varieties

Magdeburg and Brunswick Chicory
These are the best for producing roots that can be used as a coffee substitute.

Pain de Sucre (Sugarloaf)
This looks like lettuce and can be used in the same way. Does not require blanching.

Red Verona
This has crimson-red foliage and is good in salads.

Witloof (Brussels Chicory)
This is the one grown for the chicons, known as Belgian endives.

Radicchio
A red, loose-leafed chicory, rather like lettuce and not suitable for blanching.

BRAISED ENDIVES

This is just as my mother and grandmother cooked chicory. Its full flavor can be appreciated in this dish – clean and fresh with a hint of bitter. I usually serve this with boiled ham or chicken, but it is also very good with grilled tomatoes.

Serves 4

4 large Belgian endives
1¼ cups (300 ml) vegetable stock
Grated zest and juice of 1 orange
Salt and freshly ground black pepper
Grated nutmeg
1 oz (25 g) hazelnuts, coarsely chopped (optional)

Cut the endives in half lengthwise and place in a large saucepan. Pour in the stock, orange zest and juice, seasonings and nuts (if using). Bring to a boil, cover, lower the heat and simmer for 5 to 10 minutes, until the endives are tender but still crisp.

Drain the endives, reserving the cooking liquid. Place in a serving dish and keep warm. Reduce the cooking liquid over high heat to about ⅔ cup (150 ml) and pour over the endives. Serve immediately.

CHICORY AND CHEESE BAKE

The clean, bitter flavor of the chicory combined with the light saltiness of the ham and the creamy soft cheese makes this a good supper and a delicious comfort food.

Serves 4

3½ tbsp (50 ml) butter, plus extra for greasing and cooking
1 lb (450 g) Belgian endives, washed and dried
10 oz (275 g) lean cooked ham
1 tbsp (15 ml) oil
Salt and freshly ground white pepper
2 tbsp (30 ml) all-purpose flour
1 cup (250 ml) milk
⅔ cup (150 ml) dry white wine
3½ oz (100 g) soft cheese
2 tbsp (30 ml) chicory leaves, washed, dried and finely chopped
2 egg yolks, beaten
2 tbsp (30 ml) bread crumbs
1 tbsp (15 ml) chopped parsley

Preheat the oven to 400°F (200°C) and grease an ovenproof dish with butter.

Cut the endives and ham into strips about ½ inch (1 cm) wide. Heat the oil in a frying pan, add the endive and ham, season with salt and white pepper and fry, keeping to one side. Melt the butter in a medium saucepan, add the flour and cook until golden. Stir in the milk a little at a time and simmer for 5 minutes, stirring continuously. Add the wine, slowly stirring all the time until amalgamated. Add the cheese in small pieces and stir until melted, then add the chicory leaves. Remove the sauce from the heat and stir in the beaten egg yolks.

Tip the ham and endive mixture into the greased ovenproof dish. Cover with the cheese sauce, sprinkle with the bread crumbs and parsley and dot with butter. Bake in the oven for 25 minutes, until golden brown on top.

CHICORY AND STILTON SALAD

The bitterness of the chicory combined with the salty pungency of the Stilton really makes this salad.

Serves 3–6

6 Belgian endives
1 handful chicory, green leaves torn into pieces
7 oz (200 g) shelled walnuts
7 oz (200 g) Stilton (or use Roquefort)

For the dressing
7 tbsp (105 ml) olive oil
2 tbsp (30 ml) French tarragon vinegar (see page 316) or lemon juice
2 tsp (10 ml) Dijon mustard
½ tsp (2 ml) fruit (superfine) sugar

Preheat the oven to 300°F (150°C).

Remove the leaves from each endive, wash them carefully and pat dry with paper towels. Place the leaves in a shallow bowl with the green chicory leaves.

Cook the shelled walnuts in the oven on a baking sheet for 4 to 10 minutes, until toasted. Remove from the oven and leave to cool.

Remove the rind from the Stilton, crumble into small pieces and add to the cooled walnuts. Mix well, then scatter over the Belgian endive leaves. Combine the dressing ingredients until well amalgamated. Drizzle over the salad just before serving.

CHICORY AND ORANGE SALAD

Adding fruit to salad leaves (especially the clean, bitter flavor of chicory) adds more depth and flavor, particularly to this zesty salad. Serve with crusty bread and/or thin slices of smoked salmon.

Serves 2–4

¾ lb (350 g) radicchio
3½ oz (100 g) curly endive
7 tbsp (100 ml) crème fraîche
Salt and freshly ground white pepper
Generous pinch of sugar (optional)
1 tbsp (15 ml) butter
1 tbsp (15 ml) flaked almonds
1 orange, peeled and divided into individual segments, with seeds removed and broken into mouthfuls

Separate the radicchio and endive leaves, wash thoroughly under cold running water and shake dry. Tear the radicchio leaves into large pieces and cut the endive into strips.

Season the crème fraîche with salt, white pepper and the sugar, if desired. Melt the butter in a frying pan over medium heat and cook the almonds until golden brown.

Mix the crème fraîche with the radicchio, endive and orange segments, then sprinkle with the toasted almonds.

Excess chicory

Chicory can overproduce, and there is only so much chicory salad and endives one can eat. My solution to overproduction and to keep my plants producing lush young growth is to cut the plants back hard, put the excess in my compost and wait for the next lush flush.

CHIVES

(also known as Onion Chives)
Allium schoenoprasum

This was one of the first herbs I grew; it is very versatile. The leaves, having a mild onion flavor, combine well with so many dishes that it is nearly indispensable. At my childhood home my mother grew chives all along the edge of the path. It always looked stunning in mid-spring when it was in full flower. I remember thinking at that age that the flowers looked like soldiers wearing their bearskin hats on guard duty outside Buckingham Palace.

Description

Chives is a pretty, hardy perennial that dies back into the ground each winter, reappearing early in the spring. It has attractive round purple flowers in summer that are composed of individual little purpley mauve star-shaped flowers that taste of sweet onion. The green cylindrical hollow leaves have a mild onion scent and flavor.

This herb can be easily raised from seed sown in spring under protection at a temperature of 68°F (20°C). Alternatively, sow the seeds in late spring into prepared open ground. Established clumps should be divided every three years in the spring to encourage them to put out new growth. Plant in rich, moist soil in a sunny position. Keep well watered throughout the growing season. In the autumn, give the area a mulch of well-rotted manure. Both chives and garlic chives flourish in containers; plant them in a soil-based potting compost.

History in cooking

This is one of the most ancient of herbs, with records of its existence and use dating back to 3000 BC. It is the only member of the onion group to be found growing wild in Asia, Europe, Australia and North America. Historically it was used as an antidote to poison and to staunch blood flow.

Harvesting and uses

Leaves

Cut fresh leaves with scissors from early spring to mid-autumn and either use fresh or preserve by freezing as leaves or in a herb butter (see page 93). They are delicious freshly picked, snipped and included as a garnish or flavor in omelets, scrambled eggs and salads or added to sour cream as a filling for baked potatoes. They are good sprinkled on soup and on top of a thick bacon omelet or grilled meat too. The leaves should be added toward the end of cooking, because if they are cooked for too long they lose their delicious onion flavor and become bitter.

Flowers

You can pick the flowers from mid-spring until midsummer, but they are best used in early summer. They have a sweet onion flavor, which is great scattered over salads or with rice and many other dishes.

Divide the flower heads into individual bulbils and add at the end of cooking; otherwise the sweet onion flavor will disappear.

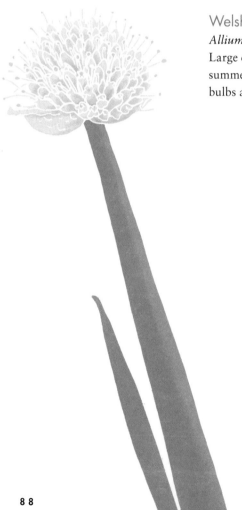

Properties

When the leaves or flowers are sprinkled onto food they stimulate the appetite by arousing the digestive juices in the mouth, therefore helping to promote digestion. They are also a beneficial antioxidant and the leaves are mildly antiseptic.

The two herbs mentioned below are hardy herbaceous perennials that die back in winter. They can both be preserved in exactly the same way as regular chives, and the flowers of both can also be eaten as you would regular chives.

Other varieties

Garlic Chives, Chinese Chives
Allium tuberosum
Garlic chives has clusters of white star-shaped flowers in summer and flat, solid thin, lance-shaped mid-green leaves that have a mild, sweet garlic flavor.

Welsh Onion, Japanese Leek
Allium fistulosum
Large creamy white globe-shaped flowers appear early in the second summer among long green hollow cylindrical leaves. Dig up the bulbs any time from early summer until early autumn.

GARLIC CHIVES BUBBLE AND SQUEAK

My mother never wasted food. There was always a set routine to meals, so that if anything was left over it became soup or was added to casseroles or used in one of my favorites: bubble and squeak. This was usually served on Saturdays – before the Sunday roast that marked the beginning of Mum's culinary week. Adding garlic chives to bubble and squeak adds a subtle flavor, and in late summer the flowers make the dish look most attractive. Perfect served with a homemade tomato sauce (see page 12) or cold meats.

Serves 2–4

2 cups (500 ml) cooked, mashed potato
½ lb (225 g) cooked cabbage or kale, cut into fine slices
4 oz (115 g) Cheddar, grated
1 egg, beaten
2 tbsp (30 ml) finely chopped garlic chive leaves
Freshly grated nutmeg
Salt and freshly ground black pepper
All-purpose flour, to coat
Sunflower or light olive oil
2 complete garlic chive flower heads (when in season), to garnish

Mix together the potato, cabbage or kale, cheese, egg, garlic chives and nutmeg and add salt and pepper to taste. Divide and shape into 8 patties.

Chill, if possible, for 1 hour in the fridge, as this helps the mixture to become firm and stops it falling apart when you fry it. Once the patties are cold, toss each in flour.

Heat some oil in a large frying pan until it is quite hot. Gently lower the patties into the pan and fry for about 3 minutes on each side. Remove carefully, as they can disintegrate at this point, and place on a plate lined with paper towels to drain off excess oil.

Serve hot and crisp, scattered with flowers, if available.

WELSH ONION, FETA CHEESE AND CUCUMBER SALAD

Scallions have larger leaves than chives and so are ideal for cooking very quickly. They add a light onion flavor to this salad, which combines well with the feta cheese to make a simple, appetizing summer dish. This salad makes a great filling for pita bread, for taking on picnics or eating at a barbecue.

Serves 4

2 bunches Welsh onions (scallions)
Extra-virgin olive oil, for drizzling
½ lb (250 g) feta
1 small cucumber
1 small romaine lettuce or 2 Little Gem, washed and roughly shredded
5 sprigs good spearmint (Moroccan or Tashkent), chopped

For the dressing
Juice of 1 lemon (plus a little zest)
3 tbsp (45 ml) extra-virgin olive oil
1 tsp (5 ml) Dijon mustard
Salt and freshly ground black pepper

Trim the scallions of any wilted greens. Heat a frying pan (do not use any oil) or use a griddle, if you have one. Place the onions in the pan and fry on each side for about 45 seconds. Remove from the pan, place on a plate and drizzle with olive oil.

Make the dressing by whisking all the ingredients together in a small bowl. Season well and set aside.

Remove the feta cheese from its package and break it up into small pieces.

Peel and halve the cucumber lengthwise. Run a teaspoon along the seed cavity to remove the seeds and discard them. Finely slice the cucumber, then toss together with the lettuce, scallions, chopped mint and dressing.

Scatter the broken feta cheese over the salad and serve.

SEA BASS WITH CHINESE GARLIC CHIVES

This is a quick stir-fry dish that is simple to make and is transformed by using garlic chives. Serve with plain boiled rice and some steamed broccoli.

Serves 2

2 sea bass (about 1 lb/450 g in total)
1 tbsp (15 ml) all-purpose flour, divided
Salt and freshly ground black pepper
3 tbsp (45 ml) sunflower oil, divided
3½ cups (825 ml) garlic chive leaves, snipped into small pieces using scissors
1 tbsp (15 ml) dry sherry or rice wine
1 tsp (5 ml) fruit (superfine) sugar
1 head garlic chive flowers, if in season, divided into individual flowers

Remove the scales from the sea bass by scraping them with the back of a knife, working from the tail toward the head. Then fillet the fish (if you cannot do this yourself, ask the fishmonger to do it for you).

Cut the fillets into large chunks and dust them lightly with the flour, salt and pepper. Heat 2 tbsp (30 ml) oil in a wok or a large nonstick frying pan. When the oil is hot, toss in the fish chunks and quickly turn the pieces to seal them. Remove from the pan and set aside. Add the garlic chives to the wok, stir-fry for 10 seconds, then add the fish and sherry or rice wine. Bring to a boil and add the sugar. Serve decorated with garlic chive flowers, if in season.

CHIVE FISH CAKES

My children were particularly fond of fish cakes, which we made and served with a homemade tomato sauce (see page 12). The chives give it a light onion flavor that is ideal for children. This is a useful recipe, as it turns a small amount of fish into a meal for four people, and it is an ideal supper for friends who drop by unexpectedly.

Serves 4

1 lb (500 g) baking potatoes, peeled and cut into large chunks
1 lb (500 g) fish (salmon, haddock, cod, hake or any large-flaked white fish)
Milk (enough to almost cover the fish)
1 bay leaf
2 tbsp (30 ml) chive leaves, cut into small pieces with scissors, divided
Salt and freshly ground black pepper
½ cup (125 ml) all-purpose flour
3½ tbsp (50 ml) butter
Sunflower or light olive oil, for frying
½ cup (125 ml) white wine
1¼ cups (300 ml) table (18%) or half-and-half (10%) cream

Preheat the oven to 325°F (170°C).

Place the potatoes in a large saucepan of cold water set over high heat, bring to a boil and cook for 20 minutes, until they are tender.

Wash the fish, place in an ovenproof dish, almost cover with milk and add a bay leaf. Place in the oven and cook for 10 to 15 minutes, until the fish is opaque and easily comes away from the bone or skin when you pull it (bearing in mind that different types of fish take varying times to cook).

Drain the potatoes, putting them back in the empty pan over moderate heat for a few minutes if they seem wet, then mash them with a potato masher.

Lift the fish from the milk, reserving the liquid, and pull the flakes away from the bones and skin. Add the fish to the mashed potato; add 1 tbsp (15 ml) chive leaves and season with salt and pepper. Mix briefly and gently, so as not to crush the flakes of fish.

Shape the mixture into patties about the size of a small ball, gently flatten, then coat each one lightly in flour. Don't panic if your patties all look different; it all depends on the size of the fish flakes. Melt a little butter and oil in a frying pan and fry the fish cakes until they are lightly golden – this should take no more than a couple of minutes for each side. Remove from the pan and keep warm in an oven set to its lowest temperature.

Wipe out the frying pan with paper towels, add the wine, bring to a boil and simmer until there are only a few tablespoonfuls left. Reduce the heat, pour in the cream and a glassful of the fish milk and bring back to a boil, turning it down to simmer so that it thickens but does not separate. Season with salt and black pepper. Add the remaining 1 tbsp (15 ml) chopped chives, then pour the sauce over the fish cakes and serve.

SMOKED MACKEREL AND CHIVE PANCAKES

I often make this recipe, especially when the chives are in flower. Smoked mackerel has a flavor that combines particularly well with Gruyère and the light onion flavor of the chives. However, you can change the fish to salmon if you wish.

Serves 4

For the pancakes
1 cup (250 ml) all-purpose flour
2 eggs
1¼ cups (300 ml) milk
2 tbsp (30 ml) snipped chives
1 tsp (5 ml) extra-virgin olive oil

2 tbsp (30 ml) butter, divided
2 shallots, finely chopped
⅓ cup (75 ml) white wine
1 bay leaf
7 oz (200 g) smoked mackerel, skin and bones removed and broken into chunks
⅓ cup (75 ml) all-purpose flour
⅔ cup (150 ml) reduced fat (2%) or 1% milk
1 tbsp (15 ml) chopped chives
Salt and freshly ground pepper
2 oz (50 g) Gruyère cheese, finely grated
½ cup (125 ml) fresh bread crumbs
Chive leaves for garnish, and flower heads when in season, divided into individual flowers

Preheat the oven to 400°F (200°C).

Start by making the pancakes. Sift the flour and a good pinch of salt into a bowl, add the eggs and half of the milk, and mix well with an electric hand mixer for 2 minutes or until the batter is smooth, with bubbles rising to the surface. Alternatively you can use a whisk, which will take a bit longer. Stir in the remaining milk and the snipped chives.

Heat an 8-inch (18–20 cm) nonstick frying pan. Add a little oil, then pour in enough batter to coat the bottom of the pan. Cook over moderate heat until golden brown on the base, then flip the pancake over and briefly cook the other side. Remove from the pan to a plate. Repeat with the rest of the batter, adding a little more oil every so often, to make 8 pancakes in all. Stack the pancakes on the plate, interleaving them with waxed paper.

Melt one-third of the butter in a large, deep saucepan and cook the shallots for 2 minutes. Add the wine and bay leaf, cover tightly and cook over fairly high heat for 3 minutes, shaking the pan a few times. Strain the cooking juices through a fine sieve and pour back into the pan. Bring to a simmer, then add the smoked mackerel chunks and poach for 2 minutes. Remove the mackerel pieces with a slotted spoon. Reserve the cooking liquid.

Melt the remaining butter in a small saucepan, stir in the flour and cook for 1 minute. Whisk in the reserved cooking liquid and the milk. Bring almost to a boil, then simmer for 3 to 4 minutes, stirring, until thickened and smooth. Add the chopped chives and season with salt and pepper to taste. Add the mackerel and stir gently.

Lay out all the pancakes and divide the mackerel mixture among them. Fold the pancakes into triangles. Arrange the filled pancakes in an ovenproof dish, then pour the remaining sauce overtop and sprinkle with the Gruyère and bread crumbs. Bake for 20 minutes or until the sauce is bubbling and the top is golden brown. Garnish with cut chive leaves and chive flowers, when in season.

Excess chives

Chives is one herb that I do like to preserve for use in the winter. Here are two methods that are quick and easy to do.

Chive butter

Useful to have in reserve, especially when you are busy, as this can be made in advance and used not only in scrambled eggs, omelets and cooked vegetables but also with grilled lamb or fish, and it is terrific on baked potatoes.

Makes about ½ cup (100 ml) butter

4 tbsp (60 ml) chives or garlic chives, cut into small pieces using scissors
7 tbsp (100 g) unsalted butter, softened
1 tsp (5 ml) lemon juice
Salt and freshly ground black pepper

Cream together the chives and softened butter until well mixed. Beat in the lemon juice. Add salt and pepper to taste.

Cover and cool the butter in the fridge until ready to use. It will keep for several days in the fridge, or alternatively it can be frozen in a labeled container and used within 3 months.

Chive ice cubes

Chives, being an herbaceous perennial, die back in winter. This is disappointing if, like me, you suddenly decide on a winter's day that you fancy a simple chive omelet with a crisp salad and some rosemary french fries, and then you remember that the chives are over. So here is a useful way of preserving a bit of summer for use in winter.

Chive or garlic chive leaves

Cut your chives in the late morning, wash and remove any brown or beige leaves, then gently dry them on some paper towels.

Using scissors, snip the chive leaves into the individual sections of an ice-cube tray. Once full, transfer to the freezer. Do not add water. Freeze for 48 hours.

Before you remove the tray from the freezer, get some freezer bags ready, because once you take the tray out of the freezer the leaves thaw very quickly. Pop the individual chive ice cubes into a few freezer bags and immediately return to the freezer. You then have portion sizes that are ideal for that winter omelet.

CORIANDER

(also known as Chinese Parsley, Yuen Sai, Pak Chee, Fragrant Green,
Dhania Pattar, Dhania Sabz)
Coriandrum sativum

I find it amazing to think that neither my mother nor my grandmother ever used this herb in any of their recipes. I remember vividly when coriander came to notice in the UK. At that time my herb farm was wholesale and Delia Smith was inspiring people to cook via her television program. She used coriander in one dish and that was it; we could not grow enough of it. Supermarkets did not sell herbs back then, so the garden centers suddenly became desperate to get their hands on it.

This is one herb you either like or dislike – there seems to be no middle of the road. Having hand-potted many thousands of plants, I must admit to disliking the scent (which is said to resemble a crushed bedbug) but I do like the flavor, which is ironic.

Description

Coriander is a tender herb and lasts for only one year, so it needs to be grown from seed each year. It has pretty clusters of small white flowers in summer. The leaves come in two forms: the first, lower mid-green leaves are broad and have a strong scent; the second to appear are the upper leaves, which are finely cut and have a more pungent scent. The whole plant is edible and this includes the root, because coriander belongs to the same family as the carrot, so the roots are most delicious. When you harvest it, pull up the whole plant so you get the roots and the leaf in one go. The seeds are also edible and, on ripening, develop a delightful orange-like scent; they are used widely as a spice and a condiment.

To grow coriander in the garden, choose light, well-drained soil that has been nourished with well-rotted manure or compost in the previous autumn, in a partially sunny position. As this herb hates being transplanted, choose your site carefully and sow it where you want to crop it. Sow the large seeds thinly, either directly into the garden or into a large pot (not a small one, otherwise you will get hardly any leaf before it flowers).

History in cooking

Coriander has been cultivated for more than 3,000 years. There are records from the 21st Egyptian Dynasty (1085–945 BC), and seeds were found in tombs of this period. It is mentioned in the Old Testament: "When the children of Israel were returning to their homeland from slavery in Egypt, they ate manna in the wilderness and the manna was as coriander seeds." It is still one of the traditional bitter herbs to be eaten at Passover, when Jewish people remember their great journey. Coriander was brought to northern Europe by the Romans, who, combining it with cumin and vinegar, rubbed it into meat as a preservative.

Harvesting and uses

Leaves

Pick the leaves from late spring until late summer when about 4 inches (10 cm) in height and bright green in color, and before the plant flowers. Alternatively, pull up the whole plant when the leaves reach 4 inches (10 cm) high. The leaf should be added to dishes just before serving, as it tends to go slimy when cooked and loses flavor. It goes well with spicy dishes and vegetables, especially carrots, and meat, chicken and fish.

Flowers

Pick when the whole cluster is in flower, from late spring until late summer, and use in salads or with rice. The flowers have a flavor that is a mixture of the seeds and the leaf – warm, aromatic and slightly scented.

Seeds

Watch the seeds carefully, as they ripen suddenly in late summer and early autumn and will fall without warning. You can cut the flower stems just as the smell of the seeds starts to change and become pleasant. Cover the seed heads with a paper bag, tie the top of the bag around the stems and hang upside down in a dry, warm, airy place. Leave for about 10 days. The seeds should come away from the husk quite easily and can then be stored in an airtight container. Coriander seeds keep their flavor well.

Roots

These are best harvested before the plant runs to flower – from late spring until early autumn. The flavor is a combination of the leaf and seed, with definite earthy undertones. Add to soups, stews, casseroles and curries.

Properties

The main medicinal use for coriander is to treat both loss of appetite and dyspeptic complaints. It is good for the digestive system, reducing flatulence and stimulating the appetite by aiding the secretion of gastric juices. The roots are high in potassium and iron.

Other varieties

None.

CARROT, ORANGE AND CORIANDER SOUP

This is a great summer and autumn soup, and as it freezes well, it is a lovely way to preserve coriander – which is notably difficult to do. Serve with fresh crusty bread.

Serves 4–6

1 large bunch coriander, with roots (if possible)
1 tbsp (15 ml) olive oil
4 large carrots, roughly chopped
1 onion, roughly chopped
1 qt (900 ml) vegetable or chicken stock
Juice of 1 orange

Cut off the roots from the coriander, wash them well and then slice. Roughly chop the greens.

Heat the oil in a large saucepan over medium heat. Sauté the carrots and onion for a few minutes until the onion has softened a little. Pour in the stock and add the coriander roots. Bring to a boil and cook until the carrots are tender, about 10 to 15 minutes. Remove from the heat and allow to cool slightly.

Add the orange juice and the roughly chopped coriander leaves. Purée the soup until smooth. Reheat before serving, but do not boil.

CORIANDER AND HERB COUSCOUS

There are many herbs in this recipe, and here coriander is included in both seed and leaf form. The seed has that lovely orange scent and the leaves a more earthy one, and when combined with the other herbs these individual flavors still shine through. This couscous goes well with grilled fish or chicken, or is delicious simply on its own.

Serves 4

1 cup (250 ml) vegetable stock
¾ cup + 2 tbsp (200 ml) orange juice
1 tsp (5 ml) paprika
½ tsp (2 ml) ground cinnamon
1 tsp (5 ml) ground cumin seed
1 tsp (5 ml) ground coriander seed
4 tbsp (60 ml) olive oil, divided
Salt and freshly ground black pepper
2⅓ cups (575 ml) instant couscous
Juice of 1 lemon
5 oz (150 g) fresh dates or 2½ oz (75 g) dried dates, pitted and chopped
1 large orange, peeled and roughly chopped
6 tbsp (90 ml) garlic chive leaves, snipped into small sections
½ cup (125 ml) coriander leaves, finely chopped
½ cup (125 ml) flat-leaf parsley, finely chopped

Place the stock and orange juice in a large saucepan with all the spices and 1 tbsp (15 ml) olive oil, season and bring to a boil. Pour the boiling liquid over the couscous, cover with plastic wrap and set aside. After 5 to 10 minutes, fluff up the couscous with a fork. Stir in the remaining 3 tbsp (45 ml) oil and the lemon juice, dates, chopped orange pieces, garlic chives, coriander and parsley. Mix well and season to taste. Serve.

VICKI'S MEXICAN ENCHILADAS

Over the past two decades I have employed many people to help me on the herb farm and nearly all have been foodies – not only enjoying cooking but also growing what they ate on their own garden plots. Vicki is a vegetarian and enjoys cooking. This is one of her favorite recipes. The coriander in the salsa combines well with and complements the tomatoes.

Serves 4 for lunch as a starter, or
2 as a main course

For the salsa
1 medium green chile pepper,
seeded and finely chopped
14-oz (398 ml) can whole tomatoes,
drained
1 red onion, finely chopped,
divided
3 heaped tbsp (50 ml) coriander
leaves, roughly chopped,
plus extra to garnish
Juice of 1 lime
Salt and freshly ground
black pepper

For the enchiladas
4 oz (110 g) Monterey Jack cheese,
grated
5 oz (150 g) mozzarella, grated
4 large flour tortillas
¾ cup (200 ml) crème fraîche
Oil for greasing

Preheat the oven to 350°F (180°C).

First make the salsa. Into a large bowl put the chile pepper, tomatoes, half the onion, all the coriander leaves and the lime juice. Season well with salt and pepper and mix thoroughly. Set aside.

Mix the two cheeses together in a bowl. Put a frying pan over high heat to preheat, and when hot, dry-fry each tortilla for 6 seconds on each side. Place 1 tortilla on a flat surface and spread 1 tbsp (15 ml) salsa over it, but not quite to the edges. Sprinkle over 1 heaped tbsp (20 ml) mixed cheeses, followed by 1 tbsp (15 ml) crème fraîche. Roll up each tortilla and place in a lightly oiled ovenproof baking dish with the seam side down. Repeat with the others, then spread the remaining crème fraîche on top of the tortillas in the dish and sprinkle the rest of the salsa overtop, followed by the remaining cheese and red onion.

Place the dish on a high shelf in the oven for 20 to 25 minutes. Garnish with extra coriander and serve immediately (if you don't, they can become soggy).

CHICKEN AND CORIANDER CURRY

This is a really great curry that has all the flavors and textures a curry should have. It is made all the better by using the coriander roots too, which bring additional texture. Serve with basmati rice.

Serves 4–6

3 tbsp (45 ml) oil
1 bay leaf
1 large bunch coriander, finely chopped, including 4–6 roots, washed and chopped (reserve some leaves to serve)
1 onion, thinly sliced, divided
Salt
3 tbsp (45 ml) water
1 tbsp (15 ml) turmeric powder
½ tsp (2 ml) chili powder, or to taste
½ tsp (2 ml) paprika
2 tbsp (30 ml) ground ginger
2 tbsp (30 ml) crushed garlic
4–6 boneless, skinless chicken breasts, cut into chunks (or use chicken thighs)
1 tomato, thinly sliced
¼ tsp (1 ml) sugar
3 cardamom pods, lightly crushed
3 cloves
1 cinnamon stick, about 1½–2 inches (4–6 cm) long
1 tbsp (15 ml) ghee or unsalted butter
1 tbsp (15 ml) ground coriander seed salt, to taste

Heat the oil in a deep casserole or large, deep frying pan with a lid over high heat. Add the bay leaf, coriander roots and three-quarters of the onion to the pan. Season with a little salt and fry until golden brown. Add a spoonful of water and stir so that the onions break down. Add the turmeric, chili powder, paprika, ginger and garlic and stir well. Reduce the heat to medium-high.

When the liquid starts to evaporate, add a spoonful of water and stir again. Add the chicken and tomato. Season with salt and sugar and stir. Add the cardamom, cloves, cinnamon, ghee or butter and another spoonful of water. Reduce the heat to low, cover and simmer for 30 to 35 minutes. Remove the lid, and if there is water left in the pan, raise the heat to medium. Add the ground coriander seed salt and cook until the water has evaporated to the consistency you require.

In another frying pan, add a little oil and the remaining onion, sprinkle a little salt and fry the onion for a few minutes or until golden brown and crispy. Remove from the oil and set aside on paper towels. Spoon the curry onto serving plates and sprinkle with fresh finely chopped coriander leaves and the fried onions.

CORIANDER, MINT AND PITA SALAD

This is an easy lunch that tastes so refreshing on a hot summer's day. The earthy flavor of the coriander leaves combined with clean spearmint makes this salad come alive.

Serves 2–4

4 large tomatoes
½ cucumber, cut into ½ inch (1 cm) dice
1 red onion, finely sliced
14-oz (398 ml) can chickpeas, drained and rinsed
2 large pita breads

For the dressing

4 tbsp (60 ml) olive oil
Juice of 1 lemon
2 tbsp (30 ml) chopped coriander
2 tbsp (30 ml) chopped spearmint (either Moroccan or Tashkent)
Salt and freshly ground black pepper

Boil a kettle, put the tomatoes in a large bowl and pour the boiling water over them. Leave them to stand for a few minutes. With a slotted spoon, remove the tomatoes one at a time and peel. Once all are peeled, slice thinly.

To make the dressing, put the oil and lemon juice into a large bowl, whisk until amalgamated and add the coriander and mint. Check the seasoning and add salt and pepper to taste.

Put the cucumber, tomatoes, onion and chickpeas in a bowl. Pour the dressing over and then toss together until well mixed. Immediately before serving, using a knife, split the pita breads in half, then toast for 1 minute, until crisp and lightly browned. Tear into bite-sized pieces and add to the salad. Mix well and serve.

Excess coriander

Fresh coriander chutney

If you have a blender or food processor this recipe is simplicity itself and will complement any curry. Alternatively it is great as a dip with pappadums.

1 bunch coriander
1 clove garlic
1 finely chopped green chile pepper
1 tbsp (15 ml) ground almonds (optional)
1 tbsp (15 ml) finely chopped spearmint leaves (either Moroccan or Tashkent)
Salt and fruit (superfine) sugar, to taste
2 tbsp (30 ml) lemon juice
Olive oil (optional)

Blend together all the ingredients in a food processor until smooth. Add a few drops of olive oil if the mixture is too dry. The flavors are best when served fresh, but at a push it will keep, covered, in the fridge for a few days.

CURRY LEAF

(also known as Curry Tree, Indian Bay, Nim Leaves, Kahdi Patta, Karapincha)
Murraya koenigii

For the past few years I have treasured a curry leaf seedling, nursed it through the winters and eaten just a few leaves each year. I am extremely proud of this plant and would love to be able to produce it here in our cold climate. So you can imagine my excitement when I saw this herb growing in a garden for the first time. I had just arrived in Sydney, Australia, and was about to give an address in the Herb Garden of the Royal Botanic Gardens. Still suffering from jet lag, I wandered into the garden to be confronted by a prolific curry leaf tree. It looked stunning, and I realized that my little plant at home was, even after a number of years, a mere baby, and I would need more patience before I could pick it regularly.

Description

The curry leaf is considered a tropical and subtropical evergreen shrub or small tree. It produces clusters of small creamy white sweetly scented star-shaped flowers from late summer, which are followed by small black fruit. The fruit is edible but its seeds are poisonous if digested. The oval soft, glossy, aromatic leaves are divided into 11 to 21 individual leaflets that have a marvelous aroma when crushed and an even better flavor when eaten, reminiscent of a mild korma. It can be grown in a garden only in the tropics or subtropics, where it prefers a fertile light soil in partial shade. If you grow it outside the tropics, it needs protection when the night temperatures fall below 55°F (13°C).

It can be grown from fresh ripe seed in the autumn, but it is easier to propagate from semi-ripe stem cuttings in late spring and early summer.

History in cooking

The use of curry leaves as a flavoring for vegetables is described in early Tamil literature dating back to the first century AD. These leaves are absolutely necessary to create the authentic flavor of southern Indian and Sri Lankan cuisine.

Harvesting and uses

Leaves

The best time to harvest leaves is either side of flowering in warm tropical climates and spring to midsummer in cold climates. The leaves when fresh have a very short shelf life; they may be stored in the freezer for up to a week. They are usually dried, so if you have a tree and wish to dry them, follow the instructions for stevia (see page 299) or lemon verbena (see page 173). In some recipes the leaves are either oven-dried or toasted immediately before use, or quickly fried in butter or oil – the scented oil is then poured over dishes to add richness and flavor. Equally, the leaves can be dropped into hot oil before adding the main ingredient. Since southern Indian cuisine is predominantly vegetarian, curry leaves seldom appear in nonvegetarian food; the main applications are thin lentil or vegetable curries and stuffings for samosas. Because of their soft texture they are not always removed before serving.

Properties

Fresh leaves eaten raw are reputedly a good cure for dysentery, and they are also used as an infusion for a drink that is said to stop vomiting. The traditional medicinal use of the curry leaf to treat diabetes has recently attracted a great deal of interest. Medical research has found special compounds that could provide the basis for an effective new medicine to treat diabetes in the near future.

Other varieties

None.

CURRY LEAF–INFUSED POACHED TROUT

I cannot describe how brilliantly the flavor of the curry leaf infuses the fish without being overpowering; it makes this a simple, perfect summer meal. Serve with new potatoes and a green salad.

Serves 4

4 trout, cleaned and gutted
Salt
6 whole black peppercorns
12 curry leaves,
plus 4 extra to garnish
1 small onion, cut into thin rings
1 lemon, cut into thin slices,
reserving 4 slices to garnish
½ cup (110 ml) white wine
⅓ cup (75 ml) butter

Place the trout in a large frying pan or heavy-bottomed roasting pan. Sprinkle with a little salt and the peppercorns. Place 3 curry leaves inside each trout. Lay the onion rings on top of each trout and arrange the lemon slices over them. Pour in the wine and enough water to just cover the fish. Bring to a boil on top of the stove, reduce the heat and let it simmer, uncovered, for 6 minutes.

When the trout are cooked, lift them out gently and place them on individual plates. Put a little pat of butter on each and top with a curry leaf and a slice of lemon.

CURRY LEAF RICE

This fragrant rice enhanced with curry leaf is lovely as an accompaniment to many dishes, for example, spinach, mushrooms or grilled fish.

Serves 4

2¾ cups (675 ml) basmati rice
3 tbsp (45 ml) virgin olive oil
20 curry leaves, finely chopped
(or use dried leaves and crumble
them into the oil)
1 onion, finely sliced
2 cloves garlic, finely chopped
Salt and freshly ground black
pepper
½ tsp (2 ml) garam masala
2 tsp (10 ml) plain bread crumbs
3 curry leaves, left whole for
garnish

Wash the rice in a colander with water that has been boiled and allowed to cool slightly, then cook it in boiling water. Once cooked, strain and run under cold water so that it does not stick. Leave it to one side.

Heat the olive oil in a large frying pan. When hot, add the finely chopped curry leaves, onion and garlic and a sprinkling of salt to stop the onions catching. Turn the heat down and fry over low heat until you can smell the curry leaves and the onions are tender, about 5 minutes. Watch that the leaves don't burn. Add the garam masala and cook for 1 minute. Add the bread crumbs and stir for 1 minute. Add the cooked rice and, with a spatula, turn over until thoroughly coated and reheated, being careful not to mash the rice. Season with salt and pepper to taste.

Garnish with the whole curry leaves and serve.

CURRY LEAF KEDGEREE

Kedgeree was a family staple that we often used to have on Fridays. I remember, when I was growing up, that the smoked haddock was always bright yellow and the dye used to come off and color the milk. Mum always added boiled eggs and peas to her smoked haddock, and just before serving she stirred in heavy cream, lots of freshly ground black pepper and a handful of chopped French parsley. I have adapted her recipe so that it includes the curry leaf.

Serves 4

1 lb (500 g) undyed smoked haddock
1 cup + 2 tbsp (275 ml) milk
3 tbsp (45 ml) vegetable or sunflower oil
3 onions, sliced and chopped, divided
12–14 fresh or dried curry leaves
4 cardamom pods, split
1 cinnamon stick (about 1½–2 inches/4–6 cm long), broken into pieces
1²/₃ cups (400 ml) water
1½ cups (340 ml) basmati rice
½ tsp (2 ml) turmeric
Pinch of salt
3½ tbsp (50 ml) butter
2 eggs
Handful of coriander leaves, finely chopped
1 lime or lemon, cut into 4 wedges

Put the fish in a deep frying pan (with a lid), pour the milk over and cover and simmer for 4 minutes. Take off the heat and leave to stand, covered, for 10 minutes to allow the fish to gently finish cooking.

Meanwhile, heat the oil in a deep frying or sauté pan (with a lid). Add one-third of the sliced onions, all the curry leaves, the cardamom and the cinnamon stick and fry until the onion is soft and golden, about 7 to 8 minutes, stirring often.

Lift the fish from the milk with a slotted spoon, discard the skin and any bones, cover to keep warm and set aside. Add the milk to the water and add extra water if necessary so that you have a total of 2½ cups (600 ml).

Rinse the rice in a colander, drain, then stir it into the onion and spices over medium heat. Keep stirring for 1 minute so the rice is coated, then pour in the milk and water mix and stir in the turmeric. Bring to a boil, then simmer for 10 minutes, covered, lowering the heat if it starts to stick on the bottom.

In a separate frying pan, fry the remaining onion with a pinch of salt (which helps to stop it burning) over medium heat, stirring occasionally, until deep golden, about 20 to 25 minutes. When done, spread on paper towels and leave to become crisp.

When the rice is tender, remove from the heat, drop the butter on top so it melts in, then lay the whole pieces of fish on the rice. Cover and leave the flavors to mingle.

Meanwhile, put the eggs in a pan, cover with cold water and bring to a boil, then boil for 6 minutes (for lightly boiled). Remove from the heat and plunge into cold water, cracking the shells against the side of the pan. Peel off the shells and quarter the eggs.

To serve, break the fish into big pieces with a fork, throw in the coriander and stir gently to mix without breaking up the fish, adding the eggs at the end. Season, scatter the crisp onions on top and serve with lime or lemon wedges.

Excess curry leaf

Curry leaf chutney

If you are lucky enough to have a curry tree or are able to source a good supply of leaves, this is an excellent chutney that will keep for a few weeks in the fridge. Serve as an accompaniment to curries or with pappadums.

½ lb (250 g) curry leaves, washed and dried
20 green chile peppers, seeded and finely chopped
2 tsp (10 ml) vegetable oil
1 tsp (5 ml) Bengal gram (obtainable from Indian supermarkets), or use chickpeas and crush them before frying
½ tsp (2 ml) white mustard seeds
Juice of 1 lemon
Salt

Grind the curry leaves and chile peppers with a mortar and pestle or in a food processor until they make a smooth paste.

Heat the oil in a pan, add the Bengal gram or chickpeas and mustard seeds and sauté until they crackle. Remove from the heat, add to the paste and mix well. Add the lemon juice and check for seasoning. Cool and transfer to an airtight jar and place in the fridge.

DILL

(Also known as Dillweed, Dill Seed, Aneto, Aneth, Sowa)

Anethum graveolens

I think this is one of the must-haves of a good family kitchen, as it is so immensely useful. The aroma and taste of dill transport me back to my childhood. My mother used dill as most households used parsley, so for me it was the norm. I grew up with the leaves being added to mashed potatoes or sprinkled over zucchini, the flowers being added to pickles and the seeds being pounded and added to soups and sauces. Today dill can be found in many prepared fish dishes from gravlax (salmon marinated with dill leaf) to pickled gherkins.

Description

This attractive feathery green annual herb, with its clusters of small yellow flowers followed by flat aromatic seeds, is a delightful addition to the garden. It is easy to muddle visually with fennel; if you are at all unsure, simply eat a tiny bit of the finely divided leaf, then you can immediately tell the difference. Fennel has an anise flavor and dill – well, it is difficult to describe. It's dill: no anise but a light aromatic flavor that combines well with so many foods.

To grow it successfully in the garden it is best to sow it in a row either in a prepared site in the garden or in a deep pot or window box in a sunny position. Dill, being an annual, will bolt to flower if transplanted or if the compost is allowed to dry out (when grown in a container). This is great if you need flowers or seed quickly, but you would miss out on the delicate flavor of the leaves.

History in cooking

Dill has a long history; it has been in cultivation for thousands of years and is mentioned in the Ebers papyrus from around 1500 BC. Historically dill was used with pickled and preserved food.

Harvesting and uses

Leaves
For the best flavor, pick before the plant starts to flower – from spring to late summer. The leaves can be used with zucchini, cucumbers, potato dishes, carrot dishes and all forms of fish.

Flowers
Pick as soon as the flowers start to form, from late spring to late summer. They have a sweeter flavor than the leaves but not as strong a flavor as the seeds. They are lovely added to salads.

Seeds
These can be harvested green from summer to early autumn to use immediately or for use in pickling. Alternatively, harvest the seeds when they turn brown and start to drop, for use throughout the year. They can be used in many dishes and for pickling.

Properties

Throughout the world dill seed is well known for its medicinal qualities. The seeds contain volatile oils, the main one being carvone, which has antispasmodic, diuretic and carminative properties. The whole plant is used not only for its flavor but also for its digestive properties, for both the seed and leaf when used in cooking are said to improve the appetite and digestion.

Other varieties

There are many forms of dill seed available from various seed merchants; some have been bred for leaf crop and some especially for seed.

Varieties worth looking out for are,

Indian Dill
Anethum sowa
This Indian variety has a more rounded, spicy flavor.

Bouquet Dill
Anethum graveolens
A popular American variety.

Dukat Dill
Anethum graveolens
A popular leaf variety.

Mammoth Dill
Anethum graveolens
Excellent for pickling.

Vierling Dill
Anethum graveolens
This variety has dark bluish green leaves that are great for salads and other vegetable dishes.

ZUCCHINI, DILL AND PARSLEY PANCAKES

Zucchini and dill was one of my mother's signature combinations. This recipe shows off how delicious the partnership is, but I've also added parsley to this mixture, which provides another level of flavor and a lovely green color. These pancakes can be eaten hot or served cold with a green salad.

Makes 6–8 pancakes

7–8 tbsp (100–115 ml) light olive oil or sunflower oil, divided
1 large onion, grated
2 zucchini, grated
2 tsp (10 ml) dill seed
2½ oz (75 g) feta
2 tbsp (30 ml) dill leaf
2 tsp (10 ml) chopped flat-leaf parsley
2 tbsp (30 ml) all-purpose flour
2 eggs
Salt and freshly ground pepper

Heat 1 tbsp (15 ml) oil and fry the grated onion gently until soft and translucent. Gently squeeze the grated zucchini in your hands to remove any surplus moisture. Add the dill seed and the zucchini to the onion and cook quickly for 2 to 3 minutes. Set aside to cool.

Whisk the feta, dill leaf, parsley, flour and eggs together in a mixing bowl, season with salt and pepper, then add the contents of the frying pan and mix well.

Wipe out the frying pan and add enough oil to shallow-fry. When hot, drop in large spoonfuls of the zucchini mixture, allowing room for them to spread. Cook until golden brown on one side before turning over.

When cooked on both sides, remove from the pan, drain on paper towels and serve.

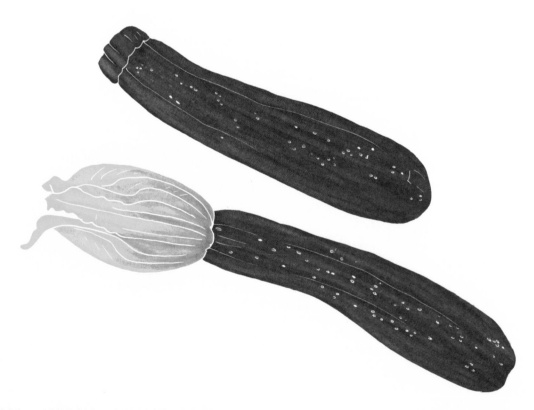

SALMON, POTATO AND DILL SOUP

Soups are a nourishing and economical way to feed a family for lunch. This recipe ticks all the boxes and is perfect on a gloomy summer's day when you want the sun to come out. The dill seed and leaf go so well with the salmon and bring out all its wonderful flavors. Serve with a green salad and/or good bread.

This is best made with fresh salmon. If possible, ask the fishmonger to give you the salmon bones and tail to make the stock with. When buying in a supermarket, try to buy a piece with the skin on, which you can then use to flavor the stock.

Serves 6–8

2 lb (1 kg) salmon, piece or fillet
2 lb (900 g) potatoes, peeled and cut into large chunks
2 tbsp (30 ml) unsalted butter
Generous handful of dill leaves, stalks removed and chopped (reserve the stalks for the stock)
¾ cup + 2 tbsp (200 ml) table (18%) or half-and-half (10%) cream
Salt and freshly ground black pepper

For the stock

8 whole black peppercorns
2 tsp (10 ml) dill seed, crushed with a mortar and pestle
Zest of 1 lemon
1 large carrot, peeled and chopped into chunks
Generous handful of celery leaves (the herb) plus stalks, washed and roughly chopped (or use 2 celery stalks, cut into chunks, plus the leaves)
3 bay leaves
Handful of flat-leaf parsley leaves, plus stalks, washed and roughly chopped
1 large onion, peeled and roughly chopped

Prepare the salmon by removing all the bones and the skin. Cut the fish into large chunks.

Next make the stock. Put 3 qt (3 L) water into a large saucepan with the salmon skin, bones, peppercorns, crushed dill seeds, lemon zest, carrot, celery leaves, bay leaves, parsley stalks, dill stalks and chopped onion. Bring to a boil, remove any scum that appears, then lower the heat and simmer for 30 minutes. Strain through a fine sieve into a clean saucepan. You need 1½ qt (1.5 L) stock; if you do not have enough, don't worry, just add some water.

Heat the stock over high heat and add the potatoes. Simmer for roughly 15 minutes, until the potatoes are just soft. Add the salmon chunks and lower the heat just to simmer for approximately 10 minutes, until the salmon is cooked. Remove from the heat, stir in the butter, chopped dill leaves and cream, to taste. Return to the heat, reheat gently (do not boil) and check the seasoning, adding salt and pepper to taste.

DILL MUSTARD

This mustard is particularly good with smoked salmon, trout or mackerel. It is also great added to mashed potato, salad dressings and sauces, or combined with either crème fraîche or cream cheese as a dip for vegetables or pretzels. A word of warning when adding mustards to hot food: remember that the pungency of mustard is destroyed by heat, so add it only to finished sauces or stews.

Makes 3 x 4-oz (125 ml) jars

3 oz (80 g) black mustard seeds
1 oz (30 g) white mustard seeds
2½ cups (600 ml) water
1 cup (250 ml) English mustard powder
¾ cup + 2 tbsp (200 ml) cider vinegar
1½ tsp (7 ml) salt
4 tbsp (60 ml) light brown sugar
1 tsp (5 ml) ground dill seeds (use a mortar and pestle)
1½ tsp (7 ml) turmeric
1 cup (250 ml) chopped dill leaves

Place both types of mustard seeds in a china or glass bowl, add the water and soak for 24 hours prior to use.

The next day, add the mustard powder, vinegar, salt, sugar, ground dill seeds and turmeric. When thoroughly mixed, place the bowl over a saucepan containing water, ensuring that the water does not touch the bottom of the bowl. Over very low heat, gently cook the mustard seed for 4 hours, stirring occasionally. Check regularly that the water has not evaporated, and never boil the mixture, as the mustard will lose its flavor and become bitter. Once cooked, allow to cool and add the chopped dill leaves.

Cover the herb mustard and keep it in the fridge. This will keep for up to 4 weeks. It will keep longer in the fridge if you put the mustard in a glass jar with a sealing lid. Once opened, use within 4 weeks.

Alternatively, you can cheat and simply mix 1 cup (250 ml) chopped dill with 3 tbsp (45 ml) good ready-made coarse-grain mustard and 3 tbsp (45 ml) ready-made smooth Dijon mustard. If it is too thick, add a small amount of white wine vinegar to obtain the correct consistency.

Excess dill

Dill freezes beautifully, so if you have a glut and want to have some leaves in winter, simply pick a bunch, wash it, pat it dry with paper towels and put it into a plastic bag and then into the freezer. When required, remove the bag from the freezer and crush the dill immediately; that way you will have crushed chopped dill with no effort. If, however, you do delay, it will thaw and go mushy.

Dill vinegar

This vinegar is lovely for making salad dressings or fish marinades.

Makes 2 cups (500 ml)

Dill leaves to fill a 1-pt (500 ml) bottle
2 tbsp (30 ml) crushed dill seed
2 cups (500 ml) white wine vinegar

Fill a clean empty bottle with fresh dill leaves and the crushed seeds. Top up with white wine vinegar and seal. (Use a plastic or plastic-lined top, as vinegar destroys metal.)

Leave on a sunny windowsill for a month, shaking from time to time, and then strain the liquid through an unbleached paper coffee filter into another sterilized bottle. Put a sprig of dill in the bottle for identification purposes and decoration.

For those who cannot wait 4 weeks for the vinegar to infuse with the herbs, here follows a quick method that is good for emergencies. Put the herbs and vinegar into a covered glass or china bowl over, but not touching, a saucepan of cold water. Bring the water to a boil, then immediately remove the bowl from the pan. Leave it to cool for about 2 hours before using the vinegar.

This vinegar will keep, bottled in the same way as above, for a number of years, whichever method you use.

ELDER

(also known as Elderflower, Elderberry, Common Elder,
Black Elder)
Sambucus nigra

Near where I live, in late spring you can see people with large black plastic garbage bags walking around the country lanes collecting elder flowers; this could be for their own use but is more commonly for the local company that makes elderflower cordial. There are also farms close by that have acres of elder trees that not only look beautiful in flower in late spring but are also magnificent in autumn, with the branches weighed down with bunches of the tiny blue-black fruit. This is one of the most useful herbs I grow in my garden; it looks good, smells good and does you good – what more can you ask of a plant?

Description

Elder is a sprawling multistemmed shrub or small tree that drops its leaves in winter. It has attractive flat clusters of lightly scented creamy white star-shaped flowers in late spring that are followed by lots of small, round blue-black fruits. The leaves are mid-green and large with saw-edged leaflets. These leaves are toxic and should not be eaten.

When growing in the garden, this plant prefers a fertile, moist soil in sun or dappled shade. Choose your site carefully, because in the right conditions elder can grow very rapidly, reaching 4 feet (1.2 m) in one season.

History in cooking

Stone Age sites in Europe reveal that elder has been valued by humans for its flowers and fruit for thousands of years. They were used by medieval monks in the kitchen and for herbal medicine, and by Native Americans, who also used the fruit as food and for medicinal compounds.

Harvesting and uses

Flowers

Pick them in the late spring just before they are fully open. They are lovely in the kitchen, not only for making the famous elderflower cordial but also for mousses, sorbets and jellies and with stewed fruit.

Berries

Pick the fruits in early autumn when they are dark purple-blue. It is advisable to cook them rather than eat them raw, as when raw they work as a good laxative and diuretic!

Properties

The berries are high in vitamins A, B and C and in the minerals calcium, potassium and iron. They are also high in anthocyanin, so are considered an antioxidant.

Other varieties

Warning Please be cautious when picking this herb in the wild and make sure you know which variety it is, for some are very poisonous. For example, the seeds inside red elder (*Sambucus racemosa*) berries are poisonous even when cooked, and the berries of dwarf elder (*Sambucus ebulus*) can cause severe diarrhea.

American Elder, Black Elder, Common Elder, Rob Elder, Sweet Elder
Sambucus canadensis
This native American shrub has numerous small white flowers in flat cymes throughout the summer and dark purple berries in early autumn. The leaves are long, sharply toothed and bright green. All parts of the fresh plant can cause poisoning (children have been poisoned by chewing or sucking on the bark). However, once cooked, the berries are safe and are commonly used in pies and jams.

ELDERFLOWER GOOSEBERRY FOOL

Gooseberries are a firm family favorite, and when we moved to the herb farm we inherited six cider-apple trees, some elder trees, gooseberry bushes, rhubarb and an amazing plum tree. This is a recipe I created using the harvest from the plants we found here.

Serves 6

1 lb (450 g) gooseberries, topped and tailed
4 tbsp (60 ml) sugar
10 elderflower heads, shaken to remove insects, then run under a cold tap

For the custard
2/3 cup (150 ml) milk
2 egg yolks
1 tsp (5 ml) arrowroot
2½ tbsp (37 ml) sugar
2/3 cup (150 ml) whipping (35%) cream
Fresh elder flowers, to decorate

Put the gooseberries in a medium saucepan with the sugar. Bring to a boil, stirring gently, and cook until the sugar is melted. Add the elder flowers, tied up in cheesecloth or a jelly bag, and simmer until the gooseberries are soft and pulpy. Leave to cool completely.

Remove the elder flowers, squeeze as much juice out as possible, then put them in the compost bin (if you have one). Keep the cheesecloth for washing later. Place the cooked gooseberries in a serving dish.

Make the custard by heating the milk in a medium saucepan to boiling point. Beat the egg yolks, arrowroot and sugar together in a measuring cup and pour in the hot milk. Mix well, then return to the pan. Heat gently until the custard thickens but do not boil. Strain through a sieve into a clean bowl and leave to cool.

Whip the cream to the same consistency as the gooseberries. Gently stir the cream into the gooseberries and then fold in the custard. Try to give it a marbled effect in the serving bowl. Place a few elder flowers on top to decorate.

ELDERBERRY SOUP

This is a wonderful spicy-sweet autumn soup that heralds the start of winter. Interestingly, it is served cold, which in my opinion enhances the unique dry and lightly fruity flavors of the berries.

Serves 6–8

2 lb (875 g) elderberries, washed and removed from the stems
1½ qt (1.5 L) water
1 cinnamon stick, about 1 inch (2.5 cm) long
4 cloves
1 large lemon, sliced, plus juice to taste
2 cups (500 ml) unsweetened grape juice
2/3 cup (150 ml) sugar, plus extra to taste
1 tsp (5 ml) arrowroot (or use cornstarch)
2 tbsp (30 ml) cold water
Sour cream, to serve
Grated nutmeg, to serve

In a large saucepan, combine the berries, water, cinnamon, cloves and lemon slices and cook slowly for about 40 minutes, until soft. Force the pulp through a sieve, pressing as much through as possible. Add enough unsweetened grape juice to make 7 cups (1.75 L) liquid and place in a large clean saucepan. Add the sugar and, stirring regularly to dissolve it, cook over gentle heat for 10 minutes.

Dissolve the arrowroot in the cold water, then add to the elderberry and grape juice mix. Keep stirring until it thickens, then adjust to taste with extra sugar and lemon juice.

Pour into a large bowl, cover and refrigerate for at least 4 hours before serving in individual bowls with a dollop of sour cream and a light sprinkle of grated nutmeg.

ELDERBERRY AND DAMSON CRUMBLE

This is a real autumn fruit crumble that I forage for every year, as we have elder growing around the farm and a large damson tree nearby. The dry fruity flavor of the elder with the intense flavor of the damsons is extremely good. Delicious served with crème fraîche or whipped cream.

It is a good idea when cooking acidic fruit not to use an aluminum pan. I suggest you use a stainless steel or nonstick pan as this will prevent a chemical reaction between the pan and the fruit.

Serves 4–6

6 bunches elderberries
1 lb (500 g) damsons, washed and pitted (you can substitute other plums if you wish)
½ cup (125 ml) fruit (superfine) sugar
1 cup (250 ml) all-purpose flour
3½ tbsp (50 ml) unsalted butter
4 tbsp (60 ml) soft brown sugar
2/3 cup (150 ml) rolled oats

Preheat the oven to 325°F (170°C).

Wash the elderberries well and then, using a fork, remove the berries from the stalks. Place them in a medium-sized saucepan.

Add the damsons and sugar to the pan, then cook over low heat for 20 minutes or until the fruit is soft. Check the surface for any missed damson stones and also check for sweetness, as both these berries can be very acidic.

Place the flour, butter and brown sugar in a bowl and rub together with your fingers until well mixed (if you have a food processor this can be done in an instant). Add the oats. (If you are using a processor, do not overprocess.)

Place the fruit in an ovenproof dish and sprinkle on the crumble mixture. Using the back of a fork, press the crumble down; this will make it crispy. Bake the crumble in the oven for 15 to 20 minutes, until the topping is golden brown. Leave to stand for 5 to 10 minutes before serving.

Excess elder

Elderflower cordial

This cordial is best made with fresh flowers that have been picked on a sunny day when they are still creamy in color, before they fade to white. At this time they have the largest amount of pollen, which contains the yeast that gives extra flavor to the cordial. The cordial can be diluted with still or carbonated water, depending on your preference, and is best served chilled.

Makes approx. 4¾ qt (4.5 L)

4¾ qt (4.5 L) water
1 lb (450 g) sugar
Juice and thinly peeled rind of 2 lemons
3 tbsp (45 ml) white wine vinegar
12 elderflower heads (shake the flowers well to remove insects prior to washing)

Bring the water to a boil in a large saucepan, then pour it straight into a sterilized container (see page 12). Add the sugar, stirring until dissolved.

When cool, add the lemon peel and juice and the vinegar and elderflower heads. Cover with several layers of cheesecloth and leave for 24 hours.

Filter through cheesecloth into strong sterilized (see page 12) glass bottles with corks or screw lids. The cordial is ready after 2 weeks. This delicious nectar will keep for weeks if given a chance, which is very rare in this household.

Elder wine

This is a recipe from my mother's *Mrs. Beeton's Household Management*. It was a revised 1949 edition with new pictures, as the original illustrations, from the edition printed in 1861, had been lost in the Blitz in 1940. The berries make a delicious wine, rich and fruity.

If you are going to make this, I advise getting a 1½-gal (5 L) fermentation jar with a rubber bung that has a hole in it, into which you can fit a glass or plastic fermentation lock. The first reason for the bung and fermentation lock is that it will stop fruit flies from attacking your wine; if they do, your wine will be sour. The second reason is that yeast produces more alcohol if fermented without air, so the lock allows the wine to ferment without letting in air but allows the gases to escape.

Makes approx. 10 x 3 cups (750 ml) bottles

3½ gal (13.5 L) water
6½ lb (3 kg) elderberries, washed

To each 4¾ qt (4.5 L) liquid, add
3 lb (1.35 kg) sugar
1 lb (450 g) raisins
2½ tbsp (40 ml) ground ginger
6 cloves
½ tsp (2 ml) dried yeast
⅔ cup (150 ml) brandy

Bring the water to a boil and leave to stand for 1 minute so that it is no longer bubbling. Strip the washed berries from the stalks and pour the water over the berries, making sure they are covered. Let them stand for 24 hours, then bruise well and push through a sieve.

Measure the juice obtained and pour it into a preserving kettle or large saucepan with the sugar, raisins, ginger and cloves. Boil gently for 1 hour and skim when necessary.

Let the liquid stand until just warm, then stir in the yeast and pour everything into a clean, dry cask or fermentation jar. Cover the bunghole with a folded cloth, let the cask remain undisturbed for 14 days, then stir in the brandy and bung tightly.

Once you notice the bubbling stop (after about 6 months), your wine is ready for siphoning. For this you will need a length of plastic tubing, as this will help leave the sediment behind in the jar. Decant into sterilized bottles (see page 12), tightly cork them and store in a cool, dry place. The wine will keep for 3 to 4 years.

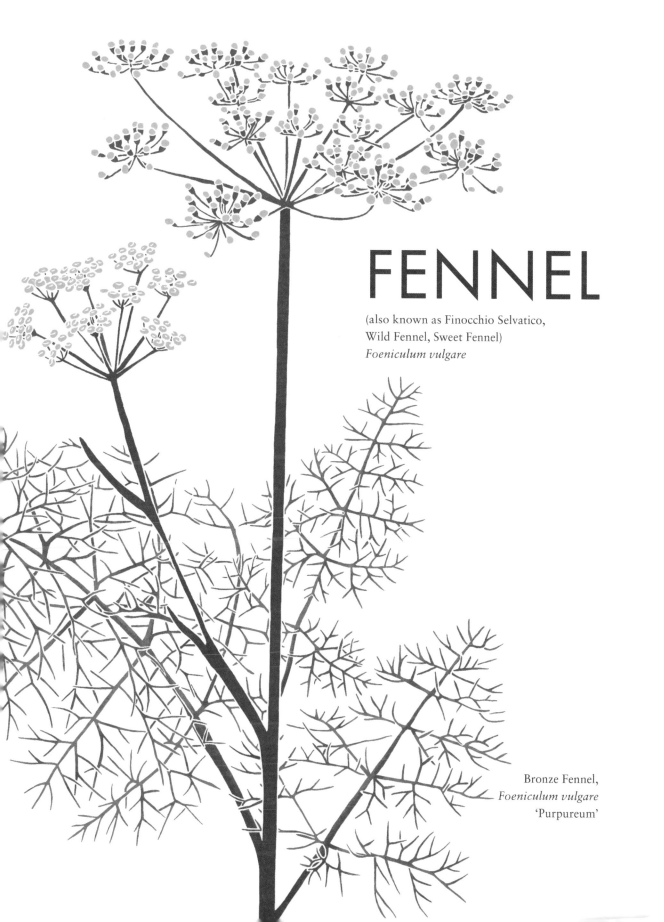

FENNEL

(also known as Finocchio Selvatico,
Wild Fennel, Sweet Fennel)
Foeniculum vulgare

Bronze Fennel,
Foeniculum vulgare
'Purpureum'

I have fond memories of a summer holiday spent on Majorca, where I either sat on the beach watching my children sail or went biking around the island, which I discovered is covered in wild fennel. One evening we got into a conversation with the proprietor of the bistro where we were eating and I mentioned the fennel. In response he gave us a glass of hierbas, which is a local liqueur made from fennel seeds and wild marjoram from the island. The predominant flavor was the anise of the fennel; it is a very strong digestive.

Description

Fennel is an attractive hardy herb that dies back in the winter, reappearing the following spring. In summer the small yellow flowers grow in flat clusters and are followed by anise-flavored, small brown seeds. The leaves are feathery and mid-green and also have an anise flavor when eaten.

In the garden, different conditions produce very different results. A hot, dry spot produces the sort of plant one sees by the Mediterranean roadside – a clump 4–5 feet (1.2–1.5 m) high with thin, highly aromatic leaves that make the whole plant look sparse. In a decent garden soil fennel looks more like a huge dome of green cotton candy.

It can be easily raised from seed sown in early summer in an open, sunny position in fertile, well-drained soil.

History in cooking

Fennel is as ancient as the Egyptian papyrus documents in which it is mentioned. The Greeks thought very highly of fennel and used it for weight loss and for treating more than 20 different illnesses. The Romans ate its leaf, roots and seeds in salads and baked it in bread and cakes. In Anglo-Saxon times fennel was used on fasting days, presumably because, as the Greeks had already discovered, it stilled the pangs of hunger.

Harvesting and uses

Leaves
The best flavor is in the new shoots as they appear from late spring until early autumn. These are lovely chopped over salads and cooked vegetables, added to soups and as a stuffing for fish.

Flowers
Pick these in summer just as they come into bloom. Add them to pickles and salads.

Stems
The young stems, produced from summer until early autumn, have a great flavor and can be used in salads or pickles. Mature stems are excellent for adding to barbecue coals.

Seeds

Gather the seeds green in late summer, or when brown in early autumn to early winter if you wish to dry them. Cut them off still attached to the stems and hang them upside down in a light, airy room. Once the seeds have dried, strip them from the branches and put them in an airtight glass jar. They can be used in sauces, fish and meat dishes and bread.

Properties

Fennel is a renowned digestive that is used to flavor many types of liquor. It also helps to ease dyspepsia and flatulence. The seeds chewed at the end of the meal not only clear the breath but also help to soothe indigestion, especially after a spicy meal.

Varieties

Bronze Fennel
Foeniculum vulgare 'Purpureum'
This is a hardy herbaceous perennial with flat umbels of flowers in summer and lovely soft, striking bronze feathery leaves. These have a milder anise flavor than the green variety but can still be used in cooking.

Florence Fennel, Finnocchio
Foeniculum vulgare var. *dulce*
This variety is grown as an annual because you dig up the sweet, anise-flavored white bulb in the early autumn. This herb is highly favored as a vegetable in Italy. If you want it to produce good bulbs you should not let it flower. The leaf is feathery and green, very similar to the green variety. It should be sown in shallow trenches during the early summer in a rich, well-composted soil for the bulbous roots to reach maturity by the autumn. When the swelling is about the size of a golf ball, draw up some soil around it. After two to three weeks the bulbs will have blanched and grown in size. The best size for harvesting is roughly the size of a tennis ball.

FENNEL AND ZUCCHINI SALAD

Anise-flavored fennel and crunchy zucchini are abundant in the garden at the same time, and when combined with oranges, this salad sings. Serve with salmon or cold pork, or simply with fresh crusty bread.

Serves 2–4

1 zucchini, grated, then drained
1 bulb fennel, finely sliced
Zest and segments of 1 orange
1 tbsp (15 ml) flaked almonds
2½ cups (625 ml) wild arugula leaves, roughly chopped
9 oz (250 g) feta, drained and roughly broken into small pieces
1 tbsp (15 ml) fennel leaves, finely chopped

For the dressing
2 tsp (10 ml) liquid honey
1 tbsp (15 ml) olive oil
1 tbsp (15 ml) orange juice
Salt and freshly ground black pepper

Combine the grated zucchini, with as much liquid squeezed out of it as possible, with the sliced fennel and orange segments and zest in a large bowl and mix well.

Toast the almond flakes in a frying pan with no oil, for about 3 to 4 minutes or until golden. Set aside to cool.

Make the salad dressing by combining the ingredients and mixing well. Pour the dressing over the fennel and zucchini, cover the bowl and put in the fridge for at least 1 hour.

Put the wild arugula leaves in a large salad bowl, then place the fennel and zucchini mixture in the center. Scatter on the feta cheese, toasted almonds and finely chopped fennel leaves.

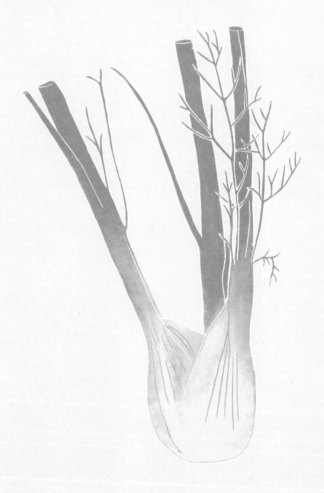

SEA BASS WITH FENNEL AND OLIVES

Serves 2

Olive oil
2 sea bass fillets, each
approximately 3½ oz (100 g)
2 tbsp (30 ml) fennel leaves, finely
sliced
Sea salt and freshly ground
black pepper
1 tsp (5 ml) fennel seeds, crushed
2 bulbs fennel, halved
and finely sliced
2 cloves garlic, peeled
and finely sliced
4 large handfuls Swiss chard, finely
sliced

For the sauce
1 clove garlic, finely sliced
6 anchovy fillets
4 tbsp (60 ml) olive oil
2 large handfuls small black olives,
pits removed
⅓ cup (75 ml) whipping (35%)
cream
2 tbsp (30 ml) flat-leaf parsley,
roughly chopped

We ate this in Majorca, where it is made with the wild fennel that grows all over the island and is served on wooden platters. This simple dish, with the anise flavor of the fennel leaves combined with the fresh sea bass, is in my opinion sheer heaven.

Preheat the broiler to medium, line a baking sheet with parchment paper and rub it with olive oil.

Using a sharp knife, score the skin side of the fish fillets (about halfway through the fish) and stuff with the fennel leaves. Place the fish, skin side up, on the baking sheet and cover with a few good glugs of olive oil and salt, pepper and crushed fennel seeds. Broil for 5 to 7 minutes, until the skin is crisp and the fish is cooked through.

Gently fry the fennel slices and garlic with a pinch of salt in 2 tbsp (30 ml) olive oil until softened and lightly colored. Add the chard and cook until the stalks are soft.

To make the sauce, gently fry the garlic and anchovies in the olive oil until soft. Chop half the olives, keeping the other half whole, and add these to the garlic and anchovies. Fry for another minute. Remove from the heat and add the cream and parsley. Check the seasoning, adding pepper if required.

Serve the fish and vegetables with the warm sauce poured overtop. Decorate with the remaining whole olives.

FENNEL AND CHICKEN STEW

The succulent fennel bulbs give a light anise flavor to this stew that gently enhances the chicken, making a delicious combination. Serve it with new potatoes and slender green beans.

Serves 4

3 tbsp (45 ml) olive oil
3½-lb (1.5–1.75 kg) chicken, cut into 8 pieces
Salt and freshly ground black pepper
12–16 shallots, peeled and left whole
4½ oz (125 g) pancetta
2 cloves garlic, finely chopped
1 tsp (5 ml) fennel seeds, lightly crushed
1 tbsp (15 ml) Pernod (optional, but good for special occasions)
1 cup (250 ml) dry white wine
1½ cups (350 ml) hot chicken stock
2 bay leaves
2 tbsp (30 ml) thyme leaves (removed from stems)
2 bulbs fennel, sliced into thick slices
2 tbsp (30 ml) butter combined with 2 tbsp (30 ml) all-purpose flour to make a smooth paste
5 tbsp (75 ml) crème fraîche
2 tbsp (30 ml) fennel leaves, finely chopped

Heat the oil in a large flameproof casserole dish. Season the chicken pieces with salt and pepper and fry, in batches, over medium-high heat until browned on all sides. As each batch is cooked, remove using a slotted spoon and set aside.

Add the shallots and gently fry until lightly browned, then remove and keep with the chicken pieces. Pour the oil out of the dish, add the pancetta and fry until golden, stirring regularly. Add the garlic and fennel seeds and fry for 1 minute, but do not brown. Add the Pernod and wine and stir well.

Once it is bubbling, add the stock, bay leaves and thyme leaves. Return the chicken and shallots to the casserole, cover and simmer gently for 10 minutes. Stir in the fennel slices, cover and gently simmer for a further 30 to 35 minutes, until the chicken is tender.

Lift the vegetables and chicken out of the casserole and place in a warmed ovenproof dish. Slowly add the butter-and-flour paste to the cooking juices, whisking all the time, until you have a smooth, thick sauce. Once mixed, cook gently for a further few minutes, add the crème fraîche, check the seasoning, then pour over the chicken, fennel and onions. Sprinkle with fennel leaves to serve.

FENNEL SEED RUB

I love the fact that when you pound the fennel seeds in the salt the lovely anise flavor is released into it, making this a very useful accompaniment for fish or meat.

Makes enough to rub into 9 lb (4 kg) meat or fish

5 tbsp (75 ml) fennel seeds
1 tbsp (15 ml) sea salt

Pound together the fennel seeds and salt with a mortar and pestle, then rub all over your chosen meat or fish. Alternatively, put the rub in a dry container with a tight-fitting lid and store in a dark cupboard for up to 3 months.

FENNEL SEED–ENCRUSTED SLOW-ROASTED PORK BELLY

To say this is a family favorite would be an understatement. I usually serve the pork rind (known as crackling in Britain) as I make the gravy, and before I have sat down, it's gone. Fennel is renowned for breaking down fatty food, which is why it is so good with the crackling – it does not just taste delicious, it also helps you digest this wonderful treat.

I am lucky enough to live near a country town that has an independent butcher. Steve purchases his pork locally; the pigs are reared outside and are free-range. It is the best pork I have ever eaten. With this cut of meat I ask him to score the skin so that it makes fantastic crackling. If you need to do this yourself, use a new, clean utility knife (box cutter) or a very sharp knife and slice the skin lengthwise at ½-inch (1 cm) intervals.

Serves 6–8

4½ lb (2 kg) pork belly, the skin pierced at intervals with the tip of a sharp knife
Olive oil
2 tbsp (30 ml) fennel seed rub (see page 126)
2 onions, peeled and cut in half
2 carrots, scrubbed and cut in half
2 bulbs fennel, cut in half
2 tbsp (30 ml) thyme leaves (common, French, compact or broad-leafed)
1 whole garlic bulb, unpeeled and divided into individual cloves
1 tbsp (15 ml) all-purpose flour
A little water or vegetable stock

Preheat the oven to 325°F (170°C).

Rub the pork all over with olive oil, then coat it in the seed rub, making sure you push it into the cuts in the skin.

Place the vegetables, thyme leaves and garlic cloves in a roasting pan and place the pork, skin side up, on top of the vegetables. Make sure the vegetables stay under the pork, otherwise they will burn. Add a little water to the bottom of the roasting pan and place in the oven for 2½ to 3 hours. Keep checking the water to make sure it does not dry out; add a little more if necessary, but keep the water away from the meat. There is no need to baste the skin; if you do, it will not become crisp.

Once the pork is cooked, remove it from the oven and put it on a serving plate or a chopping board. Remove the vegetables and put them in a warm serving dish.

To make the gravy, spoon the fat off the cooking juices, add the flour and stir well, scooping up all the juices and the bits that have stuck to the bottom of the pan. Place on the stove over low heat and, stirring all the time, add some water or vegetable stock to the pan. Keep adding the stock until you have the consistency you like. Simmer for a few minutes, then pour into a pitcher (you will not need to add extra salt and pepper because the wonderful seed marinade will automatically flavor this gravy).

If for some reason your pork rind does not crackle, using a sharp knife, simply remove the skin from the cooked pork, place it on a rack and then put it under the broiler set to the highest temperature. Keep an eye on it, as it will take only minutes to rise and bubble. Once the first side is done, turn it over and do the same on the underside. Once that is cooked, turn it over again so it is skin side up, allow to cool, then break it up into serving pieces. Put in a bowl.

Slice the meat; serve with the roasted vegetables and the gravy.

BAKED FENNEL

Both my grandmother and mother used to bake fennel. This is their recipe but with modern measurements. The flavor of fennel with cream is delicious, but that is only half of it, for fennel is also a digestive, helping one digest the richness of cream. Serve with grilled tomatoes and a crisp green salad.

Serves 2

2 bulbs fennel
1 tbsp (15 ml) unsalted butter
1 tsp (5 ml) fennel seeds, ground
¾ cup (175 ml) table (18%) or half-and-half (10%) cream
¾ cup (175 ml) crème fraîche
2 tbsp (30 ml) freshly grated Parmesan

Preheat the oven to 325°F (170°C).

Cut off the bases of the fennel bulbs, removing any remains of the roots, then cut a cone shape into each base to remove the core. (This is necessary only if you have tough homegrown bulbs that you should have pulled earlier.) Cut the fennel from top to bottom, not sideways, into ¼-inch (5 mm) slices.

Melt the butter in a large frying pan set over medium heat, add the fennel bulb and the ground fennel seeds and cook gently for about 3 minutes, then stir in the cream and crème fraîche until mixed. Transfer into a small baking dish and sprinkle with the Parmesan.

Bake in the oven for 20 minutes, until the top is golden brown and the fennel is tender. If you are unsure, check by piercing it with a fork.

Excess fennel

Fennel and cucumber pickles

This is a great way to use up an abundance of fennel stems in early autumn when you are preparing to cut back your fennel plants. This coincides well with the availability of cucumbers, which, if you grow your own, you can have in equal abundance. The great thing about combining fennel with cucumber is that some people find cucumber difficult to digest, and fennel helps this; it also counteracts the acidity of the vinegar.

I have deliberately not put quantities here, as it all depends on how many cucumbers you have.

Cucumbers
Salt
Fennel stalks and seeds
White wine vinegar
Dill seeds
Coriander seeds
Black peppercorns

Wash, dry, then sterilize some wide-mouthed jam or pickle jars in an oven, set at minimum temperature, for at least 1 hour. If you are using metal lids, cut some waxed paper to line the lid, as vinegar will in time corrode the metal.

Choose young, fresh rather than small cucumbers. These will be very crisp and, equally important, have few seeds. Wash the cucumbers, do not peel; then slice ¼ inch (5 mm) thick. Mix 2½ cups (600 ml) water per 3½ tbsp (50 ml) salt, place the sliced cucumber in the salt water, making sure it is immersed, and leave for a minimum of 2 hours.

Cut down the fennel stalks and wash and chop them into 1-inch (3 cm) pieces. The fennel stalks smell amazing when freshly cut.

Remove the jars from the oven and allow to cool until you can pick them up easily. Drain and rinse the cucumber well under a cold running tap.

Place 2½ cups (600 ml) vinegar plus 2 tsp (10 ml) salt in a pan (not an aluminum one), bring to a boil, remove from the heat and allow to cool. In each jar place a layer of fennel stalks, then some sliced cucumber and a sprinkling of the dill and coriander seeds and peppercorns. Then repeat as necessary with some stalks, some sliced cucumber and some seeds, leaving a small gap at the top. Pour in the cooled vinegar to fully immerse the cucumbers, but not to the absolute brim. Cover.

These pickles will be ready in a month and will keep for 3 months.

GARLIC

(also known as Heal-All, Aglio, Gift of the Gods)
Allium sativum

Wild Garlic, *Allium ursinum*

I cook with garlic as a matter of course, as do my children, for both my mother and grandmother used it well in cooking. It was never overpowering; it was simply part of the meal. And that is what garlic should be: a complement, not a statement.

Description

Garlic is a hardy perennial that is grown each year as an annual. Each bulb is made up of several cloves enclosed in white papery skin. The cloves vary in color from white to pink. The round heads of white flowers appear in summer only in warm climates. The mid-green flat, solid leaves smell and taste of mild garlic when broken or eaten.

Plant garlic cloves in early to midwinter in a well-drained and sunny site that has been fed with well-rotted manure or compost at the end of the previous summer. Traditionally, for the best crop, garlic cloves are planted on the shortest day of the year and harvested on the longest.

History in cooking

Garlic is one of the oldest and most valued of all cultivated plants. It was certainly known to both the ancient Chinese and the ancient Egyptians, who considered it a health-giver. Both the slaves constructing the pyramid of Cheops and Roman soldiers were given garlic cloves daily to sustain their strength.

Harvesting and uses

Leaves

Pick the leaves in spring until early summer. They can be added to salads and stir-fries or used on baked potatoes.

Flowers

Flowers are borne in summer in warm climates only. Pick the individual flowers just as they open. They have a light garlic flavor and so are good added to salads and scattered over potatoes.

Bulbs

Lift the bulbs from late summer and divide into individual cloves. To know if you should peel the clove or not for cooking, I have always worked on this rule of thumb: peel it if you are going to slice, pound, chop or fry it. Do not peel it if you are going to roast it (as this will help to stop it burning) or when you add it to boiling water. After you have roasted or boiled garlic cloves, remove them from the pan, then squish them to remove the soft pulp. The garlic will no longer be strong in flavor but creamy and sweet. Add to sauces and soups or simply mix with cooked vegetables or roasted meat.

Properties Garlic is high in many minerals, including magnesium, zinc, sodium and potassium, and in vitamins A, B and C. It aids digestion and is an antioxidant, antispasmodic, carminative and diuretic. The flavor of garlic not only enhances many meats but will also aid digestion of the meat.

Other varieties Wild Garlic, Ramson's Wild Garlic, Wood Garlic, Devil's Posy, Onion Flower, Stinkplant, Bear's Garlic
Allium ursinum
This is a hardy perennial with clusters of snow white star-shaped flowers in spring and early summer, which grow on long stalks above broad bright green leaves. It is often found growing wild in damp, shady sites, especially on the banks of streams. It is recognizable by its strong oniony smell. If you wish to grow it in your garden, choose your site carefully, because it is invasive. Plant in semi-shade in a moist, fertile soil. The leaf has its best flavor and texture before flowering. Use sparingly in salads, or wilt and cook like a vegetable. The flowers are edible and are good added to salads.

GREEN BEAN AND GARLIC SALAD

This was one of my mother's favorite salads; the combination of the garlic with the slender green beans is lovely.

Serves 2–4

1 lb (500 g) green beans
2 tbsp (30 ml) unsalted butter
2 cloves garlic, crushed
2 tbsp (30 ml) garlic leaves (when in season)

Top and tail the beans, then cook in a saucepan of boiling water (do not salt, as this will make the beans tough) for 6 minutes, until firm and crunchy. Drain using a colander.

Using the same pan, melt the butter, add the crushed garlic and stir well to just cook but not brown. Add the beans and toss. Put in a serving bowl.

Select some fresh young leaves of the new crop of garlic, finely slice and scatter over the beans. Serve.

BRUSSELS SPROUT MEZZE

The inspiration for this has come from many sources: my grandmother's book *Russian Food for Pleasure*, my mother's jottings and my travels. I love Brussels sprouts, and combining them with garlic is wonderful; they both have strong flavors but when combined they seem to balance each other.

Serves 2–4

2 tbsp (30 ml) olive oil
4 cloves garlic, peeled and sliced
1 small onion, peeled and chopped
1 oz (30 g) sun-dried tomatoes, cut into fine strips
2½ cups (625 ml) chopped tomatoes (homegrown or canned)
1 lb (450 g) Brussels sprouts, outer leaves removed and stems trimmed
Salt, sugar and freshly ground black pepper, to taste
1 tbsp (15 ml) pesto (preferably homemade but bought if the basil is over)
Freshly grated Parmesan, to serve

Heat the oil in a saucepan with a close-fitting lid over moderate heat. Slowly fry the garlic, onion and sun-dried tomatoes. When softened, add the chopped tomatoes. Cook for 5 minutes, then add the Brussels sprouts. Season with salt, a pinch of sugar and a good grinding of pepper. Cover and cook slowly for 20 minutes, until the sprouts are tender. Stir in the pesto. Scatter with the grated Parmesan to serve.

ROASTED GARLIC AND BEETS

When roasted, garlic tastes totally different to when eaten raw; it is creamy and sweet – ideal with sweet vegetables like beets. This dish can be served as an accompaniment to roast pork or chicken, or you can serve it with wild rice.

Serves 4

1 lb (400 g) fresh beets, peeled and cut into wedges
4 tbsp (60 ml) olive oil
2 tbsp (30 ml) balsamic vinegar
1 garlic bulb, cloves separated but unpeeled
1 tbsp (15 ml) thyme leaves, removed from the stems

Preheat the oven to 325°F (170°C).

Put the prepared beets in a roasting pan, add the oil and vinegar and toss well. Add the separated garlic cloves and the thyme leaves. Give another good shake to cover everything in oil and vinegar, then roast for 40 minutes, until the beets are tender.

Serve just as is or squish the garlic cloves, releasing the cooked garlic, and toss the beets in the pulp before serving.

Excess garlic   Wild garlic pesto

In spring you can certainly have a glut of wild garlic. Here is an interesting pesto recipe that can be used to stir through vegetable dishes, stews, soups and sauces, or mixed with cream and served with cold chicken.

1 generous handful young wild garlic leaves, washed, dried and finely chopped
½ tsp (2 ml) sea salt
2 tbsp (30 ml) pine nuts or ground almonds
2 tbsp (30 ml) freshly grated Parmesan
Olive oil
Freshly ground black pepper

Put the chopped garlic leaves and sea salt in a mortar and pestle and grind until you have a paste. Add the pine nuts or ground almonds and mix well, then add the grated Parmesan. Once you have a thick, smooth paste, very slowly add the olive oil until you get the consistency you require. Season with a few grindings of pepper.

Spoon into a jar with a screw top and keep in the fridge for up to 7 days.

GOOD KING HENRY

(also known as All-Good, Good King Harry,
Good Neighbour, Wild Spinach,
Lincolnshire Asparagus)
Chenopodium bonus-henricus

More than 30 years ago I was working on a herb farm in the west country that went by the name "Tumbler's Bottom," and there I met Good King Henry and his cousin amaranth, both of which come from the fat hen family. It was this herb and its family that attracted me to the herb world. I was intrigued by their names and wanted to find out the origins. The research led me into finding out about all the herbs I grew, and the more I researched, the more I was fascinated. The outcome was my first herb collection, which in turn led to starting the herb farm and writing my first book in 1994.

Description

Good King Henry is a hardy perennial herb that dies back in winter, reappearing the following spring. It has tiny greenish yellow flowers in early summer. The leaves are green and arrow- or goosefoot-shaped, depending on how you look at it.

In spring it can be either grown from seed or by division of established plants. Plant in a sunny position in a well-draining soil that has been fed with well-rotted compost or manure in the previous autumn. It will, however, tolerate any soil conditions, with the exception of waterlogged. If the soil is weak, though, the plant will be underfed and the leaves will be tough. Good King Henry can be grown in large containers using a soil-based potting compost. Feed weekly during the growing season to prevent the leaves becoming tough.

History in cooking

Good King Henry was popular for hundreds of years until the past century. Traditionally the leaves were boiled and pounded with butter, the young flowering tips were eaten with salad, and the seeds were added to gruel or dried and ground into flour for bread making. In Lincolnshire, Good King Henry was cultivated and became known as Lincolnshire spinach. It was immensely popular until the sixteenth century, when the spinach we know today arrived from Asia and quickly replaced it and all other forms of the fat hen family. There was a slight blip in its favor after the Second World War, when because of the acute food shortage it was cultivated and the wild varieties foraged.

Harvesting and uses

Leaves

In early spring you will notice the appearance of new young shoots; these are much prized by top restaurants, as they can be eaten in the same way as asparagus. In mid-spring the young leaves, which are still tender, can be eaten raw in salads. From late spring onward the leaves become tougher and need to be cooked; they are ideal for adding to stuffings, soups, purées and savory pies. Because of the plant's long tap root, they are more nutritious than spinach or cabbage.

Flowers

Pick the flowering spikes as they begin to open in summer. These can then be steamed and served either hot, tossed in butter, or cold with a vinaigrette. They are, because of their high seed content, very grainy and so not to everyone's taste!

Seeds

As the seed pods start to turn light brown, from late summer until early autumn, collect the seeds by picking whole branches and laying them on trays of newspaper in a warm, dry place out of the sun. Within a few days you will notice that the seeds are being released. Lift the flowering branch carefully and all the seeds will drop onto the tray. Leave these seeds on the tray for a further week, then sift them away from the chaff (the stems and bits) and store them in an airtight container in a dark cupboard. They can be added to soups or ground and used with flour to make pita-type breads.

Properties

The leaves of Good King Henry and fat hen (see below) are rich in iron, calcium and vitamins B_1 and C. It is recommended that they be included in the diet of anyone suffering from anemia, because of their high iron content.

Other varieties

Tree Spinach, Giant Goosefoot
Chenopodium giganteum
This is a hardy annual with tiny greenish flowers in summer and arrow- or goosefoot-shaped leaves with serrated edges. The new leaves have the most wonderful magenta color that fades to green as it ages. The young leaves can be eaten raw in salads or cooked as spinach, when the color will revert to green.

Fat Hen, Lamb's Quarters, White Goosefoot, Common Pigweed, All-Good, Muckweed
Chenopodium album
Fat hen is a hardy annual with small greenish white flowers in summer and green lance- or goosefoot-shaped leaves. This herb can be found growing wild all over Europe, and its fatty seeds have been identified at Neolithic villages in Switzerland. The seeds can be ground into flour and used to make gruel.

GOOD KING HENRY CROQUETTES

This is a lovely simple supper dish or appetizer. You can use tree spinach (chaya) or ordinary spinach leaves instead of Good King Henry leaves, if you wish, which taste like a strong version of spinach. Serve with a classic tomato sauce and baked potatoes.

Serves 2

2 lb (900 g) young Good King Henry leaves
2 tbsp (30 ml) all-purpose flour, plus extra for dusting
½ tsp (2 ml) freshly grated nutmeg
1 egg, beaten
Salt and freshly ground black pepper
Oil, for frying

Cook the Good King Henry leaves in a small amount of boiling water until reduced to a soft mound, about 5 to 7 minutes. Drain through a colander and, with the back of a wooden spoon, squeeze out as much liquid as possible. Set aside until cool.

Mix the cooked Good King Henry leaves with the flour, nutmeg and beaten egg and add the salt and black pepper. Put in the fridge to firm up, about 40 minutes, or longer if required.

Remove from the fridge, form the firm mixture into cakes or croquettes, roll in a small amount of flour, then fry briefly on either side in a pan with a little oil until uniformly golden.

GOOD KING HENRY OMELET

The flavor of the leaves of Good King Henry is enhanced when combined with eggs. This is a highly nutritious meal that is ideal for lunch or supper served with a crisp green wild arugula salad.

Serves 2

2 tbsp (30 ml) unsalted butter, divided
1 clove garlic, very finely chopped
½ lb (225 g) Good King Henry leaves, washed and chopped
Salt and freshly ground black pepper
6 eggs, beaten well with a whisk for at least 1 minute

In a nonstick frying pan, melt 1 tbsp (15 ml) butter and cook the garlic and the Good King Henry until the leaves are fully wilted, adding a little more butter if required. Season, then pour in the beaten eggs and cook until they start to solidify.

TREE SPINACH MASHED POTATOES

This recipe was inspired by my mother. She was often making interesting variations on mashed potatoes because when I was growing up we had to make food stretch a long way. She was incredibly inventive with ingredients, creating many variations on a theme, both to extend different root vegetables and to combine root vegetables with other, soft-leaved varieties. This is one of her recipes that I have adapted for tree spinach, which has a dry spinach flavor. It is especially good during the summer, when one has the start of the main-crop potatoes and a mass of tree spinach leaves to hand. This is delicious with roasted chicken.

1 lb (450 g) tree spinach (chaya) leaves, cooked, then puréed using a hand blender or food processor
2 lb (900 g) Yukon Gold potatoes, cooked and mashed by hand for a rough texture with a knob of butter and 1 beaten egg
Salt and freshly ground black pepper
Grated nutmeg

Combine the puréed spinach with the mashed potatoes by hand rather than using a mixer, which makes it too smooth and glue-like. Add the salt, pepper and nutmeg to taste.

Excess Good King Henry

If you do have a glut of this herb I suggest you cook it like spinach, squeeze out any excess water, and put it in a plastic container. Once cold, seal, then freeze. This can then be used for mashed potatoes, croquettes, sauces or soups.

HORSERADISH

(also known as Cranson de Bretagne, Rafano, Mountain Radish)

Armoracia rusticana, syn. *Cochlearia armoracia*

As a child I used to walk down the main street in Chew Magna every Sunday to get the newspapers for my parents. One Sunday I saw Mr. Bell, our neighbor, sitting outside his cottage crying. This really worried me, for I had not seen a grown man cry before. He saw me, saw my concern and called me over. Smiling through his tears, he said he was grating horseradish for the Sunday roast. As soon as I drew near, I also started crying from the pungency of the root. So every autumn as I prepare the roots for preserving, I remember Mr. Bell.

Description

Horseradish is a very hardy herbaceous perennial that dies back in winter, reappearing in the spring. It has large mid-green leaves and white flowers in summer. One should carefully consider growing this herb in the garden as it is so invasive. It spreads when you dig up the plant, for it is impossible to remove all the root, because it is very, very long, and any bit left in the soil will automatically produce a new plant. So once you begin to harvest you will start the plant spreading.

It is a most tolerant plant, liking all but the driest of soils. It prefers a sunny site but will tolerate dappled shade. If large quantities are required, horseradish should be given a patch of its own where the roots can be lifted and the soil replenished each autumn. If you have a small garden, consider growing this herb in a trash can; this makes it easy to control and very easy to harvest in the autumn.

History in cooking

Horseradish has been in cultivation for more than 3,000 years. It is said to be one of the five bitter herbs (along with coriander, horehound, lettuce and nettle) that the Jews ate during the feast of Passover.

In the Middle Ages horseradish was used as a painkiller as well as a condiment. In the sixteenth century, John Gerard, an English herbalist, noted in his book *Gerard's Herbal* that horseradish (which he calls *Raphanus rusticanus*) grew wild in several parts of England. He says: "The Horse Radish stamped with a little vinegar put thereto, is commonly used among the Germans for sauce to eate fish with and such like meates as we do mustarde."

Interestingly, this herb was not cultivated in the United States until the mid-1850s, when settlers started horseradish farms in the Midwest.

Harvesting and uses

Leaves
These can be picked and eaten in early spring, particularly in salads. However, the flavor is not to everyone's palate – and that includes mine – as it is rather dry and mustard-like.

Roots
Lift roots in autumn. The flavor of grated horseradish root is like an extremely strong radish; it can be used in coleslaw or dips or with pickled beets, cream cheese, mayonnaise and avocado fillings. Make horseradish sauce to accompany roast beef and smoked oily fish.

Properties
The reason horseradish is used in sauces and vinegars and as an accompaniment to other dishes is because the volatile flavoring oil, which is released when it is grated, evaporates rapidly, so it becomes nothing when cooked. But raw – that's a different story. The volatile oil contains vitamins A, B and C and is rich in sulfur, phosphorus, potassium, iron and magnesium. Horseradish, because of its powerful flavor, stimulates the digestion.

Other varieties

Variegated Horseradish
Armoracia rusticana 'Variegata'
This variety is a hardy herbaceous plant with white flowers in summer and large green/cream variegated oblong leaves. The edible root can be used in the same way as green-leaved horseradish.

Japanese Horseradish, Wasabi
Wasabia japonica syn. *Cochlearia wasabi*
This is a subtropical plant that has edible leaves, flowers and rhizomes. The fleshy rhizomes are finely grated and prepared to make a green paste that is widely used in Japan. As with horseradish, the flavor rapidly deteriorates once the root is cut or grated.

ICED TOMATOES AND HORSERADISH SAUCE

This is a recipe from my grandmother's notebook. She was given it by a friend of hers named Nancy Shaw, and it appears in her book *Food for the Greedy*, published in 1936:

"Very good to serve as a salad on a hot summer day with tomatoes skinned and put in the ice chest till very cold, and at the last moment some good creamy horseradish sauce poured over them. The sauce to be just slightly iced. With a joint of cold lamb this is excellent. The best horseradish sauce to use is made by grating some horseradish into mayonnaise to which has been added some cream." Here is my adaptation.

Serves 6

1 lb (450 g) cherry tomatoes
2/3 cup (150 ml) whipping (35%) cream
3 tbsp (45 ml) grated horseradish
2/3 cup (150 ml) mayonnaise
Chervil or parsley leaves, to decorate

Place the cherry tomatoes in a bowl, pour on boiling water and leave for a few minutes, then peel. Place the tomatoes in a serving dish, cover and put in the fridge until they need to be served.

Lightly whip the cream. Put the horseradish in a bowl, stir in the mayonnaise and fold into the cream. Cover and place in the fridge.

When ready to serve, spoon the horseradish sauce over the tomatoes and decorate with the chervil or parsley leaves.

HORSERADISH EGG MOUSSE

My father would eat horseradish with everything if given half a chance. I have known him to have horseradish cream with baked apples. He was extremely greedy when this mousse was served by my mother; you had to hope that the dish was not given to him first as it went around the table.

The combination of the eggs with the hotness of the horseradish and the coolness of the cucumber is delightful.

Serves 4

8 hard-boiled eggs, shelled
¾ cup + 2 tbsp (200 ml) chicken stock
1 tbsp (15 ml) gelatin
Sea salt and freshly ground black pepper
Pinch of cayenne
1 tbsp (15 ml) grated horseradish
2/3 cup (150 ml) whipping (35%) cream, lightly whipped
3 tbsp (45 ml) chopped chervil or dill
½ cucumber, peeled and coarsely grated, to garnish

Chop the eggs fairly finely and put in a large bowl.

Heat the stock and melt the gelatin in it, then strain it over the eggs and mix gently. Season with salt and pepper and add the cayenne and horseradish. Fold in the cream and chopped herbs, then turn into a food processor and blend briefly, stopping before it becomes smooth.

Pour the mixture into a 4-cup (1 L) soufflé dish and chill in the fridge for 3 to 4 hours, or overnight.

Serve chilled, with the grated cucumber scattered over the top.

STIR-FRIED BEEF IN HORSERADISH YORKSHIRE PUDDINGS

Infusing the batter with the horseradish counteracts the effect of cooking, so the flavor is wonderful.

Serves 4

¾ cup (175 ml) all-purpose flour
2 medium eggs
½ cup (125 ml) whole milk
2 tbsp (30 ml) grated horseradish (if using preserved horseradish, drain the vinegar before use; if using bought, get the relish/sauce, not the cream variety)
5 tbsp (75 ml) vegetable oil, divided
2 tbsp (30 ml) butter, divided
12 oz (350 g) beef steak, cut into thin strips
1 large onion, halved and thinly sliced
7 tbsp (100 ml) red wine
¾ cup + 2 tbsp (200 ml) beef stock

Preheat the oven to 425°F (220°C).

Place the flour, eggs and milk in a bowl. Season and mix with an electric beater for at least 3 to 5 minutes or until smooth and frothy on the surface. Mix in the horseradish. Pour the batter into a measuring cup and leave to stand at room temperature for 1 to 2 hours.

Either put 4 tbsp (60 ml) oil in a large roasting pan or use a 6-hole muffin or popover tin and put 1 tbsp (15 ml) oil in each of 4 sections. Place in the oven for about 10 minutes or until the oil just begins to smoke. Pour the batter into the pan. Cook for 15 minutes or until risen and golden.

While the pudding is cooking, melt half the butter with 1 tbsp (15 ml) oil in a large frying pan over high heat. Stir-fry the beef for 5 minutes or until brown. Using a slotted spoon, transfer to a plate and set aside in a warm place.

Return the frying pan to the heat and add the onion. Cook for 5 minutes or until golden. Pour in the wine and bring to a boil for 1 minute or until almost all the liquid has evaporated. Add the stock and boil for a further 5 minutes or until reduced slightly. Stir in the remaining butter to create a glossy gravy. Mix in the meat and season to taste.

HORSERADISH CREAM

This is a deluxe version of horseradish sauce that goes so well with meat, smoked fish and cheese. It is especially good served with cold beef, smoked mackerel or an avocado and apple salad.

Makes ½ cup (125 ml)

6-inch (15 cm) piece fresh horseradish (or use 1 tbsp/15 ml preserved horseradish in vinegar, drained, and omit the lemon juice)
1 tbsp (15 ml) unsalted butter
2 tbsp (30 ml) fresh bread crumbs
1 apple
2 tsp (10 ml) yogurt
1 tsp (5 ml) lemon juice
Pinch of salt
Pinch of sugar
1 tsp (5 ml) chopped fresh chervil, French tarragon and dill
4–5 tbsp (60–75 ml) whipping (35%) cream

Wash, peel and grate the fresh horseradish.

Melt the butter in a frying pan and add the bread crumbs. Fry until golden brown, remove from the heat and add the grated horseradish. Grate the apple into the mixture. Add the yogurt, lemon juice, salt, sugar and chopped herbs. Set aside to cool, then chill in the fridge.

Just before serving, gently fold the cream into the mixture.

Excess horseradish

Horseradish vinegar

This is the best way to preserve horseradish for use throughout the year. Always strain the grated root before using.

Freshly grated horseradish root
White distilled malt vinegar

Per jar:
½ tsp (2 ml) salt
¼ tsp (1 ml) sugar

One very good tip for how to prevent your eyes from streaming when grating horseradish is to wash and peel the root, then put it in the freezer in a plastic bag. Leave for 1 hour, then remove and grate it.

Fill a small or medium jam jar to about two-thirds full with horseradish, depending on how much you have grated. Add the salt and the sugar, cover with the malt vinegar and shake well. If using a metal lid, put a piece of waxed paper on the underside to stop it corroding.

The vinegar can be stored for at least 1 year, if not longer.

HYSSOP

(also known as Herbe Sacrée, Issopo)
Hyssopus officinalis

I love this Mediterranean herb, for in summer it abounds with bees and butterflies – they adore the blue flowers. It is one of my must-haves when I am designing a herb garden, especially if the herb and vegetable gardens are intertwined. The fact that hyssop attracts bees to the garden means that pollination of the vegetables increases, and this in turn increases their yield. In the kitchen it has been a great standby herb; it adds another dimension to food and, I believe, is underused, so its full potential has yet to be discovered.

Description

Hyssop is a hardy herb with semi-evergreen leaves, which means that some leaves can be picked throughout the winter. It is short-lived, lasting about four to five years, with attractive spikes of small dark blue tubular flowers throughout the summer. The small, lance-shaped green leaves are aromatic in scent and slightly bitter, not sour in flavor when eaten straight from the plant. Like its cousins rosemary and thyme, it prefers well-drained soil and a sunny position in the garden.

It can either be grown from seed sown in the early summer or is easily grown from cuttings taken from the new growth in late spring or early summer. This herb happily adapts to being container grown; plant in pots using a soil-based compost.

History in cooking

Historically hyssop is said to have been mentioned in the Bible, but there is some dispute about whether it is this plant or an *Origanum*. It certainly was used by Hippocrates (460–377 BC), who recommended it for chest complaints – for which it is still used today.

Harvesting and uses

Leaves
Pick young leaves from early spring until early winter to use fresh or, in summer, from nonflowering stems for drying. The leaves are quite strong in flavor, so do not be too lavish with them. Use them in salads and with meat stews, soups and stuffings. In the United States hyssop is added to apple pie.

Flowers
Pick flowers in summer just as they open to use fresh or dry – the scent becomes more intense when dried. The flowers are delicious tossed in green salads.

Properties

It is said that this herb helps aid digestion, especially when eaten with rich, oily foods. It is also a beneficial antioxidant. Medicinally it is used to treat congestion and coughs.

Other varieties

Pink Hyssop
Hyssopus officinalis 'Roseus'
Dense spikes of small pale sugar pink flowers from summer until early autumn. Small, narrow, lance-shaped aromatic green leaves.

Rock Hyssop
Hyssopus officinalis subsp. *aristatus*
Dense spikes of small dark blue flowers from summer until early autumn. Small, narrow, lance-shaped aromatic green leaves.

White Hyssop
Hyssopus officinalis f. *albus*
Dense spikes of small white flowers from summer until early autumn. Small, narrow, lance-shaped aromatic green leaves.

ROASTED PARSNIPS, HYSSOP AND DATES

The combination of the sweetness of the roasted parsnips and the dates with the bitter, aromatic leaves of the hyssop transforms this roasted vegetable dish. Serve with mashed potatoes and roast meat or boiled ham.

Serves 2–4

1 lb (500 g) small parsnips, peeled, halved lengthwise and cut into 2½-inch (6 cm) chunks (If using mature wintered stock, remove the center core, especially if it has become woody)
12 oz (350 g) small onions, cut into quarters
4 cloves garlic, peeled and sliced
4 sprigs hyssop leaves, removed from their stems
Olive oil
4½ oz (125 g) feta cheese, cubed
Handful of black olives, pitted
Handful of dates, pitted

Preheat the oven to 400°F (200°C).

Put the prepared parsnips, onions and garlic in a heavy roasting pan with the leaves from 3 of the hyssop sprigs. Drizzle with olive oil and roast for about 45 to 50 minutes until golden. During the roasting, shake the pan several times to evenly brown the vegetables and stop them sticking.

Scatter with the feta, olives, dates and remaining hyssop leaves. Return to the oven for 5 to 10 minutes.

HYSSOP-BAKED PEPPERS

This is a succulent rustic lunch or light supper. The aromatic, bitter flavor of the hyssop combined with the sweetness of the peppers and ripe tomatoes is delightful. Make sure you serve this with some crusty fresh bread so you can mop up the juices.

Serves 2–4

4 red bell peppers
3 cloves garlic
Salt
2 sprigs hyssop leaves, removed from the stems and finely chopped
Olive oil
16 ripe cherry tomatoes
8 anchovy fillets

Preheat the oven to 400°F (200°C).

Halve the peppers lengthwise, remove and discard the white core and seeds, then lay the peppers, cut side up, in a greased baking dish. They should fit snugly.

Peel the garlic, slice it finely and put a few slices in each halved pepper, together with a little salt, a pinch of hyssop leaves and 1 tbsp (15 ml) oil. (If you are using anchovies in olive oil, use this oil, as it adds extra flavor.) Halve the tomatoes – there's no need to peel these small tomatoes – and tuck them into the peppers. Bake in the oven until the peppers have almost collapsed and are full of juice.

Either drain the anchovies, if in oil, on paper towels, or if in brine, rinse and dry them. Roughly chop the anchovy fillets and stir 1 tsp (5 ml) into each of the peppers. Return to the oven for 10 minutes, then serve.

SPANISH HYSSOP TORTILLAS

Tortillas, or baked omelets, are easy and versatile; they can be eaten hot or cold, for lunch or for supper, smart or casual. My favorite way is to serve them warm with an arugula salad and a cold glass of white wine.

The use of hyssop in this recipe adds a clean, bitter, minty flavor to the dish.

Serves 3–6

1 medium onion
10 oz (275 g) small Yukon Gold potatoes
3 tbsp (45 ml) olive oil, divided
Salt and freshly ground black pepper
2 tsp (10 ml) hyssop leaves, finely chopped
5 eggs

First peel and cut the onion in half, then thinly slice each half and separate the layers into half-moon shapes. If you have a food processor, slice the potatoes thinly; if not, use a potato peeler. Doing this by hand will take time, so to stop them turning brown, fill a large bowl with cold water and thinly slice the potatoes into the water. When they are sliced, drain them and rub them dry in a clean dish towel.

Heat 2 tbsp (30 ml) of the olive oil in a heavy-bottomed frying pan that is approximately 8 inches (20 cm) in diameter and has a lid. When the oil is hot, add the potatoes and onions and toss them around in the oil to get well coated. Turn the heat down to its lowest setting and add a good sprinkling of salt and black pepper, plus the finely chopped hyssop leaves. Put the lid on the pan and let the onions and potatoes cook gently for 20 minutes or until tender. Turn them over halfway through and shake the pan from time to time, as they are not supposed to brown very much but just gently cook.

Break the eggs into a large bowl, whisk them lightly with a fork (do not overbeat) and add some salt and pepper. When the onions and potatoes are cooked, quickly add them to the eggs in the bowl.

Put the frying pan back on the heat and add the rest of the oil. Mix the potato and eggs thoroughly before pouring the whole lot into the frying pan and immediately turning the heat down to its lowest setting. Cook, uncovered, very slowly for 20 to 25 minutes. When there is virtually no liquid egg left on the surface of the omelet, turn it over to cook the other side. (The easiest way to do this is to place either the lid or a plate over the pan, invert the omelet onto it, then gently ease the omelet back into the pan using a thin metal spatula.)

Put the frying pan back on the heat and cook for a further few minutes. It should be cooked through but still moist in the center.

HYSSOP FISH CAKES

Living where I do, I cannot simply run out to the store, so I have a modern form of old-fashioned larder where I keep cans of food. These prove immensely useful on days when we are snowed in or I simply have not made time to shop. My larder includes canned tomatoes, honey, anchovies and tuna, to name but a few, and this is a great supper made from its offerings. Serve with a homemade tomato sauce (see page 12) and green beans or a fresh green salad.

Serves 4

2/3 cup (150 ml) olive oil
1 onion, finely chopped
2 x 5-oz (140 g) cans tuna, drained
1¼ cups (280 ml) leftover mashed potato (or if making specially, allow to cool before using)
1 tsp (5 ml) finely chopped hyssop leaves, removed from the stem
2 eggs, beaten, divided

Heat a little of the olive oil in a frying pan, add the onion and gently fry until soft. Add to a mixing bowl and allow to cool.

Once cool, add the tuna and mix well. Add the mashed potato and the chopped hyssop and mix again, then add half of the beaten eggs. Form the mixture into 8 flat cakes. Dip each cake into the remaining egg.

Add some extra oil to the frying pan and return it to the heat. Add the fish cakes and gently fry them for 5 minutes on each side.

Excess hyssop

Hyssop butter

This butter can be used with vegetables, soups, stews and casseroles and for grilled meat or fish.

Makes ½ cup (125 ml) butter

Handful of hyssop leaves
½ cup (125 ml) unsalted butter

Remove the hyssop leaves from their stems. Chop roughly, then add the butter and keep chopping the butter and hyssop leaves together to release the oils in the leaves into the butter.

Once you have reached the size of leaf you require, use a fork to gather up the butter. When it has been thoroughly mixed, pack it into a roll of waxed paper and place in the fridge for up to 24 hours before use. The longer you leave it, the better the flavor.

This butter can also be frozen for 2 to 3 months. Place it in a plastic bag or plastic container and don't forget to label it so you know which herb it is.

LAVENDER

(also known as Lavande, Lavanda)
Lavandula

Lavender is the quintessential herb; it smells good, looks good and does you good. It is the traditional English garden herb. Neither my mother nor my grandmother would have used it in cooking and it is a herb that I use sparingly. It is particularly useful in winter when I want another flavor than rosemary. It is also extremely good infused in sugar for making cakes, cookies and desserts.

Description

This very popular herb can be either a hardy evergreen shrub with highly aromatic gray leaves or a tender evergreen shrub with more of a eucalyptus- rather than lavender-scented leaf. It all depends on the variety. The standard lavender-scented plants have medium to long spikes of blue-mauve flowers all summer long, whereas the French forms have more of a eucalyptus scent to the leaves, with a small dark purple flower head that is topped with two colored bracts that are often called ears. The varieties with the best culinary flavors are mentioned below, and these are all hardy.

Lavenders can be raised from seed but this does take time, and even more important, it is far more reliable to raise the plant from cuttings taken from nonflowering stems in late spring. All the species need an open, sunny position and fertile, well-drained soil. They will adapt to semi-shade as long as the soil is well drained; otherwise they may die in winter. If you have very cold winter temperatures, I recommend that you grow lavender in a container that can be given protection.

History in cooking

Historically the Romans first introduced French lavender to Britain when they invaded. They brought the flower heads over dried and ground them to use as a condiment. The use of lavender as a condiment was much more common in medieval times because fresh meat was rare and difficult to keep. Condiments were used to hide the disagreeable flavors and tastes of semi-cooked or half-rotten flesh.

Harvesting and uses

Leaves
Harvest before flowering, all year round. Being evergreen, though, the best flavor is in early summer. The leaves can be used fresh or can be dried. They can be added sparingly to roast meat and used in stuffings.

Flowers
Cut the flowers in summer, just as they open, to use fresh and also for drying. Dry on open trays or by hanging in small bunches. The flowers can be used sparingly in cooking. They are good for flavoring sugar, which in turn is good for baking cookies and cakes.

Properties

I can find no other identified culinary properties for lavender than its use as a flavoring. Medicinally, the oil is antimicrobial and has sedative properties; it is used to treat insomnia, panic, shock and nervous palpitations. It is one of the best herbs for keeping flies out of the kitchen.

Varieties

Common Lavender, English Lavender
Lavandula angustifolia (syn. *L. spica*, *L. officinalis*)
This hardy perennial evergreen shrub has mauve-purple flowers on long spikes in summer and long, narrow pale greenish gray aromatic leaves. It is one of the most popular and well known of this group of lavenders. The flowers and leaves are good with meat and to infuse sugars.

Hidcote Lavender
Lavandula angustifolia 'Hidcote'
This is a hardy perennial evergreen shrub with richly scented short, rounded spikes of deep purple-blue flowers in summer and short, narrow aromatic gray leaves. The flowers and leaves are good with meat and to infuse sugars.

Old English Lavender
Lavandula x *intermedia* Old English Group
This hardy perennial evergreen shrub has aromatic long, pointed spikes of clear pale blue-purple flowers in summer and long, narrow aromatic silver-gray green leaves. The flowers and leaves are also good with meat and to infuse sugars.

French Lavender
Lavandula stoechas
This is a frost-hardy perennial evergreen shrub. It has attractive small deep purple flowers clustered around small flowering stalks topped with short mauve-purple bracts (ears) from early summer until early autumn. The short green-gray narrow leaves are camphor-scented. The flower heads can be dried and used as a condiment and are also good in baking – but use with discretion.

Lavender Viridis
Lavandula viridis
Another frost-hardy perennial evergreen shrub. This unusual lavender has green bracts with a cream center tuft. The leaves are green, narrow and highly aromatic, with a eucalyptus scent and flavor. Good with strongly flavored meats.

BROILED LEFTOVER TURKEY WITH LAVENDER BUTTER AND PIQUANT SAUCE

This recipe is a true hand-me-down. It is a great way to use up leftover Christmas or Thanksgiving turkey. That is where, I guess, it originated, as my grandmother's name before marrying was Hirsch, and I believe she was born in Hungary but lived her adult life in the United States. My mother adapted Ruth's recipe and I have adapted hers, so here is a third-generation recipe. The lavender adds an aromatic piquancy to the whole meal.

My grandmother wrote: "Take a cold roast turkey, cut it into neat joints and cover with the herb butter. Grill over a slow fire and serve with a piquant sauce." So, to be more explicit, I have written out her recipes and put in the amounts. Serve with winter green vegetables.

Serves 4

For the lavender butter
20 leaves (in summer) or 35 leaves (in winter) from Old English Group or 'Hidcote' lavender
½ cup (125 ml) unsalted butter

For the piquant sauce
3 tbsp (45 ml) unsalted butter
1 onion, finely chopped
1 clove garlic, finely sliced
Salt and freshly ground black pepper
6½ tbsp (95 ml) all-purpose flour
1¼ cups (300 ml) turkey stock (made from the bones or a good bought poultry stock)
⅔ cup (150 ml) red wine
2 bay leaves
4 cloves
2 tsp (10 ml) lavender jelly (see page 158) or red currant jelly
Generous dash of Worcestershire sauce

1½ cups (375 ml) rice
8 slices cooked turkey

Make the butter the day before you need it to allow the flavors to infuse. Remove the leaves from the stems and gently chop to release the oils. Then mix the chopped leaves with the butter. Cover and place in the fridge for at least 24 hours before use. The longer you leave it, the better the flavor.

On the day you are serving this dish, make the piquant sauce. In a small saucepan, melt the butter and gently fry the onion and garlic with a good pinch of salt until soft. Add the flour, stir until it absorbs all the juices and cook for 2 minutes, stirring regularly. In a separate pan combine the stock and the wine, bring to a boil and simmer for a few minutes to burn off the alcohol.

Turn the heat right down and slowly add about one-quarter of the infused stock to the cooked flour, stirring well to eliminate lumps. Once you have a smooth (not counting the onion) paste, slowly add the remaining three-quarters of the stock.

Add the bay leaves and cloves to the pan and stir regularly until the sauce is cooked, about 5 minutes. Do not boil. Remove the cloves and bay leaves. Add the jelly and stir well. Add a dash of Worcestershire sauce (this was my mother's secret ingredient) and check the seasoning. If necessary, add more lavender jelly so that you get a hint of lavender; it must not be overpowering or too sweet. Keep the sauce on low heat while you cook the rice and the turkey.

Cook the rice according to the package instructions. Preheat the broiler to low, smear the slices of turkey with the lavender butter and place under the broiler, turning from time to time so that all the turkey becomes slightly crispy.

To serve, place the turkey on the rice, pour some sauce over and put the remainder in a jug so everyone can help themselves.

LAVENDER AND SWEET WINE JELLY

Fruit jellies are something that were a particular favorite at children's parties when I was a child. If you went to a fancy birthday party you often had a chocolate blancmange rabbit surrounded by bright green jelly. It always looked amazing and tasted not as good as it looked! This, on the other hand, is a scrumptious dessert; the combination of the aromatic lavender with the sweetness of the dessert wine is a winner.

Serves 4–6

2 oz (55 g) fresh lavender flowers
1 cup + 2 tbsp (275 ml) water
1 cup + 2 tbsp (275 ml) white dessert wine
¼ cup (60 ml) lavender sugar (see page 159)
1 pouch (1 tbsp/15 ml) powdered gelatin
Juice of 1 orange

Put the lavender flowers, water and wine in an enamel or stainless steel pan, not aluminum or untreated metal. Heat very, very gently until it reaches just below boiling. Remove from the heat, cover and let the water, wine and flowers infuse for 10 minutes.

Strain the liquid, using a nylon sieve, into a glass or china bowl and stir in the lavender sugar until dissolved. Check the flavor and add more sugar if required.

Sprinkle the gelatin onto the orange juice and allow to soften, then warm gently until dissolved. Stir into the wine mixture and pour the jelly into 4 individual pretty glasses or bowls. Chill the jelly in the fridge until set.

Remove from the fridge when you serve the main course so that the jelly is not cold when served. Serve just as it is.

LAVENDER MERINGUE ICE CREAM

I learned this recipe from my mother, who used to have it on standby in the freezer for special meals or unexpected dinners. She became renowned for it, especially during the first Glastonbury Festival, which was held in our village, when our home became neutral ground between the show organizers and the village.

I have adapted her recipe by infusing the sugar with lavender. When cooked as meringues it is lovely, as it removes the harshness of the lavender to give one a warm, aromatic flavor. Topped with fresh fruit, this is summer on a plate.

Serves 6–8

For the meringues
3 eggs
1 cup (250 ml) lavender flower–infused fruit (superfine) sugar (see page 159)

For the ice cream
1¼ cups (300 ml) whipping (35%) cream
Dash of milk
1 tbsp (15 ml) kirsch

Seasonal summer fresh fruit (such as red currants, raspberries or strawberries), for the topping

Preheat the oven to 275°F (140°C) and line two baking sheets with nonstick baking parchment.

Make the meringues. A top tip for making meringues is to make sure that all the utensils are spotlessly clean; if there is the slightest trace of grease, your egg whites will not form those strong, firm peaks necessary for great meringues.

Separate the eggs, putting the whites in a mixing bowl. (The egg yolks can be added to mashed potatoes or omelets or used for making custard.) Using an electric hand mixer on slow speed, whisk the egg whites until they start to froth, then slowly increase the speed to maximum. Keep whisking until the egg whites form stiff white peaks. With the mixer on the fastest speed, slowly add the sugar. When all is amalgamated, turn off your machine. If you overprocess at this point the egg whites may collapse.

With two spoons, scoop the mixture onto the baking sheets to make individual meringues. Alternatively, put half the mixture in the middle of each sheet, then, using the handle of a metal spoon, in swirling movements slowly spread the mixture out into a circle about ¾ inch (2 cm) deep. I usually make half and half so I have the option of different desserts.

Place the baking sheets in the oven for 45 minutes to 1 hour. If you like gooey centers, remove the meringues from the oven immediately at the end of the cooking time, but if you like crisp centers, turn the heat off, open the door of the oven and leave the meringues to cool inside. For the meringue ice cream I prefer crisp, because when you combine it with the cream it will become a bit gooey anyway.

Whisk the cream with a dash of milk until it is very thick, then add the kirsch. Break the meringues into chunks, then fold into the cream. Immediately put the mixture in a large serving bowl, cover with plastic wrap and put in the freezer to set (about 2 to 3 hours, until firm). Remove the ice cream from the freezer just before you serve. Top with the fresh fruit. Delicious.

LAVENDER OAT COOKIES

Makes approx. 12 cookies

1/3 cup (75 ml) unsalted butter,
plus extra for greasing
2/3 cup (150 ml) all-purpose flour
3/4 tsp (3 ml) baking powder
Pinch of salt
1 cup (250 ml) rolled oats
1/3 cup (75 ml) sugar
1 tbsp (15 ml) corn syrup
1 tbsp (15 ml) milk
1 tsp (5 ml) lavender leaves,
removed from the stem and finely
chopped
1 tsp (5 ml) lavender flowers,
removed from the flowering spike
and left whole

These lavender cookies are lovely on their own, with a cup of tea or served with crème fraîche and fresh summer fruit, especially raspberries. The combination of the clean, fruity flavor of the raspberries with the aromatic flavor of the lavender cooked into a sweet oatmeal cookie, to me signals summer.

Preheat the oven to 350°F (180°C). Grease a baking sheet with butter, then line it with baking parchment.

Sift the flour, baking powder and salt into a bowl, add the oats and sugar and mix well. In a small saucepan over low heat, melt the butter with the syrup and milk and stir until well amalgamated. Add the flour, oats, sugar and lavender leaves and mix well. Remove from the heat and stir in the lavender flowers.

Scoop large spoonfuls of the mixture onto the prepared baking sheet and shape into rounds, leaving a space between each. Place in the oven and bake for 10 to 15 minutes, until golden brown. Remove from the oven, leave on the baking sheet for 5 minutes, then lift the parchment onto a wire rack and leave the cookies to cool completely.

Excess lavender

Lavender jelly

This is a great way to preserve the flavor of lavender. This jelly can be used in cakes and it is also lovely with roast lamb.

The following quantities should fill 4 x 1-pint (450 g) jam jars

4 lb (1.75 kg) cooking apples
7 cups (1.75 L) water
2 lb (1 kg) sugar
1/2 cup + 1 tbsp (140 ml) lavender flowers (stems removed, but leave the flower heads unplucked as they can be put complete into a piece of cheesecloth for cooking)
1/3 cup (75 ml) lemon juice

Wash and chop the apples and put them in a large saucepan with a lid. Add the water, bring to a boil, then simmer until the apples are soft and pulpy – this takes from 20 to 30 minutes, depending on the variety of apple. Pour carefully into a cheesecloth bag or jelly bag and leave for a day or overnight to drain into a large bowl.

Once drained, measure the juice and add 1 lb (450 g) sugar for every 2½ cups (600 ml) juice. Put the juice and sugar in a large saucepan and bring to a boil, adding the lavender flowers tied in a piece of cheesecloth. Leave 1 tbsp (15 ml) flowers, removed from the flower heads, aside to go in the jelly as decoration, if you wish. However, remember that some people do not like bits in their jelly. Boil for about 20 minutes, until setting point is reached.

At this point remove the flowers in the cheesecloth and spoon off the surface scum. Stir in the lemon juice and reserved flowers, if you wish, and pour into warmed sterilized (see page 12) glass jars. Seal when cool, date and label.

Lavender sugar

With this sugar you can make lavender cookies, cakes and desserts, including meringues.

Makes 1¾ cups (425 ml) sugar

½–1 cup (125–250 ml) chopped lavender flowers
1¾ cups (425 ml) granulated or fruit (superfine) sugar

Pick the flowers after midday, making sure they are absolutely dry before starting the sugar. If you are unsure, remove the flower heads from their stems and spread them out on a baking sheet lined with baking parchment. Place them in the oven at very low heat (225°F /110°C), leaving the door open. Put the timer on, as the flowers should be dry in 10 minutes and you do not want to bake them.

Once dry, chop up the flowers and mix with the sugar. Put the sugar and flowers in a jar or tub with a lid. After a day, shake the container to make sure that the flowers are not making the sugar sticky and lumpy. After a week, give the container another shake and check the flavor of the sugar. If you feel it is not strong enough, seal the container again and leave for a further week. When you are happy with the strength of flavor, sift the sugar and flowers through a medium sieve. If you find that the sugar is lumpy, put it in a food processor and mix until fine. Pour into an airtight container and store; it will keep for 6 to 12 months, depending on the humidity of your kitchen.

LEMON BALM

(also known as Balm, Bee Balm, Sweet Balm, Melissa)
Melissa officinalis

As a gardener you cuss this herb because, like its cousin mint, it is invasive; however, as a cook I find it incredibly useful and underused. Neither my mother nor my grandmother used lemon balm for cooking, although I found out that my grandmother kept bees and planted it around the beehives. This is a traditional thing to do, as not only are the flowers high in nectar but also it was said that rubbing a new hive with the leaves encouraged the bees to settle, while the scent of the herb stopped bees swarming.

Description

Lemon balm is a hardy herb that dies back in winter and reappears in the spring. It has clusters of insignificant pale creamy flowers in summer and intensely lemon-scented mid-green oval, toothed, textured leaves.

It can be grown from seed or division and is a tolerant plant that will grow in all soils, provided it is not waterlogged. Ideally the best situation is well-drained soil in a sunny position. A word of warning: it will be invasive in light, fertile soils, but if you want to keep it under control it happily adapts to being grown in a container in a soil-based potting compost.

History in cooking

This herb is steeped in history; records show that more than 2,000 years ago the ancient Greeks and Romans prescribed lemon balm not only for indigestion and overindulgence but also to chase away melancholy. It was also popular in Elizabethan times for use in salads, as a tea and to flavor wine.

Harvesting and uses

Leaves

The best-flavored leaves are those picked before it flowers or from nonflowering stems, and are harvestable from early spring until autumn. When added to stewing fruit, the leaves cut down the amount of sugar needed and also remove the tartness. Fresh leaves can also be added to cream cheese, vinegars, wine cups and teas and can be chopped with vegetables.

Flowers

Pick the flowers throughout summer but remove all the green parts before use, as they do not have a flavor. Add the flowers to salads – both fruit and leaf – and use in jellies and butters.

Properties

Lemon balm is high in vitamins A, B and C, and it is a natural carminative and antispasmodic and a great digestive. A tea made from the leaves is not only a digestive, it is also calming and relaxing and helps to sharpen the memory!

Varieties

Golden Lemon Balm
Melissa officinalis 'All Gold'
This is similar to the standard lemon balm with the exception of the leaves, which are golden yellow. These leaves are prone to scorch, so plant in partial shade. To maintain good leaf color, cut back in summer. This variety can be propagated only by cuttings or division.

Variegated Lemon Balm
Melissa officinalis 'Aurea'
This is also similar to the standard lemon balm but has variegated gold and green leaves.

Both varieties can be used in cooking. However, the leaf flavor is milder than that of the straight green variety.

LEMON BALM SALSA

This is good with broiled fish and meat or any barbecue dish. The lemon balm leaves have a wonderful lemon flavor when crushed, so when they are combined with the ingredients below you can imagine how delightful this salsa is.

Serves 4

3 tbsp (45 ml) lemon balm leaves, finely chopped
1 hot chile pepper, seeded and finely chopped
1 clove garlic, crushed
1 medium red onion, coarsely chopped
5-oz (140 g) jar sun-dried tomatoes, drained and chopped
Juice of ½ lemon
7 tbsp (105 ml) light olive oil
1 tbsp (15 ml) white wine vinegar

Mix together all the ingredients, adding the oil a little at a time until you have a lovely thick salsa. Spoon into a serving bowl, cover and put in the fridge for at least 30 minutes so that all the flavors blend together.

ALMOND AND LEMON BALM STUFFED APPLES

Baked apples was one of my dad's favorite dishes. He was not a cook, but if he found out that Mum was cooking this he always made brandy butter or horseradish cream, either of which goes amazingly well with all forms of baked apple. The lemon balm added to the center of the apples lends a warm lemon flavor rather than the sharper citrus flavor that a lemon would give.

Serve with whipped cream, homemade custard sauce or, especially for my father, brandy butter.

Serves 4

4 large cooking apples (preferably Granny Smiths)
3 tbsp (45 ml) unsalted butter, plus 2 tbsp (30 ml) extra for dotting
2 tbsp (30 ml) sugar
½ cup (125 ml) ground almonds
2 tbsp (30 ml) finely chopped lemon balm
Zest of 1 lemon
1 tsp (5 ml) ground cinnamon
1 oz (25 g) flaked almonds, toasted
4 tbsp (60 ml) golden syrup

Preheat the oven to 350°F (180°C).

Wash and generously core the apples. Carefully, using a sharp knife, make a shallow slit in the skin, not deep into the flesh, running all the way around the apple's diameter. Place the apples in a roasting pan.

Cream the butter with the sugar, beat in the ground almonds and stir in the lemon balm, lemon zest, cinnamon and flaked almonds. Using a small spoon, put a quarter of this mixture into each cored apple, then drizzle 1 tbsp (15 ml) golden syrup over each apple, dot with butter and bake in the oven for about 15 minutes, until the apples are soft but not mushy.

LEMON BALM, LIME AND LEMON SORBET

I make no apology for including so many sorbets in this book, for it is one of the best ways to taste the flavor of an herb and they are wonderful digestives. Historically the Romans ate sorbets between courses during their enormous banquets to cleanse their palates.

Serves 4–6

1 cup (250 ml) fruit (superfine) or granulated sugar
1 cup + 2 tbsp (275 ml) water
1 large bunch lemon balm, leaves removed from their stems and finely chopped
Zest and juice of 5 limes
Zest and juice of 5 lemons

Place the sugar and water in a small saucepan over medium heat and stir with a wooden spoon until the sugar has melted. Bring to a boil, then simmer for 5 minutes. Remove from the heat and allow to cool.

Once the syrup has cooled, mix in the lemon balm leaves and the zest and juice of the limes and lemons. Pour into a freezerproof container and place in the freezer.

Remove from the freezer after 30 minutes, break up the ice using a fork and return to the freezer. Repeat this 30 minutes later and then again 3 more times. If you are not serving this within 24 hours, cover the sorbet after the final mixing and use within a month.

Excess lemon balm

Lemon balm vinaigrette

This is a useful vinaigrette; it is delicious on salads, including seafood and chicken salads, and can also be used to marinate fish or chicken before cooking. Alternatively, it can simply be served in a little bowl for your guests to spoon over their cooked fish or chicken.

1 tbsp (15 ml) shallots, very finely chopped
2 tbsp (30 ml) lemon balm leaves, finely chopped
½ tsp (2 ml) lemon zest
7 tbsp (105 ml) fresh lemon juice
5 tbsp (75 ml) white wine vinegar
1 tbsp (15 ml) Dijon mustard
1 tbsp (15 ml) soft brown sugar
1 cup + 1 tbsp (265 ml) light olive oil

In a bowl, mix together the shallots, lemon balm leaves, lemon zest, lemon juice, vinegar, mustard and sugar, then very slowly add the oil. Decant into a bottle with a tight-fitting lid.

This vinaigrette will keep in the fridge for a week. Shake well before using.

LEMON GRASS

(Also known as Fever Grass, Bhustrina, Takrai)
Cymbopogon citratus

It is amazing to think that, when I first started my herb farm more than 20 years ago, lemon grass was only just appearing in Chinese food stores, and now it is available 52 weeks of the year in many chain supermarkets. Over the years I have become a huge fan of this herb, especially since seeing it actually growing and flourishing in South Africa. There I could appreciate how classically elegant, in true grass fashion, this plant is, rather than the small plants I raise and the small stumps of stem I first used to buy all those years ago.

Description

Lemon grass is a tropical clump-forming grass with clusters of tiny flowers that appear only in the tropics, and lemon-scented linear gray-green leaves with robust cream and beige cane-like stems.

You can raise lemon grass from seed or from division, but if you live outside the tropics you will need to do this in a warm environment. You can successfully grow lemon grass outside only where the night temperature does not fall below 46°F (8°C). So in the northern hemisphere this herb can be planted out in summer only. Plant in any soil, including heavy soil, as long as the summers are hot and wet and the winters are warm and dry.

This herb makes an excellent container plant; use a loam-based compost and do not allow it to dry out in summer. In winter, bring the plant into a frost-free environment, 40°F (5°C) minimum.

When the light levels and night temperatures drop, the plant will go dormant, the grass gradually turns brown and the outside leaves shrivel. Reduce the watering to minimal over winter and cut back the grass to 4 inches (10 cm) above the stems. In early spring, as the days lengthen and the temperatures rise, you will notice the grass starting to grow; at this time cut off all dead growth and repot if necessary.

History in cooking

Lemon grass has been used for thousands of years in Thailand, China, Malaysia, Vietnam, Indonesia and the West Indies, where it is not just considered an important culinary herb but is also highly valued for its many medicinal properties. This herb has come to the fore in European and North American cooking only during the past 20 years.

Harvesting and uses

Leaves

Pick these throughout the summer in cold climates and all year in tropical climates. Young leaves have a much fuller flavor than older ones, which tend to have a slightly bitter undertone. The fresh leaves and stalks are traditionally used in Thai, Vietnamese and Caribbean cuisine. The lemon flavor complements curries, seafood, garlic and chile peppers. Tie a handful of leaves into a knot and add to water to flavor rice or steaming vegetables. Remove before serving.

Stems

Cut the stems from mature plants throughout the summer months in cold climates and all year round in tropical climates. To prepare the swollen stems, cut at the base just where the stem joins the soil and trim off the top leaves to save for later use. Peel off the outer green sheath around the thick stem; this will reveal a white core. Slice finely or pound the white stem to release the oils and flavors before adding them to your chosen dish.

Properties

The leaves and stems are rich in iron, chromium, magnesium, zinc, selenium, potassium and phosphorus; they also contain vitamins A, B and C. The digestive properties are carminative and diuretic. A tea made from fresh leaves is refreshing as well as being a stomach and gut relaxant. It is also a good antidepressant.

Other varieties

East Indian Lemon Grass, Cochin Grass, Malabar Grass
Cymbopogon flexuosus
This is similar to lemon grass except that it grows taller and the base stems have a red rather than beige color. It has a good lemon flavor and can be used in the kitchen in exactly the same way as lemon grass.

Palmarosa, Rosha Indian Geranium
Cymbopogon martinii var. *motia*
This is a smaller tropical grass than the two lemon grasses, and the linear gray-green leaves have the most heavenly rose scent. Use the leaves to flavor cakes, desserts and syrups. Infusing the leaves in milk and then adding the milk to various desserts is a wonderful way of using this herb.

SPICY LEMON GRASS AND BUTTERNUT SQUASH SOUP

This is a great combination: aromatic lemon grass and spicy hot chile with comforting butternut squash. A soup with gusto.

Serves 4–6

2 tbsp (30 ml) light olive oil
½-inch (1 cm) piece fresh ginger, peeled and grated
½ tsp (2 ml) finely sliced red chile pepper
1 tsp (5 ml) lemon grass stems, peeled and finely sliced
1 large onion, finely sliced
1 lb (500 g) butternut squash, peeled, sliced in half, seeded, then sliced into chunks
2 cloves garlic, finely chopped
1 tbsp (15 ml) light soy sauce
1²/₃ cups (400 ml) coconut milk or reduced-fat (2%) or 1% milk
1²/₃ cups (400 ml) water
Salt and freshly ground black pepper

Heat the oil in a large sauté pan and fry the ginger, chile pepper, lemon grass, onion and butternut squash, stirring constantly until just beginning to color. Add the garlic and cook for a few more minutes. Add the soy sauce, coconut milk or milk, and water. Bring to a boil, then reduce to a simmer and cook for about 25 minutes, until the squash is tender.

Using either a hand blender or a food processor, purée until smooth. Taste and add salt and pepper as required. Reheat but do not boil, and serve.

SALMON AND LEMON GRASS PARCEL

Cooking fish in foil keeps in the moisture and all the nutrients. Combining it with lemon grass leaves is lovely, as all the aroma and lemony, spicy taste of the leaves permeate the fish. Serve with boiled rice and green beans or a fresh green salad.

Serves 4

2 tsp (10 ml) butter
1 onion, very thinly sliced
3 cloves garlic, very finely chopped
2 tomatoes, peeled and finely chopped
Pinch of salt
2 lemon grass stems, peeled, then pounded and finely sliced
1 tsp (5 ml) ground cumin
Lemon grass leaves (to line the parcel)
10½ oz (300 g) skinless salmon fillets, cut into large chunks
2 limes, sliced
1 tbsp (15 ml) coriander leaves, chopped
1 tbsp (15 ml) flaked almonds, chopped

Preheat the oven to 325°F (160°C).

Melt the butter in a sauté pan, then add the onion and gently fry on very low heat until the onion is softened. Add the garlic and cook for a further minute.

Boil a kettle of water, place the tomatoes in a bowl and pour on the boiled water. Leave for a couple of minutes, drain, then carefully (don't burn your fingers) peel the tomatoes. Add the chopped tomatoes, salt, lemon grass stems and ground cumin. Stir, then cover the pan and cook gently on very low heat for 5 minutes. Stir from time to time to make sure nothing sticks.

Place a large piece of baking parchment or foil on a baking sheet and line with lemon grass leaves. Place the salmon on one side of the sheet, spoon the mixture over the fish and top with the lime slices, chopped coriander leaves and almond flakes. Cover with the other half of the sheet of foil or parchment, sealing the edges tightly by turning them over twice. Bake in the oven for 25 minutes.

Open the parcel (beware of steam when you do this), return to the oven and bake, opened, for a further 10 minutes.

TROUT WITH LEMON GRASS STUFFING

I made this for one of my husband Mac's famous birthdays. We had friends for dinner and they were amazed at how succulent the lemon grass kept the trout and the flavor. Give it a try, as it is delicious. Accompany the fish simply with new potatoes and a crisp green salad or dwarf green beans.

Serves 4

For the lemon grass stuffing
3½ tbsp (50 ml) unsalted butter
¾ cup (175 ml) shallots, finely chopped
2 tbsp (30 ml) lemon grass leaves, finely sliced
2 lemon grass stems, peeled and finely sliced
3 cups (700 ml) fresh bread crumbs
Sea salt and freshly ground black pepper

4 whole trout
3½ tbsp (50 ml) unsalted butter
1 tbsp (15 ml) lemon juice
1 lemon, quartered, to serve

Make the stuffing first. Melt the butter in a frying pan and gently fry the shallots until golden. Add the lemon grass leaves and stems and fry for a further few minutes, until they are soft. Add the bread crumbs and stir around until well mixed. Remove from the heat and season with salt and pepper to taste. Leave the stuffing to cool completely before using.

Clean and wash the fish. Make three shallow diagonal cuts on each side, then fill each with a little of the stuffing and place on a rack in a roasting pan or baking dish. Melt the butter in a small pan, add the lemon juice and use this liquid to baste the fish as they cook.

Preheat the broiler to its highest setting. Put the pan under the broiler for 5 minutes, turning and basting the fish after 2 minutes, then lower the heat to medium for a further 6 to 8 minutes, turning and again basting the fish halfway. Take care, as they can become fragile as they cook. Serve with the lemon quarters.

Excess lemon grass

Lemon grass oil

This oil is lovely for salad dressings, mayonnaise, stir-fry dishes and soups.

For more information about preserving and the risks of using herbs in oils, see page 36.

Makes 2 cups (500 ml) oil

5 swollen lemon grass stems
2 cups (500 ml) light olive oil
2 tsp (10 ml) lemon juice

Prepare the stems by removing the outer sheath and revealing the white inner stem. Slice finely, then, using a mortar and pestle, pound the stems until you have a paste (you may have to do this in a few batches). Add a small amount of oil, mix, then spoon into a medium-sized bowl. Repeat until you have turned all the stems into paste. Once all the paste is in the bowl, add the remaining oil and the lemon juice and stir well.

Pour into a container with a sealing lid and place in the fridge. Use within 5 days; shake well before use, as the lemon juice will separate.

Alternatively, after 2 days strain the oil through an unbleached paper coffee filter, pour into a clean sterilized container with a sealing lid and keep in the fridge. Use within 3 days; shake well before use.

LEMON VERBENA

(also known as Lippia, Vervain)
Aloysia triphylla syn. *Lippia citriodora)*

The scent of this herb transports me back down memory lane. Simply rubbing its rough leaves and releasing its sharp lemon-sherbet scent lifts the spirits and reminds me of my great-aunt Ann. She had this shrub growing by her back door, so as you entered the house from the garden you automatically brought the scent of lemon verbena with you.

Description

This herb is tender, so it will need protection below 40°F (4°C). It is a deciduous shrub, which means that it drops its leaves in winter, leaving it looking like a dead twig, which it is not. The new leaves appear late in the following spring. It has clusters of tiny white flowers tinged with lilac in early summer and rough pale green lance-shaped leaves that smell strongly of lemon sherbet.

Plant it in a light, free-draining soil in a warm, sunny site, preferably against a wall. It makes an ideal container plant; use a soil-based compost with extra grit. Place the container in a warm, sunny, light and airy spot and water well throughout the growing season. Protect from frost in winter by either bringing it into a cold greenhouse or cold frame (if it is in a container) or covering it with a cloche or horticultural fleece (if it is planted out).

History in cooking

There is very little history associated with this herb. It originated in South America and arrived in Europe in the 18th century, where it was used to perfume finger bowls during banquets.

Harvesting and uses

Leaves

These can be picked all summer, but the best-flavored leaves are those picked in early summer while they are bright green and before they start to lose color and curl in the autumn. The leaves can be used to flavor oils and vinegars, fruit desserts and jellies. They can transform homemade cakes too: simply lay whole leaves on the bottom of a well-greased cake pan, pour in the cake mixture, then bake in the usual way.

Flowers

Pick flowers throughout the summer. They have an intense lemon-sherbet flavor and are lovely scattered over fruit or salads or added to jellies.

Properties

The leaves contain vitamins A, B and C and they are digestive, antioxidant, antispasmodic and a sedative. A tea made from three to five leaves last thing at night helps the digestion, and as it is a mild sedative and calmative, it also aids a good night's sleep.

Other varieties

White Brush

Aloysia gratissima

This is a half-hardy deciduous shrub with delicate small, slightly vanilla-scented white or violet-tinged flowers and rough, lance-shaped leaves.

Its leaves are lightly minty, so they are great for making tea and adding a mint flavor to many dishes.

LEMON VERBENA CRÈME BRÛLÉE

My mother made the best crème brûlée. Alistair, my son, has inherited her passion for it and always rates restaurants and cooks on how well they make this dessert. This is a wonderful recipe; the flavor, with its hint of lemon sherbet, is unique, which makes this brûlée very special.

Serves 4

1 cup (250 ml) milk
1 handful lemon verbena leaves, finely chopped (reserve a few whole ones to garnish)
7 egg yolks
½ cup (125 ml) fruit (superfine) sugar
4 tbsp (60 ml) whipping (35%) cream
¼ cup (60 ml) Demerara sugar

Preheat the oven to 275°F (140°C).

Put the milk in a small saucepan with the chopped lemon verbena leaves, bring to the simmering point, remove from the heat and leave to cool and infuse.

Place the egg yolks in a bowl with the fruit sugar and whisk until pale and thick. Add the cooled infused milk and the cream and whisk well. Pass through a fine-meshed sieve.

Ladle the mixture into 4 ramekin dishes and set them in a roasting pan. Pour in enough water to come three-quarters of the way up the side of the ramekins, put in the oven and cook for 1 hour or until set. Leave to cool, then refrigerate until ready to serve.

Just before serving, sprinkle the Demerara sugar over the top of each dessert and caramelize either with a blowtorch or by putting them under a hot broiler. Decorate with some fresh lemon verbena leaves.

LEMON VERBENA SORBET

This is my favorite way of using lemon verbena; it is summer in a bowl.

Serves 4

2/3 cup (150 ml) water
¾ cup (175 ml) fruit (superfine) sugar
4 tbsp (60 ml) lemon verbena leaves, finely chopped, plus 8 whole leaves to garnish

Place the water in a small saucepan with the lemon verbena leaves, bring to a boil and simmer for 7 minutes to infuse the water. Add the sugar then bring to a boil for 5 minutes and stir regularly so the sugar thoroughly dissolves and does not stick. Remove from the heat and cool for 30 minutes to allow the flavors to infuse.

If you wish to be fancy, strain the infusion through a sieve, but if, like me, you love the leaves, simply pour the infusion into a freezerproof container and place in the freezer. Generally sorbet takes 2 hours to set. Rather than have a solid block, stir it to break up the ice after the first 30 minutes and repeat 3 more times at 30-minute intervals.

If you are not serving the sorbet the same day, cover it and use within a month. Serve garnished with a couple of fresh lemon verbena leaves.

RASPBERRY AND LEMON VERBENA FOOL

I cannot put into words how lovely this late summer/early autumn dessert is. I am lucky enough to be able to grow autumn-fruiting raspberries, and this dessert was created because I am greedy about raspberries and passionate about lemon verbena.

Serves 4

10 lemon verbena leaves, plus 4 more, finely chopped, to garnish
2 tbsp (30 ml) vodka
1 lb (500 g) raspberries
½ cup (125 ml) fruit (superfine) sugar
⅔ cup (150 ml) whipping (35%) cream

Place the lemon verbena leaves in a small bowl and add the vodka. Using a wooden spoon, crush the leaves in the vodka and leave to soak overnight.

The next day, crush the raspberries using a fork, then add the sugar a spoonful at a time. Strain the vodka, then add it to the raspberries. Whip the cream until it forms lines but not stiff peaks, then fold in the raspberries.

Serve in individual dishes, each decorated with 1 finely chopped lemon verbena leaf.

PLUM AND LEMON VERBENA CLAFOUTI

We tend to have prolific crops of plums, and on alternate years they tend to appear when I have lots of lemon verbena leaves. The delicious combination of the slightly acidic plums and the sweet yet dry citrus fragrance of lemon verbena is just magical.

Serves 4–6

Butter, for greasing
1 lb (500 g) plums (such as Victoria), washed, halved and pitted
3 tbsp (45 ml) lemon verbena leaves, removed from the stem and finely chopped
4 eggs
⅓ cup (75 ml) fruit (superfine) sugar
½ cup (125 ml) all-purpose flour
1¼ cups (300 ml) crème fraîche
3 tbsp (45 ml) brandy (optional)
2 tbsp (30 ml) powdered (confectioners') sugar, for dusting

Preheat the oven to 350°F (180°C). Butter a large gratin dish and arrange the plums on the bottom, cut side down. Sprinkle on the lemon verbena leaves.

In a bowl, whisk the eggs, stir in the sugar, then slowly mix in the flour. Add the crème fraîche and brandy (if using) and stir until well mixed. Pour the egg mixture over the plums and lemon verbena and bake in the oven for 30 to 40 minutes, until golden brown and firm to the touch.

Remove from the oven and let stand for 5 to 10 minutes. Serve in slices, dusted with powdered sugar.

Excess lemon verbena

Dried lemon verbena leaves

I have to be honest: this is the only herb I dry. That is because, being a deciduous plant, it sheds its leaves in winter, and I really do love a cup of lemon verbena tea, which the French call *vervain*, last thing at night to help me relax and sleep.

On a warm, sunny day, pick the healthiest leaves you can from your lemon verbena, as they are the ones with the best properties. Try not to bruise the leaves, as this will not only damage the leaf but also impair the flavor. Do not be too greedy; when picking in small amounts, it is easier to control the quality.

The object of good drying is to eliminate the water content of the plant and at the same time retain the essential oil. Spread the leaves thinly on a wooden frame covered in nylon screening or cheesecloth and place in a warm, dark, dry, well-ventilated room. If you have a spare room, this is ideal, with the curtains closed; alternatively, use a cupboard with the door left ajar. Turn the herbs over by hand several times during the first week. The leaves should take only about 5 days to be totally dry; the test is that they crumble easily when crushed.

Ideally, store the leaves in a dark glass jar with a screw top that is labeled with the name and date. It is well worth checking the container during the first few days to see if any moisture has started to form under the lid. If so, this will show that the herbs have not been totally dried, in which case return them to the drying area.

The shelf life is approximately 1 year for dried herbs. They are usually 3 to 4 times more powerful in flavor than fresh, so you need to use less of them in recipes and for teas.

LOVAGE

(also known as the Maggi herb, Love Parsley, Sea Parsley, Lavose, Liveche, Smallage, European Lovage)
Levisticum officinale

I cannot remember a time in my life when I have not been able to pick fresh lovage or harvest the seeds in autumn. My mother had a prolific plant in her garden, and in both the houses where I have lived I have also had a productive plant. If you have the space, I do recommend this herb, as it is so versatile.

Description

Lovage is a hardy herb that dies back in winter and reappears in the following spring. It will form a large plant in the garden – it can grow over 6 feet (2 m) high when in flower and spread to at least 3 feet (1 m) wide – so it is not recommended for a small plot. It has clusters of pale greenish flowers in summer that are followed by dark brown aromatic seeds. The leaves are dark green and deeply divided, with toothed edges.

When planting lovage, prepare the site with well-rotted manure, as it prefers rich, moist but well-drained soil in full sun or partial shade. You can raise it from seed sown in the garden in autumn or from plants created by division of established clumps in early spring, just as the new shoots emerge. You can grow it in containers, but being a vigorous plant it will need repotting every year.

History in cooking

This herb has been cultivated for thousands of years. The Romans preserved the leaves in vinegar for year-round flavoring, the ancient Greeks chewed the seed to aid digestion and relieve flatulence and medieval monks grew it in their cloister gardens for many medicinal uses, including making a tea to treat nausea.

Harvesting and uses

Leaves

Pick the leaves from spring until autumn. They are strong in flavor (rather like a mixture of celery and beef) and so need to be added sparingly to dishes. Otherwise the flavor can, when used too enthusiastically, destroy a meal. On the other hand, used carefully they can make a meal. The sweetest-flavored leaves are the new spring shoots; the mature leaves are bitter. To maintain a supply of young leaves throughout the season, cut sections of the plant down to the ground and new shoots will appear. These can be added to stocks, stews, cheese and salads. Alternatively, crushed leaves can be rubbed over a chicken prior to roasting or around the edge of a salad bowl before adding the salad. Discard the spent leaves.

Flowers

Pick in summer just when they open, divide into individual little flowers and scatter over tomatoes. They too have a strong flavor, so use sparingly.

Seeds

The seed heads should be harvested when the seeds start to turn brown in autumn. On a dry day, cut them, tie a paper bag over the heads and hang them upside down in a dry, airy place. The dried seeds have a warm, meaty celery flavor and can be crushed and used in soups, bread and pastries, or sprinkled over salads, rice and mashed potatoes.

Properties

Lovage is a good carminative and digestive. It contains vitamins A, B and C and the minerals iron, sodium and magnesium. It is considered to be one of nature's antibiotics, with the ability to deal with bacteria and viruses. It has a cleansing effect on the body.

Other varieties

None.

SAUTÉED CHICKEN WITH LOVAGE AND CIDER

A rustic meal packed with autumnal flavors. The dry flavor of the cider and the apple, combined with the sweetness of the chicken and the celery-ish lovage seeds, is delicious. Serve with creamy mashed potatoes or plain boiled rice.

Serves 4

2 cups (500 ml) vintage cider
8 chicken legs or thighs, skin removed
1 tsp (5 ml) lovage seed, ground
3 tbsp (45 ml) unsalted butter, divided
2 eating apples (such as Pink Lady), cored and cut into wedges
8 oz (250 g) button mushrooms, washed and sliced
1 tbsp (15 ml) olive oil
2 tbsp (30 ml) lovage leaves, finely chopped (use young shoots)
4 tbsp (60 ml) whipping (35%) cream

Pour the cider into a medium saucepan, bring to a boil and simmer until reduced by about half.

Rub the chicken legs or thighs all over with the ground lovage seed. Melt half the butter in a large frying pan that has a well-fitting lid, add the apples and mushrooms and fry gently until golden brown. Remove with a slotted spoon and keep on a plate until required.

Melt the remaining butter in the frying pan with the olive oil, add the chicken pieces and fry on all sides – you may need to do this in batches. Once all the chicken has been cooked, return it to the pan, add the reduced cider and bring to a boil. Reduce the heat to a simmer and cook gently for 20 to 25 minutes, until the chicken is thoroughly cooked and beginning to fall off the bone.

Add the apples, mushrooms and chopped lovage leaves and the cream and cook gently for a further 5 minutes. Serve.

NEW POTATOES, SMOKED MACKEREL AND LOVAGE SALAD

This is a lovely early summer meal; the saltiness of the mackerel against the lovage and minted new potatoes is mouthwatering.

Serves 4

12 oz (350 g) new potatoes
Pinch of salt
6 mint sprigs
¾ cup + 2 tbsp (200 ml) crème fraîche
1 tbsp (15 ml) young lovage shoots, finely chopped
Juice of 1 lemon
2 smoked mackerel fillets, skinned and flaked
2 handfuls young spinach leaves
1 handful arugula leaves

Bring a large saucepan of water to a boil, add the potatoes, salt and mint sprigs and cook for 15 minutes, until tender.

While the potatoes are cooking, mix together the crème fraîche, young lovage shoots and lemon juice in a large bowl – there is no need to add salt because there is enough saltiness in the lovage and smoked mackerel.

Once the potatoes are cooked, drain, halve and set aside for a few minutes to cool down, then add to the crème fraîche mixture. Mix so they are well coated, then add the smoked mackerel and the spinach and arugula leaves.

CARROT, SORREL AND LOVAGE SALAD

The biting sourness of the sorrel mixed with the meaty celery flavor of the lovage and the sweetness of the carrots is an excellent combination. Do not think I have gone mad because I am using only a little lovage. As I have said before, it is a very strong herb that can make or break a dish. This amount makes it. Serve with some fresh crusty bread.

Serves 2–4

3 carrots, grated
1 apple, grated
2 tsp (10 ml) chopped lovage leaves (use young shoots, not mature leaves)
Handful of sorrel leaves, carefully washed, then torn
1 romaine or butter lettuce, washed and leaves separated
1 tbsp (15 ml) pine nuts

For the dressing
3 tbsp (45 ml) light olive oil
1 tbsp (15 ml) balsamic vinegar
Salt and freshly ground black pepper to taste

Toss together the grated carrots and apple, lovage, and sorrel leaves and pine nuts in a large bowl.

Make the dressing by thoroughly mixing together all the ingredients. Pour over the carrot and apple mixture and mix well.

Arrange the lettuce leaves on a serving plate and fill each of the leaves with a little of the mixture.

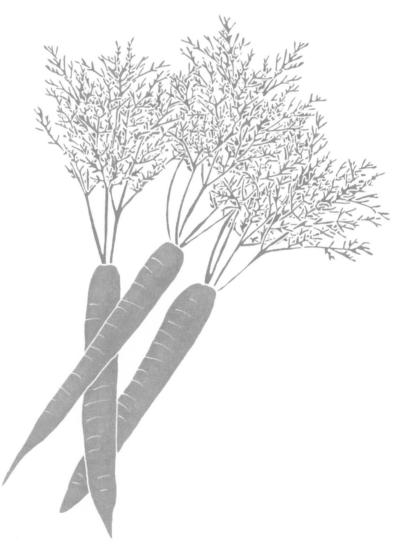

Excess lovage

Lovage as a vegetable

In spring you can often have an abundance of young lovage shoots, and fortunately this is the best time of year to cook this herb as a vegetable. You can treat lovage the same way as spinach – by cooking all the young new growth of the plant, both stalks and leaves.

As I've already said, lovage does have a strong flavor, so I have found that in order to make it acceptable to all it is best combined with a white sauce. That way everyone is happy and the plates are clean. This is lovely with grilled smoked mackerel and mashed potatoes.

Serves 2–4

1 large handful lovage stems and leaves
2 tbsp (30 ml) butter
¼ cup (60 ml) all-purpose flour
1 cup + 2 tbsp (275 ml) milk
Freshly ground black pepper
Grated nutmeg

Strip the lovage leaves from the stalks, wash and cut the stalks up into segments. Bring a medium saucepan of water to a boil and add the young lovage leaves and stalks. Bring the water back to a boil, cover and simmer for about 3 to 4 minutes, until tender. Drain.

Make a white sauce by melting the butter in a medium saucepan and stirring in the flour to make a paste. Add the milk a little at a time, whisking as you do so to avoid lumps. Season with a grating of pepper and nutmeg.

When the sauce is made, add the lovage, stir and serve.

MARIGOLD

(also known as Pot Marigold, Calendula, Garden Marigold)
Calendula officinalis

Pot marigold has been a firm family favorite throughout four generations of cooks; all of us have created or adapted recipes to incorporate this pretty herb. It is both interesting and important to note that throughout Europe pot marigold is a well-known medicinal and culinary herb. However, when lecturing further afield, I discovered that when I mentioned marigold it was automatically assumed that I was talking about 'Tagetes,' the African and French varieties, which have insecticidal properties. The flowers of these varieties can be very bitter and in some cases toxic, so please check that you have the calendula variety of marigold when making these recipes.

Description

Pot marigold is a cheerful attractive annual herb with daisy-like yellow or orange single or double flowers from spring until the first frosts. The flowers are sensitive to variations of temperature and dampness. If they are open it will be a fine day, if closed, take your umbrella with you. By dead-heading the flowers when they are over you will encourage continuous flowering. It does self-seed abundantly but never seems to become a nuisance. The lance-shaped, lightly aromatic light green leaves are edible, fresh when young or cooked when mature.

This is a tolerant plant, for it will grow in any soil with the exception of waterlogged. It prefers a sunny position in the garden or in a container, in which it will happily adapt to growing. Use a soil-based potting compost when potting it. The seed is easy to handle and reliable to grow, so it is an ideal plant to sow when encouraging children to garden. Sow the seeds in late spring until early summer, directly into a prepared site in the garden or into a large container.

History in cooking

Pot marigold has been used as an edible plant for many years. The Indians and Arabs were the first recorded users of it, followed by the ancient Egyptians. The ancient Greeks garnished and flavored food with the golden petals. In the 16th century in many countries, especially Holland, grocers and spice sellers had barrels filled with dry petals. These were sold in large quantities for use in drinks and broths, to flavor soups and stews, to color butter and cheese, and also for medications.

Harvesting and uses

Leaves

Pick young leaves in early spring to add to salads, while mature summer growth can be cooked like spinach – hence the name pot marigold, referring to cooking pots. However, be aware that the

leaves are not to everyone's taste, as they are bitter and hairy –
I have to admit to not liking them. The petals of the flowers, on the
other hand, are a different story.

Flowers

Pick these just as they open, from late spring until the first hard
frosts. The actual center of the flower is bitter; it is the petals that
are used in many culinary ways. They have a light, warm flavor that
combines well with cheese dishes and are excellent in salads and
omelets. They make an interesting cup of tea too, and as history
indicates, they make a good food dye. Simply chop the petals up
very, very finely or pulverize them using a mortar and pestle, and
add this paste to rice dishes, butter and, in fact, any foods that you
want to take on that lovely golden color.

Properties

Pot marigold flowers are believed to help improve digestion
and stimulate bile production. The herb is also considered an
antispasmodic and is said to contain vitamins A, B and C.

Varieties

Marigold Fiesta, Gitana
Calendula officinalis Fiesta Gitana Group
This is an attractive double-flowering variety of calendula; the
flowers can vary in color or range from apricot through to deep
orange. Use the petals in salads and to color rice or butter.

FARFALLE AND POT MARIGOLD

A simple and satisfying pasta dish that is quick to make and looks appetizing scattered with the marigold petals. This is delicious served with salads and cheese.

Serves 2–3

Pinch of salt (optional)
6½ oz (185 g) farfalle (or any pasta of your choice; flatter varieties are best in this recipe)
1 tbsp (15 ml) olive oil
1 clove garlic, crushed
2 tbsp (30 ml) pot marigold petals, removed from the flower head

Bring a large saucepan of water to a boil and add salt, if required. Add the farfalle slowly to the boiling water and stir. Boil for 10 to 12 minutes, until al dente. Drain well.

Put the olive oil in the pan, gently heat, add the crushed garlic and cooked farfalle and toss. Then add the marigold petals. Pour into a serving dish and serve either hot or cold.

POT MARIGOLD PIE

This is an old traditional English recipe that I found on a piece of faded paper in my mother's notebook. I have tweaked it to suit today's palate and ingredients. The marigold petals give the pastry and the filling lovely golden flecks and make this a unique dish.

Serves 4

For the pastry shell
¾ cup + 2 tbsp (200 ml) whole wheat flour
¼ tsp (1 ml) salt
2 tbsp (30 ml) unsalted butter, chilled, plus extra for greasing
2 tbsp (30 ml) lard, chilled
1 tbsp (15 ml) pot marigold petals, removed from the flower head
1 tbsp (15 ml) cold water

For the pie filling
3 eggs
4 tbsp (60 ml) pot marigold petals, removed from the flower heads
¼ cup (60 ml) organic cottage cheese (plain)
1 tbsp (15 ml) powdered (confectioners') sugar
Small pinch of salt
Freshly grated nutmeg
Zest of 1 lemon

Preheat the oven to 375°F (190°C).

Sieve the flour and salt into a bowl. Using a knife, chop the butter and lard into small chunks, then, using your hands, rub it into the flour, lifting up your hands with each movement so that the fat is cooled by the air as it falls back into the bowl. (This is exactly how my mother taught me, because she said I had hot hands and would make heavy pastry!)

When the mixture looks like fine bread crumbs, add the marigold petals, then carefully add the water as you mix the pastry with your other hand until you have a light firm dough.

Knead lightly, then place the pastry in a bowl and cover it with or just wrap in plastic wrap and put in the fridge for 1 hour before rolling out. This will help prevent it shrinking when you cook the pie.

Grease an 8-inch (18–20 cm), removable-bottom flan pan. Roll out the pastry to ¼ inch (5 mm) thick. Line the flan pan with the pastry by lifting it into place on the rolling pin. Trim the edges generously. Prick the bottom with a fork, cover the pastry shell with a circle of parchment paper, then sprinkle baking beans (or dried pasta) over the bottom and put the pan in the oven for 15 minutes.

Take the pan out of the oven, remove the beans and the paper, then put it back in the oven for a further 10 minutes, until the bottom is no longer soggy.

Lower the oven temperature to 325°F (170°C).

Separate the eggs and mix the yolks with the petals. Mix the cottage cheese with the sugar, salt and nutmeg. Add the petal mixture and lemon zest to the cottage cheese mixture.

In a separate bowl, whisk the egg whites to form soft peaks, then fold them into the cottage cheese mixture. Pour into the baked pastry shell and cook in the oven for about 25 minutes or until the pie filling feels firm to the touch. Serve when completely cold.

POT MARIGOLD AND BAY LEAF BAKED CUSTARD

Baked custards and milk desserts were a major part of my childhood; some I hated because the consistency was slimy, and others tasted of nothing in particular. This, on the other hand, was one of my grandmother's standbys and simply delicious. The flavor of bay and nutmeg with the hint of the marigold, plus the visual impact of the petals, was always a delight.

Serves 4

2½ cups (600 ml) whole milk
1 bay leaf
4 eggs
¼ cup (60 ml) fruit (superfine) sugar
8½ oz (240 g) pot marigold petals, removed from the flower head and finely chopped
Nutmeg

Preheat the oven to 275°F (140°C).

In a medium saucepan, heat the milk with the bay leaf until very hot but not boiling.

In a large bowl, beat together the eggs and sugar. Remove the bay leaf from the milk and then slowly add the hot milk to the eggs and sugar, stirring with a whisk. Strain into a 3-inch (7.5 cm) deep ovenproof dish, stir in the marigold petals and grate some nutmeg over the surface.

Place in a roasting pan containing enough cold water to come halfway up the sides of the ovenproof dish. Cook in the oven for 1½ hours, until firm.

MARIGOLD COOKIES

These marigold cookies are lovely on their own or served with lots of whipped cream and fresh greengages, if you are lucky enough to have them in midsummer.

Makes approx. 12

7 tbsp (105 ml) butter or soft tub margarine, plus extra for greasing
¼ cup (60 ml) fruit (superfine) sugar
1½ cups (375 ml) self-raising flour, plus extra for dusting
2¼ tsp (11 ml) baking powder
¾ tsp (3 ml) salt
4 tsp (20 ml) marigold petals, removed from the flower head

Preheat the oven to 450°F (230°C). Lightly grease a baking sheet with a little butter.

Cream together the butter and sugar until light, then add the flour, baking powder and salt and mix well until it forms a ball. Take this out of the bowl and knead it on a lightly floured surface.

Gently roll out the dough, then scatter the marigold petals on top, very lightly pressing them into it using a rolling pin. Cut out small rounds using a cookie cutter and place them on the baking sheet. Bake in the oven for 10 to 12 minutes, until gold and firm. Remove at once and cool on a wire rack.

Excess marigold

Marigold petal butter
The only way to save the petals of this herb for the kitchen is to either infuse them in oil or use them in a butter, the latter of which I find useful for all forms of baking.

Makes 8 oz (250 g)

½ cup + 1 tbsp (140 ml) pot marigold petals
½ lb (250 g) unsalted butter, at room temperature

Finely chop the marigold petals. Put the butter in a bowl, add the chopped petals and mix well. Cover the bowl and let the mixture rest at room temperature for a few hours.

Transfer the butter mixture to a container with a lid, place in the fridge and leave for a few days to allow the flavor to develop. This butter will keep in the fridge for about 2 weeks, or you could freeze it and then it will keep for 3 months. If you are freezing the butter, do not forget to label it.

MINT

(also known as Liu Lan Xiang)
Mentha

Before I started school I knew the difference between garden, spearmint and apple mint, as they were an essential part of my mother's kitchen, and in turn mine, for mint is without doubt one of the indispensable culinary herbs. I have a large patch of Tashkent mint, an excellent spearmint, just outside my back door, which I use virtually every day from early spring until the autumn.

Description

All the mints mentioned in this chapter are hardy herbaceous varieties that die back in winter and reappear in the spring. The flowers in summer can vary from white to mauve, and the leaves, which are all highly aromatic, especially when crushed, can vary from pointed to smooth and hairy to crinkly, depending on the variety. Common to all is that they are attractive to bees and butterflies, which is a plus. On the down side, they are all invasive in the garden, so their site needs to be chosen with care.

Being promiscuous plants (which is why there are so many different varieties), they are not good raised from seed. To get the best and most reliable flavor, grow the plants from root cuttings taken in autumn. The most flavorsome and healthiest plants are those that are grown so the plant can spread naturally, which can be difficult in a small garden, so allocate an area to them. Plant in rich, well-drained soil in a sunny position. If you do not have sufficient space in the garden for them to stretch out, mint grows well in containers in soil-based potting compost. However, to keep the plant productive, do repot every year in the autumn; this will prevent the roots rotting and enable it to produce abundant leaf in the following season.

History in cooking

Mint has been used in cooking for thousands of years. There are two stories of which I am particularly fond. The first is that the ancient Greeks believed that after nights of heavy drinking they could place a wreath of mint on their heads to exorcise an impending hangover. The second illustrates its long association with hospitality. Two strangers were walking in Asia Minor, and no one had offered them food or drink for many days until finally an elderly couple invited them in. Before laying out the food, the couple rubbed mint leaves over the table and plates and scattered it over the food. The strangers were so pleased with the hospitality shown to them that on parting they expressed their gratitude by transforming the couple's humble home into a mansion – for the strangers were none other than the gods Zeus and Hermes.

Harvesting and uses

Leaves
These can be picked to be used fresh from spring until early winter, but the ideal time for harvesting all forms of mint is before flowering, when they are at their most succulent and flavorsome. They are great not only with vegetables but also with fruit, cheese, meat, poultry and yogurt and to make a refreshing cup of tea.

Flowers
Pick the flowers in summer. The very small flowers are amazing, for they have the most wonderful mint flavor. After removing the green parts, scatter them over salads or strawberries and other summer fruit, or use in desserts.

Properties
The beneficial properties of mint in cooking are well known, these being as a digestive, antispasmodic and carminative. In addition, it also has antioxidant and antiviral properties.

Varieties
There are so many different mints that I have just chosen my favorites here and grouped them according to flavor.

Peppermints
These have the strongest flavor and are the best for making a digestive tea at the end of a meal or for adding to desserts.

Peppermint, Menthe d'Angleterre, Menthe Anglaise, Pfefferminze, Englisheminze
Mentha x *piperita*
This has pale purple flowers in summer with peppermint-scented darkish green leaves.

Basil Mint
Mentha x *piperita* f. *citrata* 'Basil'
This has purple-mauve flowers in summer and highly scented oval leaves that are green with a reddish tinge. This mint goes well with tomato dishes, especially pasta.

Chocolate Peppermint
Mentha x *piperita* f. *citrata* 'Chocolate'
This has pale purple flowers in summer with peppermint-scented dark green leaves. This variety is amazing: it tastes just like expensive chocolates. Try using it in chocolate mousse.

Spearmints These have a mid-strength flavor and are known as the classic mint that is ideal for mint sauce, with yogurt or dressings, and served with new potatoes and strawberries.

Spearmint, Garden Mint
Mentha spicata
This variety has small purple-mauve flowers in terminal cylindrical spikes in summer, with mid-green oval, lance-shaped wrinkled spearmint-scented and -flavored leaves.

Tashkent Mint and Moroccan Mint
Mentha spicata 'Tashkent' and *Mentha spicata* var. *crispa* 'Moroccan'
Both of these have mid-green crinkled spearmint-scented and -flavored leaves. They are difficult to tell apart in the kitchen, but in the garden 'Tashkent' is taller and the leaves are rounder.

Other mints
These mints have an all-round mild flavor that is good for jellies and sauces.

Apple Mint
Mentha suaveolens
This variety has mauve flowers in summer and roundish, hairy mid-green leaves.

Bowles' Mint
Mentha x *villosa* var. *alopecuroides* 'Bowles' Mint'
This has mauve flowers and round, hairy mid-green leaves. This is considered by many to be the best culinary mint. Personally I dispute that, but I do agree that it is good in cooking.

EGGPLANT AND MINT BRUSCHETTA

The flavors of the mint, eggplant and garlic combine wonderfully in these delicious bruschetta.

For those like me who like to know the meaning of words, *bruschetta* is derived from the Italian *bruscare*, which means "to roast over coals." Alternatively you could call this fancy toast. This is a lovely appetizer or first course for an early autumn meal.

Serves 4

2 firm eggplants
Sea salt and freshly ground black pepper
7 tbsp (105 ml) olive oil
2 tbsp (30 ml) balsamic vinegar
1 tbsp (15 ml) flat-leaf parsley, leaves picked and finely chopped
2 tbsp (30 ml) spearmint (Tashkent, Moroccan or garden mint), finely chopped
1 clove garlic, peeled and very finely sliced
Zest of 1 lemon
1 ciabatta

Slice the eggplants on the diagonal into ½-inch (1 cm) slices. Sprinkle with salt and set aside for about 40 minutes. Place the eggplant in a colander and wash well under cold running water, then pat dry using a clean dish towel or paper towels.

Heat a grill pan until hot. Lay the eggplant slices on it side by side. When they are charred on both sides, put them into a salad bowl. (You may need to cook the eggplant in several batches.)

While the eggplant is cooking, put the olive oil and vinegar in a large bowl and mix thoroughly, until amalgamated. Add the chopped parsley and mint, then the garlic and 1 tsp (5 ml) lemon zest. Season with salt and pepper to taste.

When the eggplant is cooked, add it to the bowl and mix it around, then check the seasoning again.

Heat the broiler to hot. Cut the ciabatta on the diagonal into 1-inch (2.5 cm) slices, then grill lightly on both sides. Once the toasted ciabatta slices have cooled, top them with the mint and eggplant mixture, pressing it down so that the juices seep into the toast. Serve immediately.

TRADITIONAL BORSCH

This recipe has been taken from my grandmother's book *Food for Pleasure*. Apparently it originally came from *Recipes of all Nations*, by Countess Morphy. I have slightly modified it by adding the mint crème fraîche, which goes so well with the sweetness of the beets. Also, I do not strain the borsch but serve it with the grated beets, which in my opinion adds texture and flavor.

Serves 4

6 tbsp (90 ml) unsalted butter
4 large raw beets
1 qt (1 L) good chicken stock, hot
1 cup + 2 tbsp (275 ml) crème fraîche
1 tbsp (15 ml) chopped spearmint (not peppermint)
2 tsp (10 ml) chopped parsley

Melt the butter in a large saucepan over low heat. Peel and grate the beets and add to the pan, cover and cook for about 20 minutes, stirring regularly. Stir in a little of the hot stock, and when this is absorbed, stir in more. Repeat this process until the beets are tender. Once the beets are cooked, add the remainder of the stock and simmer gently for another 30 minutes, then strain or not, as desired.

Mix the crème fraîche with the spearmint. Serve in individual bowls, each with 1 tbsp (15 ml) of the minted crème fraîche, and scatter a small amount of parsley over the top.

HAM, MINT AND PEA SOUP

Mint, peas and leftover ham are the basis for this simple, hearty summer soup. The use of mint cuts the saltiness of the ham and enhances the flavor of the peas. If you've cooked a ham or turkey from scratch, you can use the bones and any cooking liquid to make a batch of rich stock. Serve with fresh crusty white bread.

Serves 6

3½ oz (100 g) peas, removed from their pods (reserve the pods) or frozen (but then you miss the pods)
1½ qt (1.5 L) ham or vegetable stock
1 tbsp (15 ml) olive oil
1 medium onion, finely chopped
2 celery stalks, thinly sliced
2 carrots, finely chopped
2 tbsp (30 ml) dry white wine
7 oz (200 g) white beans, soaked overnight, or 2 x 14-oz (398 ml) cans white beans, drained
8 oz (250 g) cooked ham, cut into small pieces
2 tbsp (30 ml) spearmint leaves, chopped, but not too fine
Salt and freshly ground black pepper

Put the pea pods in a large saucepan with the ham or vegetable stock (this will add a delicious pea flavor to the stock). Bring to a boil, then simmer for 5 minutes and strain, discarding the pea pods.

Heat the oil in a large, heavy-bottomed pan over medium heat. When hot, add the onion, celery and carrots. Cover, reduce the heat and cook for about 15 minutes, until soft. Add the wine to the pan. Stir once or twice and simmer until the alcohol has evaporated. Add the beans to the pan, stir once or twice, then leave to cook for a few minutes so they start to soften and mush a little.

Pour the stock into the pan. Bring to a simmer and cook for 10 minutes; you can slightly mash the beans if you like a thick soup or leave them alone if you prefer. Add the peas and cook until the soup returns to a simmer, then add the chopped ham and mint. Stir well, allow to warm through and season to taste.

ATUL KOCHHAR'S CHUTNEY PULAO

This recipe was kindly contributed by Atul Kochhar, the wonderful Michelin-starred chef who can be found at the Benares Restaurant in Berkeley Square, London, and at Vatika, in Hampshire. He inspires me as a cook because he combines the best of the East with the best of the West and he is passionate about herbs. This dish can be served with a raita or plain yogurt.

Atul says: "This pulao is a winner. It can be served on its own or as a part of any meat dish – especially lamb and pork. There is no secret involved, except a sheer love for herbs. Mix in the chutney paste just before you serve, and that keeps the flavors alive. This rice can't be stored; it has to be made fresh and eaten on the same day."

Serves 4–6

For the chutney
2½ cups (625 ml) spearmint leaves
1¼ cups (300 ml) coriander leaves
¼ tsp (1 ml) chopped green chile pepper
½ tsp (2 ml) chopped fresh gingerroot
2 tbsp (30 ml) lemon juice
Salt, to taste
2 tbsp (30 ml) vegetable oil
Pinch of sugar
¼ cup (60 ml) water

For the rice
1½ tbsp (22 ml) vegetable oil
½ tsp (2 ml) cumin seeds
2 green cardamom pods
½-inch (1 cm) piece cinnamon stick
½ medium onion, sliced
1¼ cups (300 ml) basmati rice, washed and soaked for 30 minutes
Salt, to taste
2 cups (500 ml) water

Blitz together all the chutney ingredients, except the water, in a food processor or with a hand-held blender to make a thick paste. Add the water to bring the paste together. Transfer to a bowl and keep, covered, in the fridge until required.

To make the rice, heat the oil in a heavy-bottomed pan and sauté the spices until they splutter. Then add the onion and sauté until translucent. Add the rice and sauté for 1 to 2 minutes, then add the salt and water. Bring to a boil, then simmer very slowly for 3 to 5 minutes. Cover the rice and cook until the rice grains are properly cooked.

Just before serving, mix the thick chutney paste into the rice and stir in well.

MARIAN'S SUMMER MINTED CHICKEN

Marian is my son's godmother and my old roommate. This is one of her delicious and easy summer recipes. It works extremely well when made for a large number, and I have known her to cater for as many as 80 for a special birthday party, but it is also perfect for a few. I particularly like the combination of spearmint and mango chutney – they go together so well. Serve with a crisp green salad and some crusty French bread.

Serves 4–6

4 cooked chicken breasts
2/3 cup (150 ml) mayonnaise
2/3 cup (150 ml) sour cream
Mango chutney, to taste
4 tbsp (60 ml) spearmint, finely chopped

To serve
1 mango, peeled and sliced
1 tbsp (15 ml) spearmint leaves, finely chopped

Cut the chicken into strips.

Combine the remaining ingredients and, when mixed, fold in the chicken. Spoon into a serving dish, cover with plastic wrap and place in the fridge for a minimum of 12 hours prior to serving, to allow the flavors to develop.

Before serving, decorate with the mango and mint.

MINT AND CARAWAY MERINGUES

These meringues were an inspiration. I was sitting mulling over writing this book while cleaning my caraway seeds. I already add walnuts to meringues, and other seeds, so why not caraway? Then I thought, what would it be like to add mint to the anise and sugar? Those thoughts led to this recipe, which is magic. Serve with fresh fruit and whipped cream.

Makes 12

Oil and flour for the baking sheets (optional)
4 eggs, separated (save the yolks for making sauces)
1 cup + 2 tbsp (275 ml) fruit (superfine) sugar
2 tsp (10 ml) caraway seeds, crushed in a mortar and pestle
2 tbsp (30 ml) spearmint leaves, finely chopped

Preheat the oven to 250°F (120°C). Either line 2 baking sheets with nonstick baking parchment or brush them lightly with oil, dredge with flour, then bang the sheets to remove excess flour.

Whisk the egg whites until quite stiff – they should remain in shape when shaken from a spoon, or as some say, make stiff peaks. Add the sugar slowly, beating all the time, then add the caraway seeds and spearmint.

Using two spoons, scoop a spoonful of the meringue mixture from the bowl and then use the other spoon to place it on the baking sheet. Repeat 12 times or until you have used up all the mixture. Put the sheets in the oven, bake for 1 hour, then change the trays around, the top shelf being warmer than the lower. Bake for a further 30 to 40 minutes.

When the meringues are set, carefully lift them off the baking sheets using a thin metal spatula or sharp knife and transfer to cool on a wire rack. If you want them really crisp, turn them all over and return to the oven for a further 30 minutes.

If you do not want to serve them immediately, they will, once cold, keep in an airtight container for a few days.

Excess mint

My mum's mint sauce

Before I had even started school, Mum had taught me to make this sauce. I used to kneel on a wooden chair and chop mint using a very sharp knife. I always had a great sense of achievement and participation when I had created the sauce, which was served with our Sunday lunch, the highlight of the week.

1 bunch mint (it must be a spearmint, not a peppermint; any of these make a good mint sauce: Moroccan, garden, Tashkent, apple or Guernsey)
Fruit (superfine) sugar (enough to cover the leaves when chopped)
White wine vinegar (balsamic vinegar can be substituted; if so, use less sugar)

Remove the mint leaves from the stalks and chop them very finely. Add the sugar and keep chopping; this way the oils and flavors of the mint are amalgamated into the sugar.

Once you are happy that it is all mixed, transfer the mint and sugar to a small bowl. Stir in enough vinegar to just make it runny, but not so much that you have lots of vinegar. Check the sweetness and add extra sugar if required.

This will keep for 7 days, covered, in the fridge. Stir well before use, and if it has dried out a bit, add a little extra vinegar.

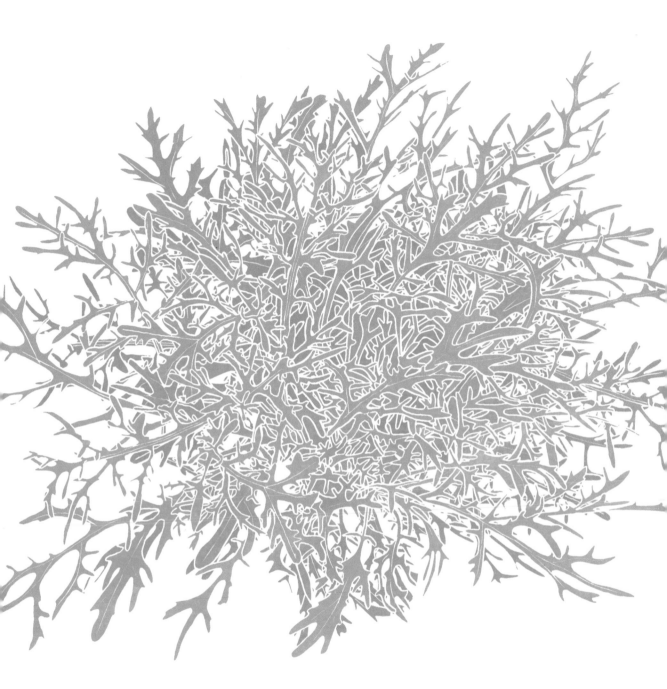

MUSTARD

(also known as Juncea, Indian Mustard, Mustard Greens,
Chinese Mustard)
Brassica juncea

I do not understand why this herb is not grown in every garden, as it is easy, rewarding and amazingly useful. I grew it as a child and remember spending hours sitting at the kitchen table extracting the dried seeds from the pods so Mum could make mustard. Homemade mustard makes a great Christmas present.

Description

Mustard is an annual herb with bright yellow flowers in summer that are followed by long, narrow seed pods. The leaves can vary from oval to deeply lobed and green, yellow or red with a purple tint – all depending on the variety.

This is a satisfying herb to cultivate because it is fast growing and the seeds can be sown from spring until autumn. The plants produced from seeds sown in spring are ideal for both seed and leaf production, while plants from seeds sown in the autumn are ideal for a late salad crop. Choose a sunny site and prepare the soil the winter before sowing by feeding it with well-rotted manure.

History in cooking

Mustard has been used for thousands of years, both medicinally and in the kitchen. Historically the Romans used the brown *juncea* mustard as a pungent salad vegetable and the seeds of the black, *nigra*, as a spice. The English name mustard is said to derive from the Latin *mustem ardens*, which translates as "burning wine," a reference to the heat of mustard and the French practice of mixing unfermented grape juice with the ground seeds.

Harvesting and uses

Leaves

Harvest brown mustard leaves from spring until late autumn – the young leaves have by far the best flavor, which is warm and peppery. Add to salads and stir-fry dishes or use to transform a plain sandwich into a delight.

Flowers

Pick for eating just as they open, from spring until early autumn. They have a mild mustard flavor that is great in salads.

Seeds

The seed pods are harvested as they change color, from summer until early autumn. Dry the pods in a light, airy room until totally dried, then remove the seeds from the pods and store in clean, dry jars with well-fitting lids. Mustard seeds get their pungency only when they are crushed and infused in a liquid. If you boil the crushed seed or overcook a sauce with crushed seed, it will become bitter.

The easiest and best way to use mustard seeds is to make your own mustard (see page 204). The seeds are also great added to salad dressings or sauces. When adding mustard to food, remember that its pungency is destroyed by heat, so add it to sauces or stews at the end of cooking.

Properties

Mustard seeds, leaves and flowers are marvelous circulatory stimulants as well as being a noteworthy alkaline food. The alkaline content aids digestion, and mustards also have antispasmodic and diuretic qualities. Eating the fresh leaves and flowers in a salad is an excellent tonic because the leaves are rich in minerals, including high levels of phosphorus as well as calcium, iron, potassium and vitamins A, B and C.

Other varieties

White Mustard, Yellow Mustard
Brassica alba
This has pale yellow flowers in summer followed by long seed pods with pale yellow seeds and rough, bristly oval deeply lobed green leaves.

Brown Mustard
Brassica juncea
Clusters of pale yellow flowers in summer are followed by long seed pods with brown seeds and oval lobed olive green leaves with pale green veins and crinkled edges.

Red Mustard
Brassica juncea 'Rubra'
This variety has yellow flowers in summer with oval red purple-tinted leaves with toothed edges and a pungent mustard flavor. Good in salads and sandwiches.

Red Frills Mustard
Brassica juncea 'Red Frills'
This has yellow flowers in summer with attractive dark red narrow, indented leaves with a mild mustard flavor. Great for salads.

Black Mustard
Brassica nigra
The pale yellow flowers in summer are followed by long seed pods with dark brown seeds and rough, bristly oval-lobed green leaves.

MUSTARD LEAF AND GREEN BEAN SALAD

Mustard leaves (especially the frilly varieties) have a unique flavor that starts off tasting of new potatoes, then changes to being warm and spicy. This flavor is excellent with many vegetables, but my favorite combination is with the small green beans that appear in profusion in the summer. My mother often added them to salads, but I am sad that she did not know of this recipe, as I am sure she would have approved. You can add tuna or anchovies to make it into a complete meal.

Serves 2–4

7 oz (200 g) fresh green beans, topped, tailed, then halved
3 tbsp (45 ml) olive oil or basil oil (see page 36)
1 tbsp (15 ml) balsamic vinegar
1 clove garlic, crushed
2½ cups (625 ml) mixed mustard leaves

Put the prepared green beans into a pan of boiling water and cook until just tender. Drain and set aside to cool.

Mix together the oil, vinegar and garlic. Wash, if necessary, the mustard leaves and shake dry. Place them in a serving bowl with the cooled green beans, toss, add the dressing, toss again and serve.

WENDY'S FETA AND MUSTARD COTTAGE LOAF

For the past few years Wendy has been in charge of the show and garden plants on the herb farm. This is one of her favorite recipes. The aromatic mustard leaves go so well with the feta cheese and potato, enhancing all the flavors. Serve it with homemade tomato sauce and a crisp green salad.

Serves 4

1½ cups (375 ml) all-purpose flour
2¼ tsp (11 ml) baking powder
1 tsp (5 ml) salt
Pinch of cayenne pepper
4–5 Welsh onions (scallions), finely sliced
1 tsp (5 ml) finely chopped sage
1 tbsp (15 ml) roughly chopped mustard leaves
4 oz (115 g) feta
1 largish potato, peeled and grated
1 egg
1 tsp (5 ml) French mustard
2–3 tbsp (30–45 ml) milk

Preheat the oven to 375°F (190°C).

Sift together the flour, baking powder, salt and cayenne pepper. Mix in the scallions along with the sage and mustard leaves and two-thirds of the feta – which will need to be broken up into small pieces. Add the potato to the mixture, making sure it is well covered in flour.

In a separate bowl, mix together the egg, mustard and milk, beat well, then slowly add it to the flour and herb mixture to make a dough.

Remove from the mixing bowl and place on a baking sheet that has been greased or lined with baking parchment. Shape into a 6-inch (15 cm) round.

Break up the remaining feta into small chunks and push them into the surface of the loaf. Sprinkle with flour and bake in the oven for 35 to 40 minutes or until golden brown. Serve warm.

MUSTARD-LEAF SAUCE

This is a lovely, spicy, warm-flavored sauce that can be adapted by adding other ingredients. I often stir in hard-boiled eggs or bread crumbs soaked in vinegar, which add different textures. Serve with fish, cooked meats, cheese and salads.

Serves 2–4

2½ cups (625 ml) mixed mustard leaves (red or yellow), washed and roughly chopped
1 clove garlic, crushed
2–3 tbsp (30–45 ml) white wine vinegar or herb vinegar
2/3 cup (150 ml) olive oil
Salt and freshly ground black pepper

Put the mustard leaves and garlic into a food processor and blend with 2 tbsp (30 ml) vinegar. With the motor running, add the olive oil in a slow stream, season to taste, then add the remaining vinegar if required.

RABBIT IN MUSTARD SAUCE

Coney pie and coney stew were part of my childhood, because where I lived in the West Country this was the name for rabbit. The name coney originates, I believe, from the medieval French word *connis*, meaning wild rabbit.

I notice that rabbit is coming back into the kitchen. My wonderful butchers in Chipping Sodbury, Steve, Chris and John, often have it for sale, and this is a delicious way to cook it. Serve with plenty of boiled potatoes to mop up the sauce, and a crisp green salad.

Serves 4–6

1¼ lb (575 g) rabbit, removed from the bones
Seasoned all-purpose flour, for dusting
3 tbsp (45 ml) butter
½ lb (225 g) shallots, halved (or use 1 large onion, sliced)
1 clove garlic, sliced
1¼ cups (300 ml) vegetable or chicken stock
Small handful thyme leaves
Salt and freshly ground black pepper
1 bay leaf
1 tbsp (15 ml) thyme mustard (or any herb mustard you have, see page 205)
2/3 cup (150 ml) whipping (35%) cream

Cut the boned rabbit meat into neat pieces, then toss it in the seasoned flour. Set aside.

In a large pan or casserole dish, melt the butter and add the shallots or onion and cook until golden, not dark brown. Add the garlic for the last few minutes of cooking. Add the floured rabbit pieces, stir until lightly cooked all over, then pour in the stock and bring to a simmer. Turn the heat down and add the thyme and salt and pepper. Cover and cook very slowly for 1½ hours, until the meat is tender. Stir during cooking to make sure nothing sticks.

Once the meat is tender, lift out the meat and onions, leaving the cooking juices behind, and place on a warmed serving dish. Remove the sprigs of thyme and reheat the cooking juices, stirring well to remove any pieces stuck to the bottom of the pan. Add the thyme mustard and cream, then stir until blended, but do not boil, as this will destroy the mustard flavor. Check the seasoning.

Serve the rabbit with the sauce poured over it.

Excess mustard

Mustards (the condiment) are increasingly popular and easy to make. The different-colored mustard seeds – white or yellow, brown and black – are substantially different in character and produce a huge number of different-tasting flavors depending on the combinations. When blended with other ingredients, such as wine, vinegar and herbs, they can create the perfect mustard for you, your friends and your family.

Herb mustards are particularly good when combined with crème fraîche or cream cheese as a dip for vegetables or pretzels. They are also great added to salad dressings or sauces.

This is the basic mustard recipe, to which you can add the herb of your choice. I mention some on page 205.

Quick-and-easy basic mustard recipe

My mother always made her own mustards, but her recipe took nearly two days to complete. With the advent of food processors and blenders I have found that I can make a good basic mustard in an hour. It is great fun and the herb combinations are endless: the final flavor can be sweet, hot, pungent, tangy or herby, depending on your personal taste. The whole process is surprisingly straightforward, involving simply grinding and mixing mustard seeds with a few other ingredients. The seeds themselves are not hot until they are ground and moistened with some sort of cold liquid, but do be warned that freshly made mustard is searingly hot. It should be allowed to stand for 10 to 30 minutes to allow the flavor to develop and the heat to subside slightly. The longer it stands, the more mellow it becomes.

Makes 2 x 3½ oz (100 ml) jars

⅓ cup (75 ml) white mustard seeds
3 tbsp (45 ml) black mustard seeds
¼ cup (60 ml) light brown sugar
1 tsp (5 ml) salt
1 tsp (5 ml) turmeric
½–1¼ cups (125–300 ml) herbs (see herb list below; if using dried, use half the amount)
¾ cup + 2 tbsp (200 ml) white wine vinegar, or white wine and cider vinegar, or a herb vinegar, or a combination of these

Put the mustard seeds, sugar, salt, turmeric and herbs into a blender or use a mortar and pestle to blend them together until you have the consistency you require – this can be grainy or smooth.

Gradually add the vinegar, 1 tbsp (15 ml) at a time, blending well between each addition and continuing to blend until you have a coarse paste.

Leave to stand for 10 to 15 minutes to thicken slightly. Spoon the mustard into sterilized small jars (see page 12). Seal, label and date the jars and place in a cool, dark cupboard or old-fashioned pantry for 2 weeks before using, to allow the flavors to develop. Use the mustard within 6 months. Once opened, the flavor will start to deteriorate, so refrigerate it and use it within 1 month.

Herbs for mustards

Try any of the herbs mentioned below, either singularly or mixed, to make your own delicious condiment.

All the herb measurements are for about ½ cup (100 ml) of mustard.

Dill: Add 1 cup (250 ml) of chopped dill leaves and 1 tsp (5 ml) crushed dill seeds. This is particularly good served with smoked salmon.

Horseradish: Add 2 tbsp (30 ml) grated root. This is lovely with red meats.

Oregano: Add ½ cup (125 ml) of chopped leaves. This is particularly good with goat cheese and tomatoes.

Rosemary: Add ½ cup (125 ml) of chopped leaves. This combines well with cold lamb – there is a saying that mustard with mutton is the sign of a glutton, but in this case it's worth it.

Thyme: Add ½ cup (125 ml) of chopped leaves. Try this with cheese, meat and fish.

Winter Savory: Add ½ cup (125 ml) of chopped leaves. This is lovely used in dressing for a bean salad.

Tarragon: Add ½ cup (125 ml) of chopped leaves. This goes well with fish and cold chicken, and is also great for adding to sauces.

MYRTLE

(also known as Common Myrtle, Mirto)
Myrtus communis

I fell in love with myrtle after I saw it being used as formal hedging at the Alhambra Palace in Granada, Spain, and then growing wild in the hills of Sardinia, where it can be found clinging to craggy rocks and smelling absolutely heavenly in the baking sun. Over the years myrtle has become one of my top must-haves for the herb garden, as it looks wonderful grown in the garden or in containers, and it is, in my opinion, a very underrated and underused culinary herb. It can transform an English summer barbecue into a Mediterranean feast.

Description

This lovely Mediterranean aromatic evergreen plant has leaves all year round, as well as pretty, fragrant white flowers throughout the summer, which are followed by dark purple-black berries in late autumn. The dark green oval leaves are aromatic when crushed, smelling of sweet spice.

Being a Mediterranean herb, it will grow in fertile, well-drained soil in full sun. Where winters are borderline, plant it against a south- or west-facing wall, as this will not only protect it from cold winter winds but also cut the rainfall by 25 percent, thereby restricting the amount of water the plant receives. Alternatively, if temperatures in your garden regularly reach below 23°F (-5°C), grow myrtle as a container plant, using a soil-based potting compost, and bring it under cover for the winter months.

History in cooking

Myrtle has been used for more than 2,000 years as a flavoring, a perfume and a medicine. The ancient Romans made myrtle wine by immersing the ripe fruits in *mosto* – fermenting grape juice. The fruits were also used in Roman cooking, especially with wild boar. In Chile, myrtle seeds and flower buds were dried and used to make a type of coffee.

Harvesting and uses

Leaves

Being evergreen, the leaves can be picked all year round, but the best-flavored leaves appear in midsummer on new shoots that have started to change color from light bright green to dark green. They have a warm, spicy, slightly bitter, aromatic flavor. They need to be used carefully, as they have a strong flavor that can overpower a meal, but when mastered they can transform soups, casseroles, stews and vegetable, poultry or meat dishes into feasts. Like bay, the leaves are not eaten but used only to flavor and should be removed before serving. Foods flavored with the smoke of myrtle leaves are common in rural areas of mainland Italy and Sardinia.

Flowers

These can be picked throughout the summer and have a warm and spicy flavor. Add sparingly to rice and pasta dishes.

Berries

The ripe berries can be harvested from late autumn to midwinter. They have a dry, spicy flavor and go well with strong meat dishes, boar, duck and quail. The dried berries can be ground like pepper – they are known as mursins in the Middle East, where they are used as a spice.

Properties

Myrtle leaves and berries are an antiseptic; the buds and flowers contain vitamin C and citric acid. Medicinally the leaves and berries have been used to treat diarrhea and dysentery.

Varieties

Variegated Myrtle

Myrtus communis subsp. *tarentina* 'Variegata'
This variety has fragrant white flowers with a hint of pink in summer, followed by dark purple-black fruits. The leaves are oval and dark green with silver variegation, developing a pink tinge in autumn.

Tarentina Myrtle

Myrtus communis subsp. *tarentina*
This has small, fragrant white flowers in summer followed by small dark purple-black fruits. The leaves are small, oval, dark green and aromatic. The branches of this myrtle are very straight, making them ideal for using as natural barbecue skewers for grilling kabobs (both meat and vegetable), sausages, fish and peppers.

Variegated Tarentina Myrtle

Myrtus communis subsp. *tarentina* 'Microphylla Variegata'
Small, fragrant white flowers with a hint of pink in summer are followed by dark purple-black fruits. The leaves are small, oval and dark green with silver variegation, developing a pink tinge in autumn.

ROAST BUTTERNUT SQUASH AND MYRTLE SOUP

The warm spice of the myrtle combined with the comforting sweetness of butternut squash (especially when roasted) makes this a lovely winter soup – particularly when one has been working outside. Serve with Sage Rotis (see page 265).

Serves 4

2 lb (1 kg) butternut squash
3 tbsp (45 ml) olive oil, divided
4 myrtle sprigs
Salt and freshly ground black pepper
4 whole, unpeeled and 2 finely chopped cloves garlic
2 onions, finely chopped
2 carrots, finely sliced
2 qt (2 L) vegetable or chicken stock

Preheat the oven to 475°F (240°C).

Cut the butternut squash in half, scooping out the seeds using a large spoon. Slice the flesh, including the skin, into 3-inch (7 cm) wedges and brush them with 1 tbsp (15 ml) olive oil. Place the wedges in a roasting pan on top of 2 of the myrtle sprigs and season with salt and pepper.

Place in the oven and roast for 45 minutes or until the squash is soft and caramelized. After 25 minutes of cooking, add the 4 unpeeled garlic cloves and the remaining sprigs of myrtle, which can be pushed under the cooking squash.

Meanwhile, heat the remaining olive oil in a large saucepan. Add the onions, carrots and chopped garlic and cook gently for 10 to 15 minutes, until soft but not brown. Pour in the stock, bring to a boil and simmer for 20 minutes or until the vegetables are tender.

Allow the cooked squash to cool for 5 minutes. Using a large spoon, remove the flesh from the skin and add to the stock. Squeeze the roasted garlic from its skin into the stock and discard the myrtle. Simmer the stock and vegetables for a further 5 minutes or until the squash begins to break up.

Place the soup in a food processor or use a hand-held blender and mix until smooth. Return the soup to the pan and gently reheat. Check the seasoning. Pour the soup into bowls and serve.

BEEF STEW WITH MYRTLE, CINNAMON AND RED WINE

There are two great tips in this recipe that I picked up from my mother. First, marinating meat not only makes it taste wonderful but also tenderizes it. Second, the salty flavor of pancetta adds another dimension to the dish. So combine these tips with the spicy myrtle and you have a great stew. Delicious served with noodles or mashed potatoes.

Serves 4

1 lb (500 g) rump or braising steak, cut into 1½-inch (3–4 cm) pieces
2 cloves garlic, crushed
2 cinnamon sticks, approx. 2 inches (4–6 cm) long
2 x 3-inch (8 cm) sprigs myrtle, plus 6 myrtle leaves
2½ oz (70 g) cubed pancetta
2½ tbsp (37 ml) salted butter, divided
6 small shallots, peeled but left whole
3 large carrots, cut into sticks
1 tbsp (15 ml) all-purpose flour
1¼ cups (300 ml) beef stock
1¼ cups (300 ml) red wine

Mix the prepared meat with the garlic, cinnamon sticks and myrtle sprigs in a large bowl, cover and leave in the fridge overnight.

The next day, preheat the oven to 300°F (150°C). Drain the meat, reserving the marinade after removing and discarding the cinnamon and myrtle sprigs.

Fry the pancetta in a casserole dish over medium heat until it starts to brown. Add half the butter and all the shallots and carrots. Sauté until the carrots and shallots start to brown.

Pat the meat dry with paper towels. In a separate pan, melt the remaining butter, add the meat to the pan and cook until brown, then transfer to the casserole dish. Add the flour to the dish, stir well, then add the reserved marinade and myrtle leaves. Bring to a boil. Add the stock, return to a boil, cover, and put in the oven for 1 hour 20 minutes or until the meat is tender and the sauce has thickened.

Remove from the oven and let stand, covered, for 20 minutes before serving.

HOT MEAD AND MYRTLE PUNCH

Although red wine is most popular for punches, mead blends well with sweet spice and myrtle berries, resulting in an unusual medium-sweet, full-flavored drink. Excellent at Christmas or on a cold winter weekend when you have been for a long walk with friends.

Makes approx. 1½ qt (1.5 L)

25-oz (750 ml) bottle mead
2½ cups (575 ml) cider
2½ cups (575 ml) apple juice
2 oranges
12 cloves
5-inch (12 cm) piece cinnamon stick
4 myrtle berries
3 tbsp (45 ml) honey, or to taste

Put the mead, cider and apple juice into a large saucepan. Thickly slice the oranges and stick the cloves into the slices. Put them in the pan with the cinnamon stick and myrtle berries. Stir in the honey. Heat the punch to just below simmering point and keep it at that temperature for 20 minutes.

Strain the infused mead through a sieve. Serve hot, in warmed mugs or thick heatproof glasses.

APPLE, WALNUT AND MYRTLE BERRY CHUTNEY

I often make chutneys for Christmas presents. This is a particularly good one that is always popular, as it goes well with cheese and cold meats.

Makes approx. 5 lb (2.25 kg)

3¾ cups (900 ml) malt vinegar
1 lb (450 g) light soft brown sugar
12 myrtle berries (fresh, if possible)
2 lb (900 g) cooking apples
1 lb (450 g) onions, chopped
1½ cups (375 ml) raisins
3½ tbsp (50 ml) English mustard powder
2 tbsp (30 ml) freshly grated gingerroot
2 tsp (10 ml) mild curry powder
1½ tbsp (20 ml) salt
1 cup (250 ml) walnut pieces

Put the vinegar and sugar in a large saucepan and bring to a boil. Peel, core and roughly chop the apples and add to the pan with all the other ingredients, except the walnuts. Bring back to a boil. Cook, stirring more regularly as it thickens, until it is well reduced and thick (remember, it will thicken even more once cold).

Remove the pan from the heat and stir in the walnuts. Spoon the mixture into warm sterilized jars (see page 12) and seal with vinegar-proof lids.

This will keep for up to 1 year.

Excess myrtle

Myrtle salt

Being an evergreen herb that can be used for most of the year, a surplus of myrtle is something that occurs less than for annual herbs. However, if you do not have a myrtle bush growing in your garden and you are given a branch, the best way to preserve the flavor of the leaves is to make myrtle salt, which is great with fish and for barbecues.

Makes 1 cup (250 ml)

1 cup (250 ml) noniodized salt
20 myrtle leaves

Using a mortar and pestle, pound together the salt and the myrtle leaves – the salt will pick up the flavor of the herb.

Bottle the salt and crushed leaves and keep in a dark cupboard. It can be used immediately or stored, but it is best used within 3 months.

NASTURTIUM

(also known as Garden Nasturtium, Indian Cress, Large Cress)

Tropaeolum majus

This herb is recognizable in many gardens but it is rarely acknowledged as the useful culinary and medicinal herb that it is. For me it brings back many childhood memories, from using the flowers when creating miniature gardens to astonishing school friends with the flavor of the leaves. Neither my grandmother nor my mother believed they were worthy of the kitchen. I, on the other hand, find them useful not only for the flavor but also for the flamboyancy that the flowers can add to a meal.

Description

Nasturtiums are half-hardy, meaning that they die as soon as there is any threat of frost, and so last only one year. Despite this brevity, they are seriously worth growing for the wonderfully brazen flowers they produce all summer – the colors can vary from orange to amazing mahogany and deep crimson. The round mid-green leaves have a peppery flavor.

Sow the large, easy-to-handle seeds directly into small pots in early spring. Alternatively, sow the seeds in late spring in prepared well-drained soil in sun or partial shade. A word of warning: if the soil is too rich there will be an abundance of leaf and little flower, so be stingy with your feed, fertilizer or compost if you want a profusion of flowers.

History in cooking

This herb was introduced into Europe from Peru in the 16th century. It was first known as Indian Cress (*Nasturtium indicum*) on account of the pungent watercress-like flavor of its leaves. The custom of eating its petals and using them for tea originated in the Orient, and from the early 17th century onward there are references to nasturtium flowers being used in salads. Even the famous Mrs. Beeton, in the mid-1800s, suggested that they should be used to dress a summer salad.

Harvesting and uses

Leaves

Pick the young leaves from late spring until the first frosts or late autumn. Their peppery flavor combines well with salad greens, especially when served with a vinaigrette dressing, potatoes, crème fraîche or cream cheese.

Flowers

Pick from early summer until the first frosts or late autumn. These also have a light peppery taste that is ideal in all forms of salads and served with mustard and fruit, especially strawberries.

Seeds

The best-flavored seed pods are those that are small and green, and they can be pickled or added to salads fresh; they are quite strong in flavor, so use sparingly. The seeds that are turning brown, which can be harvested from midsummer until early autumn, should be saved for drying and sowing in the following spring.

Properties

Medicinally all parts of the plant appear to be antibiotic. It also contains large amounts of sulfur and the leaves contain vitamin C and iron, as well as an antiseptic substance that is at its strongest before the plant flowers. Nasturtiums are reputedly good for the skin as an antiseptic wash.

Varieties

There are many different varieties of *Tropaeolum majus*; some are bushy, some are trailing and some are climbing, but all have edible leaves and flowers. Here are just a few varieties that are easily available from good seed suppliers.

Alaska Nasturtium
Tropaeolum majus Alaska Series
Red/orange flowers with variegated cream/white and green leaves.

Empress of India Nasturtium
Tropaeolum majus 'Empress of India'
Dark red flowers with dark green leaves.

Peaches & Cream Nasturtium
Tropaeolum majus 'Peaches & Cream'
Pale pink/orange/cream flowers with mid-green leaves.

Tom Thumb Black Velvet Nasturtium
Tropaeolum majus 'Tom Thumb Black Velvet'
Deep red/scarlet flowers with mid-green leaves.

Double Gleam Nasturtium
Tropaeolum majus 'Double Gleam'
Mixture of golden yellow, orange and scarlet flowers with mid-green leaves. This is a semi-trailing variety.

Jewel of Africa Nasturtium
Tropaeolum majus 'Jewel of Africa'
Mixture of yellow, red, cream and pink flowers with variegated cream and green leaves. This is a climbing variety.

NASTURTIUM SALSA

This is a great way to serve nasturtium leaves and petals. The pepper flavor of the leaves goes so well with the fiery chile, and the whole thing looks amazingly pretty in the serving bowl.

Serves 4

2 large tomatoes, peeled
1 small chile pepper, seeded and finely chopped
½ red onion, finely sliced, then chopped
1 tbsp (15 ml) nasturtium leaves, chopped
1 tbsp (15 ml) balsamic vinegar
Juice of ½ lime
Salt
2 nasturtium flowers (petals only)

Cut the tomatoes in half, remove the seeds and discard them. Chop the tomatoes finely, then place them in a small bowl. Add the chopped chile pepper, onion, nasturtium leaves, vinegar and lime juice and season with salt.

Scatter the nasturtium petals over the top and serve.

NASTURTIUM MUSHROOM BAKE

When I was growing up, garlic mushrooms were considered *de rigueur*. I still have a soft spot for them. This dish combines the mushrooms and garlic with the peppery flavor of nasturtium leaves, creating a lovely depth of flavor. It makes a good summer first course that can be served with crusty homemade bread or toast and a cold glass of cider.

Serves 2–4

6 tbsp (90 ml) olive oil
3 cloves garlic, crushed
20–30 fresh young nasturtium leaves
8 oz (225 g) fresh mushrooms, washed and sliced
1 tbsp (15 ml) thyme leaves (common, French, Porlock or broad-leafed), removed from the sprigs and finely chopped
Salt and freshly ground black pepper
Freshly grated nutmeg

Put the olive oil in a bowl and add the garlic to infuse for 1 hour.

Preheat the oven to 400°F (200°C). Wash and dry the nasturtium leaves and add to the infused garlic oil.

Place the mushrooms in another bowl and sprinkle with the thyme, salt and pepper and a grating of nutmeg. Gently stir the mushrooms well so they are well coated in the herbs and seasonings.

Remove the leaves one by one from the garlic oil, reserving the oil, and place one-third of the leaves on the bottom of a shallow 6-inch (15 cm) baking dish. Cover the leaves with half the mushrooms, then cover those in turn with more leaves, followed by the remaining mushrooms and ending with a layer of leaves. Add a sprinkling of garlic oil, cover well and bake in the oven for 20 minutes. Serve.

BROILED SALMON WITH NASTURTIUM BUTTER

The nasturtium butter is not only colorful but also packs a punch. Its piquant flavor enhances the flavors of the salmon, making this an attractive and appetizing meal.

Serves 4

For the nasturtium butter
7 tbsp (100 ml) unsalted butter
10 nasturtium flowers
Juice of ½ lemon

For the salmon and salad
4 wild or organically
farmed salmon steaks
1 red onion, finely sliced
1 sweet red pepper,
seeded and finely sliced
1 iceberg lettuce, finely sliced

For the salad dressing
3 tbsp (45 ml) olive oil
1 tbsp (15 ml) lemon juice
Salt and freshly ground
black pepper

Start by making the butter. Put all the ingredients in a food processor and mix until totally mixed. Transfer to a small container with a lid and place in the fridge until required.

Preheat the broiler to high. When hot, broil the salmon until it is cooked through.

Combine all the dressing ingredients and mix together well. Mix the onion, pepper and lettuce in a bowl and pour on the salad dressing. Arrange the dressed salad on 4 plates and top each with a piece of cooked salmon, then place a quarter of the nasturtium butter on each piece and serve.

STUFFED NASTURTIUM LEAVES

This French recipe is lovely and unusual; the first time I had this I was 13 years old. I was staying with my Aunt Pippa, who then lived in La Garde Freinet in the hills above St. Tropez. I was amazed to learn that I was eating nasturtium leaves. This recipe transforms them.

Serves 4

1 tsp (5 ml) capers, rinsed and chopped
1 small gherkin, finely chopped
1 tsp (5 ml) parsley, finely chopped
1 tsp (5 ml) chervil, finely chopped
24–30 nasturtium leaves
2-oz (50 g) can anchovy fillets, drained and cut into narrow strips
2/3 cup (150 ml) dry white wine
1 tbsp (15 ml) French tarragon vinegar (see page 316)
1 thyme sprig
1 bay leaf
2 tbsp (30 ml) olive oil

Preheat the oven to 300°F (150°C).

In a bowl, mix together the capers, gherkin, parsley and chervil. Remove the stems from the nasturtium leaves. Place a little of the herb mixture in the center of each leaf and cover with a strip of anchovy. Fold in the sides of the leaf and then roll it up, rather like a cigar, with the seam underneath.

Arrange the stuffed leaves in a shallow ovenproof frying pan and pour the wine and vinegar over. Add the thyme and bay leaf, then transfer to the oven for 15 minutes.

Remove from the oven and transfer the stuffed leaves to a serving dish. Keep warm. Reduce the remaining wine and vinegar over high heat until there are about 2 spoonfuls left. Put the olive oil in a small bowl and strain into it the warm reduced wine, discarding the bay and thyme leaves. Whisk well, then pour over the stuffed nasturtium leaves.

Chill until ready to serve.

Excess nasturtium

Pickled nasturtium seed pods

These pickled seed pods make a good substitute for capers. They have a light, peppery flavor and add crunch to salads and sauces and are great with cheeses.

Enough nasturtium seed pods to fill a standard jam jar
2 tbsp (30 ml) salt to 2¼ cups (560 ml) water, repeated 3 times (see recipe)
2 tbsp (30 ml) French tarragon leaves, finely chopped
1 onion, finely chopped
1¾ cups (425 ml) white wine vinegar
12 black peppercorns
1 chile pepper, seeded and finely chopped
1 tsp (5 ml) salt
Generous grating of fresh nutmeg

Before putting the seed pods in the jam jar, place them in a bowl and cover with salted water. Leave them for 1 day, strain, then cover with clean salted water. Repeat this for 3 days. On the final day, drain, place in a dry dish towel and pat dry.

Place the dried seed pods in layers in the jam jar with the tarragon and onion.

In a saucepan, combine the vinegar, peppercorns, chile pepper, salt and nutmeg, bring to a boil, then simmer for 10 minutes. Allow to cool, then strain and pour the liquid over the seed pods.

Seal with the lid and store in the fridge for at least 1 week before using.

OREGANO, MARJORAM

(also known as Maggiorana, Origano, Wild Marjoram, Mountain Mint, Oregano, Winter Marjoram, Winter Sweet, Marjolaine)

Origanum vulgare

I feel quite strongly about this subject – when is a plant oregano and when is it marjoram? In my understanding the only true marjoram is *Origanum majorana*, which is known as sweet marjoram, whereas oregano is *Origanum vulgare* (the *vulgare* part means common). Both are great in the kitchen and in the garden. Grandmother used oregano sparingly, whereas my mother, who was enamored with Mediterranean cooking, used sweet marjoram with gusto and at times rather too liberally.

Description

In summer this plant is a joy for the bees and butterflies that surround the flowers. All the varieties of *Origanum vulgare* are hardy, with clusters of tiny tubular mauve flowers in summer and dark green aromatic hairy leaves, which in winter form a tight mat. Sweet marjoram, on the other hand, is an annual in cold climates. It has tiny white flowers that grow in a knot-like cluster and pale gray-green leaves that are highly aromatic.

The vigor and aroma of all forms of *Origanum* vary greatly depending on where it is planted and in which country. In the Mediterranean you can smell the oregano before you see it, but in the damp, cool northern European climate you see it, but only smell it when you either crush a leaf or cook with it. So for the best results, plant in full sun in free-draining soil. Standard oregano and marjoram can both be grown from seed; however, the seed is very fine, so mix with sand or flour before sowing so that you do not sow too thickly. Both varieties can be grown from cuttings taken from the new growth in summer, and established plants of oregano can be divided in the spring or after flowering in late summer.

All oreganos can be grown successfully in containers. Use a soil-based potting compost mixed with additional sharp grit or sand and place the container in a sunny position.

History in cooking

In medieval times marjoram was combined with alecost (costmary) to flavor ale – this was before hops were introduced into Britain during the reign of Henry VIII (1491–1547). *The Englishman's Flora*, by Geoffrey Grigson (1905–85), is illustrated with woodcuts from the 16th century, and one of these shows an Italian lady watering marjoram. Under the woodcut are the following words: *confortat cerebrum et omnia viscera*, which translates as "comforts the head and all internal organs."

Harvesting and uses

Leaves

The leaves of oregano are available all year round, while those of marjoram are available in the northern hemisphere from spring until early autumn. For both, the best-flavored leaves can be picked either side of flowering. The summer leaves are much more strongly flavored than the winter, mat-forming ones because the warmth of the sun brings the oils in the leaf to the surface. The leaves can be used in salads, with eggs and vegetables, cooked with meat and in marinades, and they are also lovely with grilled fish.

Flowers
Pick these just as they open throughout the summer and scatter over salads, soups, baked potatoes and roast vegetables.

Properties

Marjoram and oregano have a soothing effect on the digestive system; they stimulate the digestive juices that help to break down rich and heavy foods. They are also highly valued for treating dyspepsia, loss of appetite, colic and nausea.

Other varieties

There are many varieties of oregano available. Here I have simply chosen my favorites for the kitchen.

Greek Oregano
Origanum vulgare subsp. *hirtum* 'Greek'
This variety is a very strong flavored, with hairy dark olive green leaves and white flowers. Excellent with meat and casseroles.

Oregano Acorn Bank, Marjoram Acorn Bank
Origanum vulgare 'Acorn Bank'
This is a golden-leaved variety with clusters of tiny tubular pink flowers in summer. The leaves have a mild flavor and are good with vegetables and in salads.

French Oregano, French Marjoram
Origanum onites
The green leaves turn gold in the sun and it bears clusters of light pink flowers in summer. This oregano has a light, spicy flavor that is good with vegetable dishes.

Sweet Marjoram, Knotted Marjoram
Origanum majorana
This aromatic marjoram is often grown as an annual. It has clusters of tiny white flowers with oval pale green soft, aromatic leaves, which have an excellent culinary flavor that goes well with tomatoes and tomato sauces, vegetables and meat dishes.

BAKED SWEET MARJORAM GOAT CHEESE WITH ROAST VEGETABLE SALAD

This is a rustic summer salad. The marjoram and mint, being cousins, combine beautifully with the salty goat cheese.

Serves 4

2 small or 1 large zucchini, sliced into ½-inch (1 cm) rounds
2 red bell peppers, halved and seeded
4 tbsp (60 ml) olive oil, divided, plus extra for drizzling
1 bulb fennel, halved and very finely sliced
1 bunch arugula leaves
2 tbsp (30 ml) sweet marjoram leaves, removed from their stems
7 oz (200 g) goat cheese, cut into 4 round slices
Sea salt and freshly ground black pepper
Juice of ½ lemon
10 spearmint sprigs, finely chopped (pick from the top so you have the new growth; choose Moroccan, garden or Tashkent mint, not peppermint)

Preheat the oven to 325°F (170°C), and preheat the broiler to hot. (If you have a combined oven, heat the broiler first, then preheat the oven once you have finished with the broiler.)

Line the bottom of a broiler pan with a piece of foil, lay the sliced zucchini and the pepper halves on the rack, drizzle with olive oil and place under the hot broiler. Cook for about 3 to 4 minutes, turning the vegetables over halfway through. Remove from the heat. Place the peppers on a chopping board to cool and place the zucchini in a large bowl with the finely sliced fennel and the arugula leaves.

Chop the marjoram leaves finely and place in a small bowl with 1 tbsp (15 ml) olive oil. Add the goat cheese to the bowl and season with pepper. Make sure the goat cheese is coated all over with the herby oil, then place on a baking sheet lined with baking parchment or foil. Place in the preheated oven and cook for about 10 minutes, until golden brown. (The oven is better than the broiler, which will burn the marjoram and destroy the flavor.)

Peel the peppers, slice into ribbons and add to the salad.

Make a dressing by combining the remaining olive oil with the lemon juice, salt and pepper. Pour the dressing over the salad and toss well, then divide among 4 serving plates. Top with the goat cheese, sprinkle with chopped mint and serve.

SPINACH, TOMATO AND SWEET MARJORAM GALETTES

Using aromatic sweet marjoram both in the pastry and with the tomato and spinach topping lets the herb's wonderful warm, spicy flavor permeate right through these small pastries.

This is a useful dish; you can make it for two, then freeze the rest of the pastry raw, interleaved with foil. You can then use it at a later date to make a meal quickly.

I have to be honest – pastry and my gardening hands have never been a good mix, but recently I was introduced to a wonderful technique: you freeze the butter, grate it into the flour, then mix it with a thin metal spatula, thus keeping warm physical touch to the minimum. Ever since I adopted this tip these little tartlets (or, if you want to be fancy, galettes, as the pastry shell has no sides) have been a great success.

Serves 3–6

For the pastry
½ cup (125 ml) unsalted butter
1 cup + 2 tsp (260 ml) all-purpose flour, plus extra for dusting
Pinch of salt
1 tsp (5 ml) finely chopped sweet marjoram leaves
Cold water

For the topping
8 oz (225 g) young leaf spinach
2 onions, peeled and thinly sliced
1 knob unsalted butter
1 tbsp (15 ml) chopped sweet marjoram leaves, plus a little extra to decorate
6 medium-ripe tomatoes, peeled and thinly sliced
1 tsp (5 ml) olive oil
2 tbsp (30 ml) freshly grated Parmesan

Preheat the oven to 425°F (220°C) and lightly grease 2 baking sheets.

To·make the pastry, measure and freeze the butter prior to use, wrapped in foil or plastic wrap. Sift the flour into a large bowl with the salt. Remove the butter from the freezer, fold back the covering and grate over the flour, using the coarsest side of the grater.

Once you finish grating, add the sweet marjoram leaves and fold in with the butter and flour using a thin metal spatula. Once the butter is well covered, add 2 tbsp (30 ml) cold water – don't overadd water, as the dough should not be too wet. (I do use my hands for the last bit.) Having made the dough, remove it from the bowl, place it in plastic wrap or a plastic bag and put in the fridge until you are ready to use it.

Wash the spinach and place it in a saucepan, cover with a lid, then cook on the stovetop over medium heat. You only need the spinach to wilt down, which takes 2 to 3 minutes. Give it a turn, then drain off all the excess liquid through a colander, pressing the spinach with the back of a serving spoon to make sure all the liquid is squeezed out. Put to one side.

Fry the sliced onions in the butter until translucent. Add the sweet marjoram leaves and stir them into the onions. Remove from the heat and drain off any excess liquid.

To peel the tomatoes, simply place them in a bowl, cover with boiling water, leave to stand for 1 minute, then drain. The skins can now be removed easily – however, they will be hot, so do protect your fingers.

Remove the pastry from the fridge and roll it out on a lightly floured surface to ⅛ inch (3 mm) thick. Cut out 6 x 6-inch (15 cm) circles and place them on the prepared baking sheets. Chop the spinach, then divide it among the 6 circles, leaving a narrow rim clear around the edge of the pastry. Scatter with the onion and marjoram mix, then cover with overlapping slices of tomato. Sprinkle over a little marjoram and olive oil.

Place the baking sheets in the oven for 10 to 12 minutes. If you are using 2, you will need to switch their position in the oven halfway through the cooking time. Remove from the oven, sprinkle with Parmesan and serve warm, or allow to cool and then serve.

FISH PIE WITH SWEET MARJORAM CRUMBLE

As a child I was always served fish on Fridays. Mum usually cooked a pie, as this made a small bit stretch a long way. As a treat she would buy smoked haddock, and today the aroma of this fish cooking transports me back to my childhood. I have added the marjoram crumble to augment the flavor of the pie. Serve simply with carrots and boiled new potatoes.

Serves 4

14 oz (400 g) smoked haddock fillets (try to get the undyed version)
1 onion, finely sliced
1¼ cups (300 ml) reduced fat (2%) or 1% milk
2 bay leaves
Salt and freshly ground black pepper
3 tbsp (45 ml) unsalted butter
½ cup + 2 tsp (135 ml) whole wheat flour
3 tbsp (45 ml) freshly grated Parmesan
2 tbsp (30 ml) sweet marjoram leaves, chopped
4 tsp (20 ml) cornstarch
2 tbsp (30 ml) flat-leaf parsley, finely chopped

Preheat the oven to 325°F (170°C).

Put the fish in a roasting pan and add the onion, milk and bay leaves. Season with salt and pepper to taste, then cover with foil. Place the pan in the oven and cook for 15 to 20 minutes.

Remove from the oven and check that when you touch the fish it is still firm but easily breaks up. Lift the fish out of the milk with a metal spatula and put it on a plate. Set aside the milk in the roasting pan and discard the bay leaf. Remove the skin from the fish and flake the flesh, discarding any bones.

In a mixing bowl, make the crumble by using your fingertips to rub the butter into the flour to make fine crumbs. Add the Parmesan, marjoram and seasoning to taste.

Mix the cornstarch to a smooth paste with a little water. Put the infused milk in the roasting pan on the stove top over low heat, add the cornstarch paste and bring to a boil, stirring until the sauce has thickened. Gently stir in the flaked fish and chopped parsley and season with salt and pepper to taste.

Pour the fish mixture into an ovenproof dish. Spoon the crumble mixture overtop and press down with the back of a fork. Bake for 35 minutes or until the top is golden. Serve at once.

OREGANO COTTAGE PIE

In my grandmother's notebook I came across this description: "Cottage pie is made with beef, shepherd's pie is made with mutton or lamb." As soon as I read this it became an "of course"; I guess I had never stopped to think about the two names and why they had them.

When I was growing up, this dish was a Wednesday meal and was made with what was left from the Sunday roast. Adding oregano to the dish spikes up the flavors of the pie. Serve with green beans, peas or Brussels sprouts.

Serves 4

For the topping
1½ lb (680 g) potatoes (Yukon Gold or red)
4 tbsp (60 ml) milk
2½ tbsp (35 ml) unsalted butter

For the pie
10–12 oz (285–340 g) cold cooked beef, mutton or lamb
6–8 oz (180–225 g) carrots, thinly sliced
1 tbsp (15 ml) unsalted butter, plus extra for greasing and dotting
1 small onion, finely chopped
1 tbsp (15 ml) oregano or sweet marjoram leaves, finely chopped
2 tsp (10 ml) all-purpose flour
Salt and freshly ground black pepper

Preheat the oven to 375°F (190°C) and grease an ovenproof dish.

First make the topping. Cook the potatoes in boiling water, drain, then mash with the milk and butter and set aside.

Prepare the meat by removing the fat, then either slice and dice it finely by hand, which makes nice chunky bits, or use a food processor to ground the meat. Do not overprocess or it will become a mush.

Cook the carrots for 5 minutes, drain, reserve ⅔ cup (150 ml) of the cooking water and set aside. Fry the onion in the butter for 5 minutes until it is translucent, then add the meat and the oregano or sweet marjoram. Cook for a few more minutes, stirring all the time. Add the flour and cook for 1 minute to blend in any of the fat and juices. Add the carrot water plus any remaining gravy you might have, stir well until all is blended, then add salt and pepper to taste.

Turn the contents into the prepared ovenproof dish. Lay the sliced carrots on the surface of the meat, then cover with the mashed potato. Using a fork, make lines in the potato, then dot with a small amount of butter.

Cook in the oven for 30 to 35 minutes.

OREGANO AND LEMON PAN-FRIED CHICKEN

This is a simple, healthy meal that is quick to prepare and cook, only needing a little time to marinate. Using oregano and lemon as a marinade before cooking the chicken infuses it with their flavors. Delicious served with boiled rice and a crisp green salad.

Serves 2

2 boneless chicken breasts
Zest and juice of ½ lemon
2 tsp (10 ml) oregano leaves, finely chopped
1 tbsp (15 ml) olive oil
1 tbsp (15 ml) parsley leaves, finely chopped
Salt and freshly ground black pepper

Make shallow cuts in the chicken breasts. Mix the lemon zest and juice with the oregano leaves and rub into the chicken breasts. Leave in the fridge for 30 minutes to marinate.

Heat the olive oil in a small frying pan on medium heat. When hot, remove the chicken from the marinade, fry for 8 to 10 minutes on each side until cooked, then add the marinade and increase the heat until it is bubbling. Add the parsley leaves and turn off the heat. Toss everything around, season and serve.

OREGANO YORKSHIRE PUDDINGS

Adding oregano to Yorkshire pudding batter transforms a family favorite into a treat. It also makes it ideal for vegetarians; when I make the individual desserts I serve them with a rich, thick homemade tomato sauce (see page 12) in the center, topped with a slice of grilled goat cheese.

Makes approx. 6–9 puddings, depending on the size of the tray

1 cup (250 ml) all-purpose flour
Salt
2 eggs
1 cup + 2 tbsp (275 ml) milk
1 tbsp (15 ml) oregano leaves, finely chopped
2–3 tbsp (30–45 ml) vegetable oil or good dripping or lard

Preheat the oven to 450°F (230°C).

Make the batter by sieving the flour and salt into a bowl, then make a well in the center and add the eggs, breaking the yolks with a spoon before you start stirring. Add the milk gradually, stirring into the flour little by little until half the milk is added; keep going until all the flour is taken up and the mixture is smooth. Then add the rest of the milk and the oregano and beat for 5 to 10 minutes. Stand the batter in a cool place for 1 hour.

When the batter is ready, heat the oil or dripping in a roasting pan or popover pan until it is just beginning to smoke; check that there is ½ inch (1 cm) of oil in each section. Pour the batter into the pan or into the individual sections. Cook for 5 minutes at 450°F (230°C), then turn down to 400°F (200°C) and cook for 35 to 40 minutes, until crisp and puffy. Individual Yorkshire puds will take less time, about 15 to 20 minutes. Don't open the door of the oven too soon, otherwise you will get flat puds.

Excess sweet marjoram

Sweet marjoram butter

This can be used to fry vegetables, to put on broiled tomatoes or for making pastry.

Makes ½ cup (125 ml)

3 tbsp (45 ml) sweet marjoram leaves, finely chopped
½ cup (125 ml) unsalted butter, softened to room temperature

Mix the chopped leaves with the butter. The simplest and easiest way of blending the herb and butter together is to use a fork. Once thoroughly mixed, pack the butter into a roll of waxed paper and place in the fridge for up to 24 hours before use. The longer you leave it, the better the flavor.

This can also be frozen. Place it in a freezerproof container, label it, and use within 3 months.

PARSLEY

(also known as Persil, Prezzemolo)
Petroselinum crispum

This is one of the most widely used herbs throughout the world. In the main it is used as a garnish, but it is also a great root vegetable and a terrific leaf herb that can make bland food come alive. All four generations of my family that have contributed to this book have loved, respected and used this herb in the kitchen. I have deliberately chosen recipes from my grandmother and mother that show how this herb can make a meal.

Description

Parsley is a hardy biennial, which means that it produces leaf in the first year and flowers in the second. The flowers appear in creamy white clusters, while the leaves are a bright green (which can vary in depth of color depending on variety) with toothed edges (again this can vary according to variety, from being straight to amazingly tightly curled).

This herb has to be grown from seed. For the most productive crops, sow where you want to crop it, as it hates being transplanted; so either sow seed directly into the garden once the soil has started to warm up, in mid-spring, or into a large, deep container. Be patient, as germination can vary from 10 days to six weeks. Parsley is a hungry plant and likes a good deep soil, not too light and not acid. Always feed the chosen site well in the previous autumn with well-rotted manure.

If you wish to harvest parsley all year round, the ideal arrangement is to have two different sites prepared. For summer supplies, a western or eastern border is perfect because the plant needs moisture and prefers a little shade. For winter supplies, a more sheltered spot will be needed in a sunny position, like next to a south-facing wall. Remember to water well during hot weather.

Only Hamburg or turnip-rooted parsley differs, as it is a root crop not a leaf crop. The soil should be prepared in exactly the same way and the seed should be sown in shallow drills in mid-spring. Water well all summer. The root tends to grow more at this time of year and, unlike a lot of root crops, the largest roots taste the best. Lift the roots from the ground in late autumn until early winter.

History in cooking

Parsley has been popular since records began; the Romans ate it as a deodorizer, whereas the ancient Greeks believed that the plants grew from the blood of their heroes, so it was fed in abundance to their athletes. During the Middle Ages the monks grew parsley to treat the sick. John Gerard (1545–1612), the English herbalist and surgeon, said of parsley: "It is delightful to the taste and agreeable to the stomache."

Harvesting and uses

Leaves

Pick the leaves from early summer of the first season to the early spring of the second. Parsley is a widely used culinary herb, valued for its taste as well as its rich nutritional content (see Properties, below). Cooking with parsley brings out the flavor of other foods and herbs. In bland food it is always best to add parsley just before the end of cooking to get the best flavor.

Seeds

The seeds can be harvested from midsummer of the second season. They are hardly ever used in cooking but, like those of its cousin caraway, they are delicious ground and used to flavor soups, stews or casseroles.

Roots

If you want to use the roots of parsley, grow separate plants for this purpose so you can get the seeds in the second year from the other plants. Dig up roots from autumn to early winter of the first season. The roots of Hamburg parsley make a great alternative to carrots or celeriac; they are lovely cooked on their own or added to soups, stews or casseroles.

Properties

Parsley is a most beneficial culinary herb; it helps clear the toxins from the body and is also well known for its digestive properties and for being a diuretic, carminative, antispasmodic and good antioxidant. It is renowned for its high vitamin and mineral content, due to its long tap root; the leaves are high in beta-carotene and vitamins A, B, B_2, B_3, C and E, plus the minerals calcium, iron, sodium, phosphorus and magnesium. So, all in all, this is a must-have culinary herb that should be eaten regularly.

Varieties

French Parsley, Broad-leafed or Flat-leaf Parsley
Petroselinum crispum 'French'
This hardy biennial has umbels of small creamy white flowers in the second summer and flat mid-green toothed leaves that are strongly flavored.

Italian Parsley
Petroselinum crispum var. *neapolitanum*
This is a hardy biennial with umbels of small creamy white flowers in the second summer and flat dark green large-toothed leaves that are strongly flavored.

Hamburg Parsley, Turnip-rooted Parsley

Petroselinum crispum var. *tuberosum*

This is a hardy biennial that is usually grown as an annual, with flat umbels of white flowers in summer, green leaves that are similar to French parsley and creamy white roots that have a similar flavor to celeriac. This variety was probably first developed in Holland, since it was once called Dutch parsley. It was introduced into England in the early 18th century but was only popular until the early 19th century. The plant is still frequently found in France and Germany in the vegetable markets.

FRIED PARSLEY

This is one of my grandmother's recipes from her handwritten notebook, which I have reproduced here with my comments in parentheses. It is interesting that this dish has come right back into fashion as an appetizer. It is a wonderful way to use parsley, especially if you have a glut.

Get everything ready before you pick your parsley, as this dish is useless once the parsley has started to wilt. Serve with freshly ground salt. This goes well with pâtés or aperitifs.

Serves 4

1 large bunch curly parsley
Cooking oil, for deep frying

Unless it is absolutely essential, refrain from washing the parsley. If it is necessary do so, do it some hours beforehand and see that it is perfectly dry before lowering it into the hot fat; otherwise the fat splashes in a violent way and is dangerous.

Pick the sprigs from the main stalks of the parsley. Allow a really large handful of sprigs for 4 people. Set a pan of oil over high heat. Put the parsley sprigs in a frying basket, and when the oil shows a faint blue haze, plunge it into the fat-bath. Do not be deterred by the noise it makes. As soon as the hissing stops, lift out the parsley (it is ready in seconds), which should be bright green. (It should be crisp, bright green and not greasy, limp or brown.) Once cooked, place on paper towels to mop up the oil.

PARSLEY AND HERB SPREAD

The parsley enhances the spinach in this tasty spread, which is wonderful served with toasted pita bread, freshly baked crusty bread or cheese crackers.

Serves 4–6

1 lb (450 g) young spinach leaves
1 lb (450 g) flat-leaf parsley leaves, roughly chopped
9 oz (250 g) coriander leaves, roughly chopped
9 oz (250 g) celery leaf, roughly chopped
4 cloves garlic, peeled and halved
¼ cup (60 ml) extra-virgin olive oil, divided
1 tsp (5 ml) smoked paprika
¼ tsp (1 ml) cayenne pepper
1 tsp (5 ml) ground cumin
1 tbsp (15 ml) lemon juice
Salt and freshly ground pepper

Wash the spinach, parsley, coriander and celery leaf and shake dry, but do not towel dry.

Place all the washed herbs and spinach in a large saucepan with the garlic. Cover and heat gently until all the greens have sweated down. Drain in a colander and remove the garlic cloves; put them on a plate and squish into a purée using a fork.

When cool enough to handle, squeeze the excess water out of the herbs and spinach. In a medium frying pan, heat 1 tbsp (15 ml) olive oil. Add the mashed garlic, paprika, cayenne and cumin to the pan and stir over medium heat for 30 seconds or until fragrant. Add the spinach and herb mixture and cook together, mashing and stirring at the same time until soft and smooth, for about 8 minutes.

Remove from the heat and transfer to a small bowl, add the remaining oil, mix well and cover. Once cool, put the bowl in the fridge for at least 24 hours.

Just before serving, stir in the lemon juice and check the

seasoning, adding extra salt and pepper if needed. Serve as an appetizer or first course.

This spread will keep for 3 days in the fridge.

SALSA VERDE

Parsley comes into its own when used with salty dishes, and it is excellent when combined with anchovies. This is a useful summer sauce that goes well with so many dishes, particularly fish, boiled ham and new potatoes.

Makes approx. 1 cup (250 ml)

1 large bunch flat-leaf parsley
1 clove garlic, crushed
4 anchovy fillets, chopped
1 tbsp (15 ml) capers, drained and chopped
¾ cup + 2 tbsp (200 ml) olive oil
Salt and freshly ground black pepper

Wash and dry the parsley and cut off the bottom ½ inch (1 cm) of the stems but leave the rest. Check the leaves for any spoiled ones and remove.

Place the parsley in a food processor with the garlic, anchovies and capers. Process for a few minutes, then, with the motor running slowly, add the oil in a steady stream. Season to taste.

PARSLEY AND LEMON ICE

Here is another interesting recipe from my grandmother's notebook (my notes are in parentheses). I would never have thought of using parsley in a dessert, but it has a refreshing green flavor. We would call this sorbet, my grandmother called it ice. I find this a really good summer dessert.

Serves 4

Juice and pared rind of 1 lemon
2 cups (500 ml) water
¼ cup (60 ml) sugar
2 large handfuls parsley

Put the lemon rind in a saucepan with the water and sugar, bring to a boil and infuse for 5 minutes (or until the sugar has melted, stirring with a wooden spoon). Add the lemon juice, strain and cool. (I don't strain it, as I like the lemon bits, so I simply fish out the pared lemon peel with a slotted spoon.)

Boil the parsley (bring a small pan of water to a boil and add the parsley) for 5 to 10 minutes (5 minutes is sufficient), then drain and press through a sieve. Add this to the lemon mixture and freeze. (I recommend that you thoroughly stir this ice with a fork to form a slush. Do this twice during the first 2 hours of freezing; this way it will not be a solid lump when you come to serve it.)

PARSLEY HONEY

This recipe I found fascinating – it is one of my grandmother's recipes that she recommended during the Second World War, when honey was difficult to obtain. It makes an interesting form of spread for bread! And, again, it is a unique way of using parsley. The flavor is, strangely, rather like honey, but perhaps that is word association. Great with yogurt, crème fraîche and fruit.

Makes 2 x 1-pint (450 g) jars

4 1/3 cups (175 g) fresh parsley
3½ cups (850 ml) water
Juice of 1 lemon
1 lb (450 g) sugar

Wash and dry the parsley. Roughly chop, stems included, and put into a saucepan with the water. Bring to a boil and simmer gently for 30 minutes.

Strain through a jelly bag and measure the resulting juice. Put the juice into a clean pan with the lemon juice and 1 lb (450 g) sugar for every 2 1/3 cups (570 ml) parsley juice. Stir well over low heat until the sugar has dissolved, then bring to a boil. Reduce the heat and simmer gently for 30 to 45 minutes, until the mixture is clear and syrupy, very like thin honey.

Pour into warm sterilized jars (see page 12) and cover and seal while hot.

Excess parsley

Frozen parsley

This is one herb that freezes well and is an easy way to harvest an excess.

For a good harvest one needs to pick the leaf at its optimum flavor, which is in the first year in late summer and after the plant has been well fed. Pick the leaves as soon as the dew has evaporated but before the height of the day. If the leaf is harvested late in the day, after it has been in the sun, all the essential oils will have evaporated. Freezing the leaves does destroy some of the beneficial essential oils, but it does not impair the flavor.

Pick the leaves with the stems. Wash if necessary, dry well, then place in a freezer bag and put in the freezer.

When you require the parsley, remove the bag from the freezer and crush it immediately; do not hesitate or leave the bag for a few minutes, because the parsley will thaw. By crushing the bag when the parsley is still frozen you will break it into small pieces, giving you instant, easy-to-use chopped parsley.

PURSLANE

(also known as Kulfa, Baql, Pigweed, Horse Money, Pussley)

Portulaca oleracea

This scrumptious culinary and medicinal herb can be found growing wild throughout Europe and India. It is, in many countries, considered a pernicious weed. When I was a child, it was one of the plants that my mother taught me to forage for when on holiday in France and Italy.

One of the funniest references I found for this herb is a mention in Matthew Biggs's *Complete Book of Vegetables*. I discovered that its name in Malawi translates as "buttocks of the wife of a chief," obviously referring to its succulent round leaves and juicy stems! The mind boggles.

Description

Purslane is a hardy annual with small yellow stalkless flowers in summer that open in the sun and close in the shade. It has thick, fleshy, spoon-shaped mid-green leaves that to me taste of fresh snow peas with a hint of salt.

It prefers to grow in a sunny position in a moisture-retentive light soil that has not been fed in the previous autumn. It is more attractive and more productive if grown in thick rows or clumps in the garden rather than as an isolated plant. It can be easily grown from seed sown in spring once the soil has warmed. It will adapt to growing in a container but it does not fare as well as when grown in the garden.

History in cooking

Historically this plant has been grown for culinary and medicinal use for more than 2,000 years; it was used as an antidote to wasp stings and snakebite. Before the days of vitamin C pills, this herb was valued for its ascorbic acid content and was used to treat and prevent scurvy.

Harvesting and uses

Leaves

Pick for use fresh throughout the growing season, from summer until early autumn. Always pick from the top, not the sides, to encourage new growth. Purslane does not dry or freeze well, so preserve it by extracting its juice or pickling it in vinegar. In the Middle East purslane is an ingredient of a traditional salad called fattoush.

Flowers

Pick flowers as they appear from summer until early autumn. The stems and flower buds add a delightful crunch to a mixed salad.

Properties

This is an important culinary herb as it is one of the few vegetable sources of omega-3 essential fatty acids. It also contains vitamins A, B and C and minerals such as magnesium, calcium and potassium.

It has antidiarrheal and antibacterial properties and is also considered an aphrodisiac.

Varieties

Golden Purslane

Portulaca oleracea var. *aurea*

This variety is a hardy annual. It also has small yellow flowers in summer with large golden disk-shaped succulent leaves. Golden purslane is ideal for container growing.

PURSLANE AND FLAGEOLET SALAD

Purslane transforms the texture of this salad by adding crunch to the soft beans – a wonderful mix.

Serves 4–6

1½ cups (375 ml) dried flageolet or cannellini beans (or canned)
1 garlic head, cut in half horizontally
1 large lemon, cut in half
2 bay leaves
1 bunch celery leaf (with stems)
2 handfuls purslane leaves
6 tbsp (90 ml) tbsp olive oil
1 tbsp (15 ml) lemon juice
3 anchovy fillets
2 cloves garlic, finely chopped
1 tbsp (15 ml) finely chopped spearmint, Tashkent, Moroccan or garden mint
1 tbsp (15 ml) chopped celery leaf
1 tbsp (15 ml) chopped flat-leaf parsley

Soak the beans overnight in cold water, if using dried ones, then drain.

Put the beans in a large saucepan with lots of cold water and the garlic head, lemon, bay and celery leaves and stems, and bring to a boil. Simmer for 30 to 45 minutes until they are cooked; by which I mean soft, with no hardness left. Do not add salt until they are cooked, otherwise you will make the skins very tough. As soon as they are cooked, add a pinch of salt, stir, then drain. (If you are using canned beans, just drain them.)

Pour into a bowl and, while still warm, add the purslane leaves, olive oil and lemon juice, anchovies, garlic and chopped herbs. Toss and leave for 30 to 40 minutes before serving to allow time for the flavors to infuse.

PURSLANE AND SPINACH SALAD

This is an adapted French recipe. When on a barge on the Canal du Midi I found masses of purslane growing wild. The children and I would forage for it for our lunch and add it to all forms of salad. This was our favorite recipe, especially when combined with the almonds, which were also abundant in all the local stores.

Serves 3–4

2½ cups (625 ml) purslane
2½ cups (625 ml) young spinach leaves
3½ oz (100 g) feta
1 tbsp (15 ml) almonds, peeled
3 tbsp (45 ml) olive oil
1 tbsp (15 ml) white wine vinegar or herb vinegar
1 clove garlic, crushed
Salt and freshly ground black pepper
Pinch of brown sugar

Wash and dry the purslane and spinach leaves and remove these from their stems. Mix together in a bowl. Break up the feta and scatter over the leaves.

Toast the almonds under a hot broiler, shaking from time to time until they are golden but not dark brown.

Mix together the oil, vinegar, garlic, salt, pepper and sugar in a glass measuring cup and whisk until all amalgamated. Pour the dressing over the herbs and cheese, toss, and scatter on the almonds, then serve.

PURSLANE, BREAD, TOMATO AND OLIVE SALAD

A hearty rustic salad that is an excellent way to use up any leftover bread. It is even better made with slightly stale bread. The purslane adds crunch and a clean flavor, which is lovely when combined with the tomatoes and bread. Accompany with a chilled glass of white wine.

Serves 4

2½ cups (625 ml) purslane, succulent leaves removed from the stems
1 lb (500 g) ripe tomatoes
Salt
1 large red onion, halved and finely sliced
4 tbsp (60 ml) red wine vinegar, divided
1 lb (500 g) stale, 2-day-old white traditionally baked bread
4 tbsp (60 ml) flat-leaf parsley, chopped
1 handful lettuce or sweet basil leaves, torn
½ cup + 1 tbsp (140 ml) extra-virgin olive oil

Wash and dry the purslane.

Cut the tomatoes into small chunks, put them in a colander, sprinkle with a little salt and leave for 10 minutes to allow the juices to be drawn.

Put the onion slices in a small bowl of cold water with a splash of red wine vinegar and a pinch of salt.

Break the bread up into chunks and place in a large bowl with just enough cold water to cover it. Set aside for 10 minutes. Drain the bread, then, using your hands, squeeze out all the water. (If it is not squeezed well enough you will have a soggy meal.) Crumble the bread into a large serving bowl.

In a small bowl, combine the purslane leaves, tomatoes, drained onions, parsley and lettuce or basil leaves. Mix the oil and the remaining vinegar in a glass container and check the seasoning, adding extra if required. Pour the dressing over the salad, toss well and then add to the bread. Mix all the ingredients well and serve.

Excess purslane

This is the only way I know of preserving purslane; it is a French delicacy that can be found in some markets in the south of the country. It is excellent with cold meats and cheese and in sandwiches.

Pickled purslane

2 lb (1 kg) purslane leaves and stems
3 cloves garlic, sliced
10 black peppercorns
1 qt (1 L) apple cider vinegar

Wash and dry the purslane and cut it into 1-inch (3 cm) pieces. Fill a clean, sterilized (see page 12) glass jar with the purslane to just below the rim. Choose a jar with a well-fitting lid that is not metal, as that would be corroded by the vinegar. Add the garlic and peppercorns, then pour in the vinegar, making sure that the leaves and stems are immersed in the vinegar.

Put in the fridge or a dark, cold cupboard and leave for a minimum of 2 weeks before eating. It will keep for 3 months.

ROCK SAMPHIRE

(also known as Sea Fennel)
Crithmum maritimum

The first time I saw this herb growing in profusion was on the island of Gozo, near Malta, where it is often cooked with the local fish. Since then I have managed to happily grow it in containers so that I can use it in my kitchen at home.

A number of times I have read recipes for rock samphire only to discover that the chef/cook is actually referring to marsh samphire (*Salicornia europea*), which is sometimes known as glasswort or pickleweed. This samphire grows on muddy flats or salt marshes at, or close to, standing water. The scale-like leaves of this plant are bright green in spring and lie flat on the succulent stems. Rock samphire, on the other hand, is related to fennel and grows, as its common name suggests, in the rocks.

Having cleared that up, I must admit to being a fan of both, but I am more excited by rock samphire, as it can be grown away from the sea.

Description

This hardy perennial has flat clusters of tiny pale yellow flowers in summer and aromatic succulent sea gray–green triangular leaves with long, rounded, linear lance-shaped segments that grow in small groups along the branch.

As this is commonly a seaside plant that grows literally in the crevices between rocks, it is essential, when growing it in a garden, to prepare the site well prior to planting. Make sure the soil is well drained and add extra grit if necessary. Plant rock samphire in a sunny position and protect from cold winds. In winter, cover the crown with straw, not mulch or compost, which would cause it to rot. This herb can be raised from fresh seed sown under protection in the autumn.

History in cooking

Rock samphire was at one time cultivated in English gardens for its seed pods and sold in London, where it was called crest marine. In John Gerard's (the 16th-century herbalist) time it was considered a very good condiment. He wrote in 1597: "The leaves kept in pickle and eaten in sallads with oile and vinegar is a pleasant sauce for meat, wholesome for the stoppings of the liver, milt and kidnies. It is the pleasantest sauce, most familiar and best agreeing with man's body."

Harvesting and uses

Leaves
The best time for harvesting the leaves is in late spring and early summer before the plant flowers. They can be eaten fresh or cooked as a vegetable. Prior to cooking, remove any leaves that have begun to turn slimy and any hard parts of the stalk, and soak in salt water for an hour. The leaves have an aromatic, salty flavor that is

delicious in salads or when cooked in butter. The leaves can also be used to make sauces and aromatic pickles.

Flowers
The flowers can be picked throughout the summer, and the buds taste similar to fennel flowers but with slightly less anise. Add the flowers to salads, fish dishes or sauces.

Properties
This herb is high in vitamin C; it also has digestive and purgative properties. It is being used in current research to treat obesity and there are now a number of herbal products available using rock samphire that claim success.

Other varieties
None.

SHRIMP AND ROCK SAMPHIRE RISOTTO

Using rock samphire in this recipe adds not only the complementary aromatic, anise and salt flavors but also texture.

Serves 4

1²/₃ lb (750 g) unpeeled cooked pink shrimp or North Atlantic prawns
2½ cups (625 ml) rock samphire
¹/₃ cup (75 ml) unsalted butter, divided
½ onion, chopped
1 qt (1 L) fish stock
1 blade mace
2 shallots, finely chopped
1 clove garlic, finely chopped
1²/₃ cups (400 ml) risotto rice
½ cup (125 ml) white wine
2¼ tbsp (35 ml) Parmesan, freshly grated
Salt and freshly ground black pepper

Peel the shrimp and set them aside, reserving the shells. Wash and clean the rock samphire, removing any hard, woody bits or any soft, slimy bits. Put the samphire in a bowl, cover with cold salted water and leave for 1 hour.

Melt one-third of the butter in a large saucepan, add the onion and fry for 5 minutes, until soft and lightly browned. Add the shrimp shells and fry for 3 to 4 minutes, then add the stock and mace and bring to a boil. Cover and simmer for 20 minutes.

Pass the stock through a sieve into a clean saucepan, pressing out as much liquid as you can with the back of a ladle. Bring back to a simmer and keep hot over low heat.

Melt the rest of the butter in a large saucepan and add the shallots and garlic; cook gently for a couple of minutes. Add the rice and stir until all the grains are coated with butter. Pour in the wine and simmer, stirring constantly, until it has all been absorbed, then add a ladleful of the hot stock, stir until it has all been taken up, then add another. Continue like this for about 20 minutes, stirring constantly, until all the stock has been used and the rice is tender but still a little al dente.

Before the risotto is ready, bring a large saucepan of water to a boil, drain the soaking samphire and wash under cold water. Add to the pan, simmer for 8 minutes, until just tender, then drain well. Stir the shrimp, Parmesan and some seasoning into the risotto. Heat for 1 minute, then stir in all but a handful of the samphire.

Divide the risotto among 4 warmed bowls and serve, garnished with the rest of the samphire.

ROCK SAMPHIRE AND MUSSEL SALAD

Mussels equal summer holidays in Devon, where I was taught by my mother to collect and cook them; and in turn I taught my children the sheer delight of eating them. This they did with gusto one summer holiday in Brittany when they were only seven and eight, much to the astonishment of the proprietor of the restaurant.

This recipe includes the sea from rock to shore; it is flavorsome and full of texture, from the softness of the mussels to the crunch of the rock samphire. Serve it on a bed of crisp green lettuce with some fresh crusty white bread.

Serves 3–4 (depending on how greedy you are)

1 cup (250 ml) white wine
1 cup (250 ml) water
3 cloves garlic, finely crushed
1 small onion or shallot, finely sliced
1 bay leaf
2 lb (900 g) mussels, scrubbed and debearded
8 oz (225 g) rock samphire, washed, picked over, all tough old stems and slimy leaves removed, then soaked in cold salted water for 1 hour prior to use
4 tbsp (60 ml) olive oil
2 tbsp (30 ml) white wine vinegar
1 tsp (5 ml) French tarragon, finely chopped
Salt and freshly ground black pepper

Combine the wine, water, garlic, onion and bay leaf in a large saucepan, bring to a boil, reduce to a simmer, then cover and cook for a few minutes. Add the mussels, increase the heat and cook for 4 minutes. Remove all the mussels and discard any that have not opened. Strain the cooking liquid and return it to the pan. Remove the mussel meat from the shells and set aside.

Drain the soaking rock samphire and rinse it under cold water. Dry and lightly chop it, then add to the reserved mussel cooking liquid. Bring to a boil, reduce the heat and simmer for 4 to 7 minutes, until the rock samphire is tender. Drain and set aside.

Whisk together the oil, vinegar and tarragon and season with salt and pepper to taste. Mix together the rock samphire and the mussels, add some of the vinaigrette, toss and serve.

ROCK SAMPHIRE AND LAMB STEAKS

This is a great combination; the crunchy, salty, slightly anise flavors of the samphire work well with the sweetness of spring lamb.

Serves 4

2 tbsp (30 ml) olive oil
4 x 8-oz (225 g) lamb rump steaks
½ cup (125 ml) unsalted butter, divided
7 oz (200 g) young rock samphire leaves, washed and thoroughly checked, all tough old stems or soft, slimy leaves removed
6 oz (175 g) young fava (or lima) beans
Salt and freshly ground black pepper
1 shallot or small onion, finely diced
1 clove garlic, finely chopped
¼ cup (60 ml) flat-leaf parsley, roughly chopped
2 tbsp (30 ml) balsamic vinegar
2 tbsp (30 ml) stock (preferably made from lamb bones)

Preheat the oven to 400°F (200°C).

Heat an ovenproof casserole dish or frying pan until hot, add the olive oil and the lamb steaks and cook for 2 to 3 minutes on each side. Transfer the casserole dish or pan to the oven and cook for 12 to 15 minutes, uncovered, or for 20 minutes if you prefer your meat well done. Remove from the oven and place the lamb on a plate to rest. Reserve the casserole dish or pan with the juices in it for later.

Meanwhile, heat a clean frying pan or saucepan with a tight-fitting lid and add 2 tbsp (30 ml) of the butter and the samphire leaves. Gently fry, covered, for 4 to 7 minutes, until the leaves become tender. Add the beans and stir well, then gently cook for a further 2 to 3 minutes. Check the seasoning and remove from the heat. Mix together the shallot, garlic and parsley in a bowl and set aside until ready to serve.

Using the casserole dish or frying pan that the meat was cooked in, drain off any meat juices into a clean bowl and reserve. Place the dish or pan over medium heat and add the balsamic vinegar. Bring to a boil and stir, scraping up the bits on the bottom. Add the stock and simmer for a further minute. Add the remaining butter and stir gently until melted and combined. Add the reserved meat juices and bring to a simmer. Check the seasoning and add salt and pepper if needed.

To serve, slice the lamb thickly and arrange on 4 serving plates. Place the rock samphire around the sliced lamb, then pour the sauce over the lamb. Finally, scatter on the parsley mixture.

Excess rock samphire

Pickled rock samphire

Raw rock samphire has a unique salty, aromatic flavor that, when cooked and pickled, changes into a more fennel-like flavor that is great with salads, cheese and cold meats.

Makes approx. 3 x 1-pint (500 ml) jars

Enough young rock samphire leaves to fill a standard colander
3 cups (750 ml) white wine vinegar
1 cup (250 ml) water
1 tsp (5 ml) salt
2 bay leaves
1 tsp (5 ml) ground mace
5 black peppercorns

Check the rock samphire leaves, removing any hard main stems or mangy soft pieces. Wash the leaves, then place in a large bowl of salted water and leave to soak for 1 hour or more.

Wash thoroughly in a colander to remove the salt. Place in a large saucepan with enough cold water to cover the leaves, bring to a boil and cook for 4 to 7 minutes. Drain.

In a separate saucepan, add the vinegar, water, salt, bay leaves and spices, bring to a boil, reduce the heat and simmer for 5 minutes. Strain into a pitcher, set aside and allow to cool.

Put the cooled rock samphire in sterilized wide-necked jars (see page 12), leaving a gap at the top, and pour on the vinegar until it covers the leaves. Leave a small gap at the top of the jar.

Seal with a non-metallic lid and store for 4 to 5 months before using. Will keep for a minimum of 2 years if not opened. Once the jar is opened, keep in the fridge and use within a month.

ROCKET (ARUGULA)

(also known as Wild Rocket (Arugula), Ruccola, Rucola, Rocquette)
Diplotaxis muralis

I love arugula. It is so versatile, as it goes well with meat, fish and vegetables, and therefore I must have it in my garden. Well over a decade ago I had a large crop of rocket salad (see page 249) growing on the herb farm for a garden center, but it ran to flower, so I could not sell it. While I stood next to it, pondering what to do, I started eating the flowers. They were wonderful – so wonderful that they became the inspiration for my book *Good Enough to Eat*, which is all about growing and eating flowers.

Description

Wild arugula is a perennial herb that is often grown as an annual, especially in cold, damp climates, where it hates the winter. It has yellow four-petaled flowers in summer with green deeply divided aromatic leaves that form a rosette as the plant matures. It can be easily raised from seed sown in late spring, either directly into a prepared site in the garden when the air temperature at night does not fall below 45°F (7°C), or alternatively into a large, deep container (as it has a long tap root) filled with soil-based potting compost. When growing it in the garden, for an ideal crop plant it in light shade in a well-fed soil that does not dry out in summer.

History in cooking

For hundreds of years arugula was collected in the wild and sold in markets in southern France, Italy and Egypt. Both the leaves and seeds of arugula were used as flavoring by the Romans. In England the Elizabethans were extremely partial to it when used in salads.

Harvesting and uses

Leaves
Pick leaves from early spring until early winter. The best culinary flavored leaves are those that have reached full size but have not yet turned dark green – from spring to early summer and again in autumn. Summer leaves tend to be tough and bitter, especially if the weather is very hot. The peppery leaves are lovely when added to salads and are a common ingredient in the salad-leaf mixtures that can be bought in supermarkets. Dress with salt, oil and vinegar, or simply serve on their own with a little fresh Parmesan.

Flowers
These can be picked in summer as they appear. The whole flower is edible, although any excessive green should be removed. The swelling behind the flower, where the seeds are formed, adds the crunch when eating them, so you can use just petals, whole flowers or whole flowers plus crunch, depending on your taste or the recipe.

Both wild and rocket salad stimulate the appetite and digestion.

Properties   The leaves are high in sulfur, which is good for healthy skin, hair and nails. They also contain vitamins A, B, C and E.

Other varieties

Rocket Salad
Eruca vesicaria
This is a half-hardy annual with cream-colored flowers that, as they mature, become pale with purple veins. The leaves are oval and lance-shaped with a peppery/nutty flavor.

Dame's Rocket, Sweet Rocket
Hesperis matronalis
This is a short-lived perennial herb with pink, white, purple or mauve sweetly scented flowers all summer. The leaves are lance-shaped, green and slightly hairy. This rocket can be eaten – the flowers are delightful in all forms of salad – however, the leaves are only good for emergencies when one runs out of both rocket salad and wild arugula. But then, if I am honest, there is no comparison, so change your recipe.

OMELET ARNOLD BENNETT AND WILD ARUGULA

My grandmother, in her cookbook *Lovely Food*, credits this recipe to the Savoy Grill, where this omelet, it is said, was created for the author Arnold Bennett. I, on the other hand, credit it to the Sloane Club, which to me is the most wonderful, quintessential English club, where Mac and I stay during the Chelsea Flower Show. It is within staggering distance of the show, and as we reappear each evening from building our display, exhausted, muddy, wearing our steel-toe boots and fluorescent Day-Glo safety vests, no one bats an eyelid. To be able to come down to a bar that feels exactly like a comfy country living room, order a long, cold drink and wild arugula and omelet Arnold Bennett with pommes frites (no, they don't serve french fries) is sheer heaven.

The strong, peppery taste of the wild arugula truly balances the flavors of the omelet and the smoked haddock.

Serves 2

3 tbsp (45 ml) crème fraîche
8 oz (225 g) smoked haddock, skin and bones removed and cut into ½-inch (1 cm) chunks
5 large eggs
½ tsp (2 ml) cornstarch
Salt and freshly ground black pepper
2 tsp (10 ml) unsalted butter
1 tsp (5 ml) olive oil
1¾ oz (50 g) Gruyère, grated
Wild arugula leaves, to serve

Pour the crème fraîche into a medium saucepan and bring it to a simmer over low heat, then add the smoked haddock and gently poach it for about 5 minutes.

Next, start making the sauce; this is what makes this dish, so don't skimp. Separate one egg and place the yolk in a small bowl and the white in another. Whisk the yolk with the cornstarch.

When the fish is cooked, use a slotted spoon to lift it out of the pan and place it in a sieve over the pan. Using a wooden spoon, gently press the fish, allowing the juice to drip back into the pan. Place the fish on a plate. Bring the fish liquid back to simmering, not boiling, then pour it over the egg yolk and cornstarch, whisking all the time. Return to the heat and simmer until the sauce thickens; this should take only a few minutes.

Remove from the heat and add the cooked haddock. Check the seasoning and add pepper and maybe salt, depending on the saltiness of the fish.

In a bowl, whisk the egg white to the soft peak stage and fold it into the haddock. Set aside while you make the omelet, for which you will need an 8-inch (20 cm) frying pan. However, before you start the omelet, turn on the broiler to its highest setting.

In another bowl, beat the remaining eggs and season with salt and pepper. Melt the butter and oil in the frying pan and, when hot, add the eggs and cook, drawing the sides slowly into the middle and tipping the pan to ensure that all the egg is being cooked but the top is still soft. Add the haddock mixture, spreading it over the surface of the omelet, sprinkle with the Gruyère and place the omelet, in the pan, under the broiler. Cook for 2 to 3 minutes, until it becomes puffy and golden brown.

Remove from the under the broiler and let it stand. Cut it in half and carefully slide each half onto a plate. Serve with the wild arugula leaves scattered on top of the omelet.

BEEF TENDERLOIN AND FLORENTINE ARUGULA

Hannah, my daughter, and I went on holiday to Florence where we ate some beautiful meals. This was one of them, so simple and so nourishing, so flavorsome and so attractive. Again, it is the peppery flavor of the arugula that is essential to this dish.

Serves 4

14-oz (400 g) beef tenderloin, left in one piece and trimmed
½ tbsp (7 ml) olive oil
Sea salt and freshly ground black pepper
1 tbsp (15 ml) balsamic vinegar
1/3 cup (75 ml) extra-virgin olive oil
2 oz (60 g) Parmesan
3½ oz (100 g) rocket salad or wild arugula, washed and roughly chopped

Preheat a ridged grill pan, broiler or barbecue.

Rub the beef with the ½ tbsp (7 ml) olive oil, season it, then cook on the heated grill or under the broiler for about 4 to 5 minutes for rare, turning it every so often so that it cooks evenly. If you prefer your meat medium or well done, cook for a further 3 to 5 minutes, depending on your taste and the thickness of the beef. Once cooked, place on a plate to cool. If there are any juices in the grill pan or broiler, keep them for later.

Make the dressing by whisking together the balsamic vinegar and 1/3 cup (75 ml) olive oil with any juices from the beef. Season with salt and pepper to taste. With a potato peeler, shave slices of Parmesan as thinly as possible onto a plate. Slice the beef into ¼–½-inch (0.5–1 cm) slices, dress the arugula leaves and arrange on a large plate or individual serving plates, and arrange the slices of beef on top. Scatter the Parmesan shavings on top and eat immediately.

ROCKET PASTA SALAD

A simple cold salad that is so useful, especially when one has guests who appear and need feeding. The rocket salad has a gentler flavor compared to its cousin wild arugula. In fact, you could call it more nutty than peppery, but that is a matter of taste. What I do know is that this dish works because of the rocket salad.

Serves 4

11 oz (320 g) pasta (any of the following: fiorelli, cocciolette, farfalle or francesine)
3 cloves garlic, whole and peeled
1 lb (500 g) red cherry tomatoes
½ cucumber
1 tbsp (15 ml) pitted black olives
2 tbsp (30 ml) fresh chives
⅓ cup (75 ml) rocket salad leaves
Sea salt and freshly ground black pepper
3 tbsp (45 ml) extra-virgin olive oil
1 tbsp (15 ml) balsamic vinegar

Bring a large saucepan of salted water to a boil, add the pasta and garlic, bring back to a boil, then simmer until cooked and al dente. (This could be 5 minutes for fresh or 7 to 10 minutes for dried pasta.)

Drain in a colander and fish out the garlic, keeping it to one side for the dressing. While the pasta is still in the colander, hold it under cold running water to stop it sticking and to allow to cool down. Drain well, then put the pasta in a large serving bowl.

Cut the tomatoes, cucumber and black olives into small pieces that are about the size of the pasta, then toss with the pasta. Using scissors, snip the chives over the pasta, then roughly chop the rocket salad and fold it into the pasta.

Using a fork, mash the cooked garlic on a chopping board with a little salt. Make the dressing by combining the oil and vinegar and whisking well. Add the mashed garlic, whisk again, add salt and pepper to taste, then pour over the salad. Toss well and serve.

Excess arugula

It is so easy to have a sudden glut of arugula leaves that you need to use up; you want to pick them to keep the plants productive but you do not want yet another arugula salad, so here is an easy and delicious solution.

Arugula pesto

This can be used to stir through cooked pasta, as a dip or added to potato salad.

Makes enough for a small jar

8 oz (250 g) wild arugula or rocket salad leaves, washed, dried and roughly chopped
1 cup + 2 tbsp (275 ml) extra-virgin olive oil
1 tbsp (15 ml) lemon juice
1 tsp (5 ml) lemon zest
¼ cup (60 ml) pine nuts
2 cloves garlic
Salt
2 oz (60 g) Parmesan, grated

Blend the arugula leaves, olive oil, lemon juice and zest, pine nuts, garlic and salt until smooth. This can be done most easily in a food processor or blender, stopping a couple of times to push the ingredients down the sides of the bowl. Alternatively, you can use a large mortar and pestle.

When evenly blended, scrape into a bowl and stir in the grated Parmesan, check the seasoning and add extra to taste if needed. Cover the bowl and put in the fridge. Alternatively, if storing for some time, put into a screw-top jar and put a layer of olive oil on the top before sealing. This will then keep for 4 to 6 weeks in the fridge as long as the olive oil layer is maintained. You may need to top it up if you keep dipping into the jar.

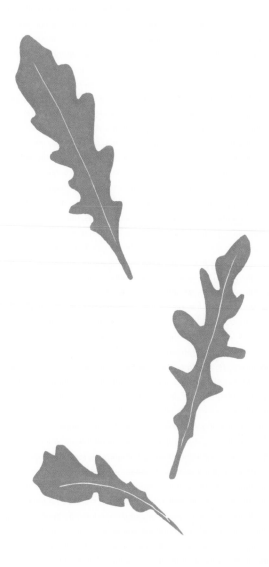

ROSEMARY

(also known as Rosmarino, Rosmarin)
Rosmarinus officinalis

No herb garden should be without this plant; it is one of the most versatile and useful herbs in the kitchen, in the home and medicinally. It is associated with love, friendship and remembrance. Both my children took a large rosemary plant with them when they went off to university, to cook with and to drink as a tea – which, it is said, not only revives the memory but allegedly is also one of the best cures for a hangover!

Description

Rosemary is a hardy evergreen, so the leaves are available all year round. It has attractive small pale blue flowers in spring and again in late summer and short needle-shaped, highly aromatic dark green leaves.

The most reliable way to grow this herb is from cuttings taken in summer from new nonflowering growth. You can raise plants from seed, but they have a nasty knack of keeling over once they reach their first birthday. Rosemary prefers to be planted in well-drained soil in a sunny position; however, I have found, with patience, that it will adapt to growing in heavy soil as long as it is in full sun. All forms of rosemary will happily adapt to being grown in a container in soil-based potting compost.

History in cooking

This herb has been used for hundreds of years in the kitchen, as a preservative and medicinally. I love the story that in medieval times rosemary was used at banquets as an edible table decoration; large branches were dipped in egg white, sprinkled with grated tree resin to make them glisten, then placed on the table set in bread or lard.

Harvesting and uses

Leaves
This is a useful herb because it can be picked all year round. The flavor is versatile and goes well with many forms of food, from roast vegetables, meat, soups, fish and eggs to all forms of bread.

Flowers
Harvest the small flowers as they appear from spring to late summer. They taste of sweet rosemary and are lovely added to salads and scattered over cooked vegetables.

Properties

Rosemary is excellent for treating stomach cramps and flatulence. When used in cooking, it helps to stimulate the appetite and secretion of gastric juices. The leaves have antioxidant and antibacterial properties.

All forms of rosemary bearing the name *Rosmarinus officinalis* are edible. They can vary in flavor from the standard form to very eucalyptus or very pine. As there are so many different rosemaries available, I have limited the following list to my favorite culinary ones.

Varieties

White Rosemary
Rosmarinus officinalis var. *albiflorus*
This is the very hardy form of rosemary that adapted to my heavy soil to produce a good round flavor.

Green Ginger Rosemary
Rosmarinus officinalis 'Green Ginger'
This variety is really worth looking for; the leaves have a rosemary-ginger flavor, great with meat and vegetables.

Tuscan Rosemary
Rosmarinus officinalis 'Tuscan Blue'
This variety has a very straight habit, so the stems make ideal barbecue skewers.

Prostrate Rosemary
Rosmarinus officinalis Prostratus Group
This variety has a trailing habit, which is ideal for growing over walls or over the side of a container.

MEDITERRANEAN TOMATO AND ROSEMARY SOUP

My mother was a great soup maker, and this is one of her recipes. Mum always used a pinch of sugar with tomatoes, even when making salads or a dressing to go over tomatoes, because she said it brings out their flavor. This is particularly true if you are using supermarket rather than homegrown tomatoes.

What transforms this soup from being run-of-the-mill to good is the rosemary; it truly brings out the flavors of the tomatoes. Serve with some fresh crusty white bread.

Serves 4

2½ cups (600 ml) vegetable or chicken stock
3½ tbsp (50 ml) unsalted butter
1 tbsp (15 ml) olive oil
1 large onion, finely sliced
1 large red bell pepper, seeds removed and finely sliced
1 clove garlic, finely chopped
1½ lb (675 g) tomatoes, peeled and chopped
2 rosemary sprigs (each 1 inch/ 3 cm long)
Salt and freshly ground black pepper
Pinch of soft brown sugar
1 tbsp (15 ml) orange juice

Gently heat the stock in a saucepan over medium heat.

In another large saucepan, melt the butter with the olive oil and gently sweat the onion and red pepper until soft (try not to color them). Add the garlic, stir and cook for a minute. Add the chopped tomatoes, stir for a few minutes, then pour in the heated stock and add the rosemary sprigs. Simmer for 20 minutes, add the salt and pepper to taste and, as my mother always did, a pinch of soft brown sugar.

Remove the rosemary sprigs – it does not matter if some of the leaves fall off. Using either a hand blender or a food processor, mix for a few seconds. If you are being a purist you can sieve the soup over a large bowl so that it is perfectly smooth.

Return to the pan, add the orange juice and check the seasoning. Gently reheat but do not allow to boil. Pour into serving bowls.

WINTER VEGETABLES AND ROSEMARY

This is a most satisfying and comforting winter meal that warms the cockles of one's heart. Rosemary infuses the vegetables and fills the kitchen with an appetizing aroma. Serve with baked potatoes and broccoli.

Serves 6–8

1 cup (250 ml) dried red kidney beans or 14-oz (398 ml) can, drained
3 tbsp (45 ml) light olive oil or sunflower oil, divided
1 large onion, finely chopped
2 small turnips, sliced
2–3 parsnips (depending on size), sliced
2–3 carrots (depending on size), sliced
4 oz (110 g) button mushrooms, cut in half
1 tbsp (15 ml) whole wheat flour
1¾ cups (425 ml) hot vegetable stock
14-oz (398 ml) can Italian tomatoes
2 tbsp (30 ml) parsley, roughly chopped
2 tbsp (30 ml) celery leaf, roughly chopped
1 tbsp (15 ml) rosemary leaves, removed from the stem and finely chopped
Salt and freshly ground black pepper

Place the dried kidney beans in a large bowl and cover with boiling water, making sure you add an extra inch (2.5 cm) of water so the beans are submerged. Leave for an hour to soak. Pour into a colander, rinse under cold water and place in a large saucepan. Cover with water (plus an extra inch/2.5 cm) and 1 tbsp (15 ml) oil to stop it boiling over. Bring to a boil and cook for 10 minutes, then simmer, covered, for 45 to 60 minutes or until the beans are tender. Alternatively, which is my preferred method, place the beans in a pressure cooker, add enough water to cover, plus an extra inch (2.5 cm), bring to high (15 lb) pressure and cook for 8 to 10 minutes. (I do advise following your pressure cooker's instructions, as they can vary.) Of course, if you are using canned beans, miss all this out!

Preheat the oven to 325°F (170°C). Heat the remaining oil in a large casserole dish, add the onion and cook for 5 minutes, then add the sliced vegetables. Toss them in the oil so they are well covered, then add the mushrooms and stir well. Reduce the heat to low, stir in the flour and add the stock, a little at a time, stirring well. Once all the stock has been added, increase the heat to the simmering point and cook for 2 to 3 minutes.

Add the tomatoes, the cooked and drained kidney beans, the parsley, celery leaf and chopped rosemary leaves, and cover and cook in the oven for 1½ hours.

ROSEMARY LAMB HOTCHPOTCH

Rosemary is renowned for use with lamb; it is not only the flavor that suits the meat so well, it is also the fact that it helps one digest fatty meat. This lovely warming dish is equally delicious cold, in the unlikely event that you have some leftovers. Serve with mashed potatoes.

Serves 4

7 tbsp (105 ml) olive oil
1 large onion, sliced
2 cloves garlic, finely chopped
8 lamb cutlets
2 carrots, diced
4 baby turnips, diced
2 bay leaves
3 rosemary sprigs
(approx 4 inches/10 cm in length)
3²/₃ cups (900 ml) warm vegetable stock
Salt and freshly ground black pepper
1 lb (500 g) spinach, well washed and torn into large pieces

Preheat the oven to 325°F (170°C).

Heat the oil in a frying pan, add the onion and gently cook until it is translucent. Add the garlic and cook for a few minutes. Remove from the frying pan. Add the cutlets and gently sauté on both sides to seal the meat.

Place the onion and seared cutlets in a large casserole dish; add the prepared vegetables, bay leaves, rosemary sprigs and warm stock and season to taste. Place on the stovetop and bring gently to a boil.

Cover and place in the oven for 2 hours. Check the stock level occasionally; if it is beginning to look dry, add a little water. Twenty minutes before the end of the cooking time, take the casserole out of the oven, remove the bay leaves and rosemary sprigs and add the torn spinach. Stir well, making sure that the spinach leaves are well covered with stock.

Return the casserole to the oven and cook for a further 20 minutes.

DELUXE ROSEMARY ROASTED POTATOES

These are known as "Mom's posh chips," and are always very popular. I never seem to make enough of them.

Serves 4 after a day's gardening or 6 for a dinner party

2 lb (1 kg) potatoes, washed but not peeled
2 tsp (10 ml) sea salt, divided
1 tbsp (15 ml) rosemary leaves, removed from the stem and finely chopped
Olive oil

Preheat the oven to 400°F (200°C).

Cook the potatoes in a large pot of salted boiling water for about 12 minutes, or until your knife slides easily through them. Drain and leave for 5 minutes. Once cool enough to handle, cut the potatoes into narrow wedges.

Put 1 tsp (5 ml) sea salt in a mortar and pestle, add the chopped rosemary leaves and crush them together. (This will infuse the salt with the oil from the leaves.) Add the remaining salt and crush to mix together but not too fine.

Put a small amount of olive oil into a roasting pan and add the potatoes, toss well, add the salt and rosemary, toss again, add 2 more tbsp (30 ml) olive oil and place in the oven. Roast for 40 to 50 minutes, until crisp and golden.

ROSEMARY BREAD

Until recently I have been very sniffy about bread machines, but I have now used one and I am hooked. They are wonderful when you are running just to stand still. This bread can be made by hand or in a machine, and it is lovely with soups or salads. The flavor of the rosemary leaves gently infuses throughout the bread, so do not be tempted to use more than the recommended amount, as it would be overpowering. If you are using a bread machine, follow the manufacturer's instructions. This is a handmade recipe, but I know that the ingredients happily adapt to being used in a machine.

Makes 1 large loaf, 2 small loaves or 6 rolls

1 oz (25 g) fresh yeast
Pinch of sugar
1¹/3 cups (310 ml) warm water
5 cups (500 g) white bread flour, plus extra for dusting
1 tsp (5 ml) rosemary leaves, stripped from the stems
2 tsp (10 ml) salt
4 tbsp (60 ml) olive oil

Preheat the oven to 400°F (200°C).

Put the yeast in a bowl with the sugar, stir in the warm water and leave to activate.

Put the flour in a large, wide bowl or onto your work surface. Make a well in the middle of the flour, add the yeast and most of the rosemary leaves, plus the salt and most of the olive oil. Mix well, then knead the dough for about 10 minutes, until it is smooth and elastic and makes a compact ball.

Put the dough into a bowl, cover with a damp dish towel, and leave to rise in a warm place for approximately 1½ hours or until it has doubled in size.

Lightly dust the work surface with flour. Divide the dough in half and shape into ovals or rounds or small individual balls. Sprinkle the tops with the remaining rosemary and drizzle with the remaining oil. Dust a baking sheet with flour and place the loaves on it, leaving a space between each one for spreading. Cover loosely with a dish towel and leave in a warm place for a further 30 minutes to an hour, until the loaves have risen.

Put in the oven and bake for about 35 minutes, until the top is golden. Remove once cooked and place on a wire rack to cool before serving.

Once cold this bread can be placed in a freezer bag and frozen.

ROSEMARY, GARLIC AND LEMON MARINADE

To me this sums up the Mediterranean. When you smell the food cooking that has been infused in this marinade, you will be transported to the warmth of the sun, the loud buzzing of the cicada and the scent of the pine trees.

Makes enough for a roast, a large fish or a whole chicken

2 tbsp (30 ml) rosemary leaves, pounded in a mortar and pestle
6 cloves garlic, peeled and crushed
¾ cup (175 ml) olive oil
Zest and juice of 3 lemons
Salt and freshly ground black pepper

Mix together all the ingredients in a large bowl, cover and leave to infuse for 1 hour while you prepare your chosen meat or fish.

Rub the marinade into the meat or pour it over a fish that has had slices cut into the flesh. Cover and set aside for 1 to 3 hours; the longer the better for meat, as the lemon will act as a tenderizer. Cook your marinated fish or meat accordingly.

Excess rosemary

Rosemary oil

I know that rosemary is an evergreen and available all year round, but occasionally it is great to have oil infused with rosemary for making bread or for using in stir-fries.

For more information about preserving and the risks of using herbs in oils, see page 36.

Makes 1 cup (250 ml)

3 good handfuls rosemary leaves
1 cup (250 ml) light olive oil or sunflower oil
2 tsp (10 ml) lemon juice

Wash the leaves and dry on paper towels. Finely chop the leaves (this can be done in a food processor), add the oil and the lemon juice and mix well. Pour into a container with a sealing lid and place in the fridge. Use within 5 days; shake well before use, as the lemon juice will separate.

Alternatively, after 2 days strain the oil through an unbleached paper coffee filter, pour into a clean, dry container with a sealing lid and keep in the fridge. Use within 3 days; shake well before use.

SAGE

(also known as Common Sage, Garden Sage, Shu Wei Cao, Sauge)
Salvia officinalis

Sage is one of those herbs that is so well known you think you can imagine the flavor. However, until you have had fresh pasta tossed in sage butter (see page 269), you have not known its true wonderful taste. It is also an archetypal herb for the cottage garden, especially when it is in full flower, when it becomes a magnet for bees and butterflies.

Description

Sage is a hardy evergreen herb with very attractive mauve-blue flowers in summer. The oval gray-green leaves are textured and highly aromatic when crushed. Although predominately a Mediterranean plant, it is sufficiently hardy to withstand an ordinary winter outside without protection, as long as the site is warm, dry and well drained and the soil is not acid. The flavor of the leaf is more intense when grown in full sun in free-draining low-nutrient soil.

Sage can be grown from seed or from cuttings taken in late spring from nonflowering shoots. It does adapt to being grown in containers, but I advise using a loam-based potting compost, as it does not thrive for more than a few months in peat.

History in cooking

The generic name *salvia* comes from the Latin *salvere*, which means to save, cure or to be in good health, which certainly reflects its historical reputation. Traditionally, before fridges were invented, sage was combined with salt and used to preserve meat. Before it became a culinary delight in the Middle Ages, it was dried, powdered and scattered over food much as we use pepper today.

Harvesting and uses

Leaves
Pick fresh leaves from this evergreen herb throughout the year. In spring (before the plant flowers) the leaves have a mild, warm flavor; after flowering the leaves have a stronger, tannic flavor.

Flowers
Harvest flowers as they appear throughout the summer. The flavor of the flowers is similar to that of the leaves, with a slight hint of sweetness, which makes them an ideal accompaniment for rice, meat, duck and stir-fry dishes where one wants extra zing.

Properties

Sage is a digestive, antispasmodic and carminative herb and it also eases flatulence and is a useful antioxidant. A tea made from three to four leaves can be used to alleviate upset stomachs and diarrhea.

Other varieties

There are many different sages available so I have simply identified my favorites. If you want a quick guide as to whether or not your sage is edible, the most reliable check is to look at the name: if it mentions *officinalis* you can be sure that the variety is safe to eat. Even so, there are some non-*officinalis* sages that are safe, such as the one identified below.

Narrow-leaved Sage, Spanish Sage
Salvia lavandulifolia
This hardy perennial evergreen has attractive blue flowers in summer. The small, narrow, oval textured and highly aromatic leaves have an excellent and very strong culinary flavor. In my opinion this is the best culinary sage.

Purple Sage, Red Sage
Salvia officinalis Purpurascens Group
This is a hardy evergreen perennial that bears mauve-blue flowers in summer. The aromatic oval purple/red/gray textured leaves have a milder flavor than common or narrow-leaved sage and are good with vegetable dishes such as stuffed peppers and zucchini.

Greek Sage
Salvia officinalis 'Greek'
This variety is a hardy evergreen perennial with very attractive pale mauve-blue flowers in summer. The aromatic oval gray textured leaves have a unique extra lobe at the base. When grown in full sun this sage has a strong flavor that goes well with meat and tomato dishes.

CRISPY SAGE, APPLE AND WALNUT SALAD

This is an old family recipe, the origin of which I am unsure. What I am certain about is that the combination of sage, apple, walnut and lettuce has everything a salad should have.

Serves 2

¾ cup + 2 tbsp (200 ml) walnuts, coarsely chopped
5 sage leaves, torn into small pieces
1 crisp eating apple, cored and cut into small slices
3 tbsp (45 ml) walnut or olive oil
1½ tsp (7 ml) white wine vinegar
1 sage leaf, finely chopped
Salt and freshly ground black pepper
1 shallot, finely minced
Good mix of lettuce leaves

Place a small nonstick frying pan over low heat and toast the walnuts, shaking the pan often. After the first 5 minutes, add the torn sage leaves and apple slices and keep shaking the pan gently, so that nothing sticks, until the walnuts and sage become gently cooked. Tip out into a bowl and set aside.

In a large bowl whisk together the oil, vinegar, finely chopped sage and enough salt and pepper to taste. Once amalgamated, add the shallot and mix well.

Tear the lettuce leaves into bite-sized pieces and add them to the bowl. Using a spoon, gently toss to coat the lettuce well with the dressing. Arrange the salad on a plate and sprinkle with the toasted sage, apple slices and walnuts.

SAGE ROTIS

These small unleavened bread rolls are quick to make and extremely useful. They are ideal with soups or for filling with salad and popping into a lunch box. The sage subtly infuses the bread and is not overpowering.

Makes 6

¾ cup (175 ml) whole wheat flour, plus extra for dusting
Small pinch of salt
2 tsp (10 ml) finely chopped sage leaves (narrow-leafed sage has the best flavor but either purple or common sage can be used)
1 tsp (5 ml) sunflower oil
4 tbsp (60 ml) warm water
Unsalted butter

Sift the flour and salt into a large bowl and add the sage. Make a well in the middle of the flour, add the oil and then the warm water and, using your hands, blend into a pliable dough. Remove from the bowl and knead on a floured work surface for about 2 minutes, or preferably 5 minutes; the more you knead the dough the softer the rotis.

Divide the dough into 6 portions and roll into balls. Dust the work surface with plenty of flour and roll out the dough into flat disks 4 inches (10 cm) in diameter.

Heat a grill pan or frying pan. Cook the disks on high heat until the surface becomes bubbly. Turn over and press the edges down with a metal spatula to cook evenly. As soon as brown spots appear, the roti is done.

Remove each roti from the pan and smear with butter. Keep warm by enclosing in a dish towel or foil. Cook all the rotis in the same way. Serve warm or reheat under a hot broiler, taking care not to burn them.

LAMB AND SAGE STEW

The aroma of this warming winter dish as it permeates the house brings the family to lunch without any extra shouting that it's on the table. Sage adds an earthy flavor to lamb and it is particularly good in this recipe – while also stopping me from continually using rosemary, which in winter is my herb of choice. Serve with mashed potatoes and purple sprouting broccoli.

Serves 4

2 tbsp (30 ml) olive oil
8 meaty lamb chops
(about 3 lb/1.3 kg in total)
2 sage sprigs, leaves removed from the stems and chopped
3 cloves garlic, finely chopped
Salt and freshly ground black pepper
2 tsp (10 ml) all-purpose flour
½ cup (125 ml) white wine vinegar
½ cup (125 ml) water
4 salted anchovy fillets

Heat the olive oil in a large casserole dish over medium-high heat. When hot, add the lamb chops and brown them all over.

Add the sage, garlic, salt and pepper. Stir to release the flavors and coat everything in the oil. Sprinkle the flour over the meat, stir well, then continue to cook over medium heat, stirring from time to time until the meat is quite dark (8 to 10 minutes). Be careful not to burn the garlic. Add the vinegar and water, scraping up the bits at the bottom of the casserole. Bring the liquid to a simmer, then reduce the heat to low, cover the casserole and cook for 40 minutes or until the meat is tender.

Just before serving, take a ladleful of juices from the casserole and mash the anchovy fillets into it until quite dissolved before pouring it back over the meat.

SAGE TOAD-IN-THE-HOLE

This is the best form of comfort food and appeals to all ages. Using the sage in the batter brings this dish alive. Serve with homemade gravy or simply with a crisp green salad.

Serves 4

2 eggs
1¼ cups (300 ml) all-purpose flour
2/3 cup (150 ml) milk
2/3 cup (150 ml) cold water
1 tbsp (15 ml) sage leaves (narrow-leaved, purple or common), finely chopped
Salt and freshly ground black pepper
6 large pork sausages (preferably 70–85 percent meat)
3½ oz (100 g) bacon
3 tbsp (45 ml) dripping or lard

Preheat the oven to 425°F (220°C).

Mix together the eggs, flour, milk, water, sage, salt and pepper and whisk well, making sure there are no lumps of flour. The final consistency should be similar to that of whipping (35%) cream. Leave to rest at room temperature for at least 15 minutes to give the flour time to expand.

Remove the skin of each sausage by using a sharp knife, slicing the side, then peeling the skin off. Wrap each sausage in a slice of bacon. Put the dripping or lard in a roasting pan (I use my meat roasting pan which is 11 x 12½ in/28 cm x 32 cm) and place in the oven until the fat begins to smoke.

Pour in the batter – it will sizzle, but don't panic – arrange the sausages and bake for 25 minutes. Check that it has risen and is beautifully golden; if not, leave for a further 5 minutes.

SALSICCE E FAGIOLI

The title for this recipe in Italian sounds so wonderful compared to "sausages and beans." I ate this in Tuscany on holiday with my daughter. It was a cold February and the wind was bitter; this dish was so nourishing and warming and such a brilliant use of sage that I asked for the recipe. Admittedly we cannot get the same sausages, but you can buy great sausages with 80 percent meat content or more in any good supermarket, and they make perfectly good substitutes.

Serve with fresh pasta or fresh bread, a crisp green salad and a glass of good red wine.

Serves 4

2½ cups (625 ml) dried cannellini or other white beans, soaked for 12 hours or overnight in cold water
3 cloves garlic, peeled and left whole
2 sage sprigs
2 tbsp (30 ml) olive oil
6 large pork sausages, Italian or 80 percent plus meat content
14-oz (398 ml) can chopped tomatoes with juice
Salt and freshly ground black pepper

Rinse the soaked beans in cold water, put them into a large pot, cover with cold water and bring to a boil. Skim the surface of the water to remove the scum during boiling. Add 2 of the garlic cloves and 1 sage sprig and cook for 1 to 1½ hours, until the beans are tender.

In another large pan, heat the olive oil. Prick the skin of the sausages with a fork to stop them splitting. Fry over medium heat to brown on all sides and add the remaining garlic clove and the remaining sage sprig. As soon as the herbs begin to sizzle, add the tomatoes and simmer for about 15 minutes to allow all the flavors to combine.

Drain the cooked beans, reserving a couple of cupfuls of the cooking liquid. Add the drained beans to the sausages and tomatoes, check the seasoning and add salt and pepper if needed. Simmer for a further 10 minutes; if the sauce is becoming too thick, dilute with the reserved bean water.

SAGE POTATO BAKE

This is another of my culinary accidents; I started making roast potatoes, then friends turned up and the potatoes would not stretch in time. So I took the potatoes out of the roasting pan and put them in with herbs, milk and egg and turned it into a bake. The trick with this dish is to keep the potatoes poking up above the milk mix so that they become crispy, which is wonderful when combined with the herb-custard mix. Serve with roast chicken or as a vegetarian meal with grated cheese sprinkled over the top.

Serves 4–6

2 lb (900 g) boiled potatoes, peeled and diced
2 tbsp (30 ml) light olive oil or canola oil
2 tbsp (30 ml) unsalted butter, plus extra for greasing
½ cup (110 ml) whipping (35%) cream
¾ cup + 2 tbsp (200 ml) reduced-fat (2%) milk
1 egg
1 tbsp (15 ml) sage leaves, finely chopped
1 tbsp (15 ml) flat-leaf parsley, finely chopped
1 clove garlic, crushed

Preheat the oven to 325°F (170°C).

In a frying pan, sauté the potatoes in the oil and butter until golden. Grease a large dish (I use a lasagne dish) and add the potatoes.

In a large glass measuring cup, mix together the cream, milk, egg, sage, parsley and garlic and pour over the potatoes. Bake in the oven for about 1 hour, until golden.

MUM'S SAGE BREAD SAUCE

Mum always made the best bread sauce; it was thick, creamy, fragrant and scrumptious. Her use of sage was in those days original. We enjoyed this sauce with many dishes, from roast chicken to baked onions.

Serves 4–6

2 1/3 cups (570 ml) milk
10 cloves
1 small onion or ½ large onion
Nutmeg
Salt and freshly ground pepper
10 fresh sage leaves, torn
1¾ cups (425 ml) fresh white breadcrumbs
2 tbsp (30 ml) unsalted butter (optional)
2 tbsp (30 ml) whipping (35%) cream

Pour the milk into a saucepan, press the cloves into the onion and add it to the pan. Grate some nutmeg onto the surface of the milk along with some pepper, turn the heat on to very, very low and slowly simmer, uncovered, for 30 to 40 minutes to allow all the flavors to infuse.

Remove the onion and take out the cloves, then put it to one side. Add the sage leaves and stir. You will find that there is a layer on the bottom of the pan, so stir well, scraping the bottom of the pan, then increase the heat slightly, add the bread crumbs, stir well, turn the heat down and gently simmer for 10 minutes, stirring to make sure nothing sticks. If the sauce is too thick, add the butter. Stir well.

Finely chop the infused onion, add to the sauce, stir, then check the seasoning. Serve in a warmed bowl, adding the whipping cream just before serving.

Excess sage

Sage butter

This is incredibly useful. One of the best ways to use it is to toss it, melted, with cooked fresh pasta; serve it with no other sauce, just some Parmesan and a crisp salad. Heaven.

Makes ½ cup (125 ml)

Handful sage leaves
½ cup (125 ml) unsalted butter, slightly softened

Remove the sage leaves from their stems. Once removed, tear them into pieces, then chop with the butter to release the oils. You do not need the sage leaves to be fine, just small enough not to overpower the taste of the food it is being combined with.

Finish the blending with a fork. When it has been thoroughly mixed, pack it into a roll of waxed paper or plastic wrap and place in the fridge for up to 24 hours before use. The longer you leave it the better the flavor.

This butter can be frozen; put it into a freezerproof container and label it. It will keep for up to 3 months.

SALAD BURNET

(also known as Meadow Pimpernel, Garden Burnet, Small Burnet)

Sanguisorba minor syn. *Poterium minor*

At the primary school I attended in the village of Chew Magna there was only one teacher, Miss Woods, and she was formidable. I have mixed memories of that school, for when I started I was left-handed. As Miss Woods did not like an untidy classroom, she changed me over to being right-handed. On a happier note, what I do remember with fondness and gratitude are the nature walks; she taught us to recognize birdsong, trees and wild plants. One of the many plants we saw was salad burnet, which grew on Dundry Common, which was part of our weekly walk. We used to pick the young leaves and chew them as we marched along in single file.

The leaves have a bitter yet cooling cucumber flavor, and today, when I eat them in salads, I remember those walks.

Description

This is one of the most useful herbs because the soft gray-green leaves, which are divided into neat ovals with toothed edges, belie their strength. They are evergreen, surviving most winters in the UK; in hard winters they die back only for a short time before reappearing in early spring. This makes them useful in the kitchen, especially in winter, when all other salad herbs have finished. In summer tiny magenta flowers appear around small, compact thimble-shaped flower heads that stand about a foot (30 cm) above the leaves. Interestingly, these flower heads are male at the bottom, bisexual in the middle and female at the top.

Plant salad burnet in well-drained soil in partial shade; semi-shade is important when growing this plant for culinary use because the leaves become very bitter in summer when grown in full sun.

History in cooking

Traditionally this herb was used in the Mediterranean to flavor wine, which was drunk as a tonic. Nicholas Culpeper (1616–54), the herbalist, wrote that it was "a most precious herb, the continual use of it preserves the body in health, and the spirits in vigour." Salad burnet was taken to the New World by the Pilgrim Fathers. In 1865 Matthew Robinson, in *The New Family Herbal*, wrote, "The continual use of it preserves the body in health and the mind in vigour. Pick two or three of the stalks, with leaves put into a cup of wine, especially claret, are known to quicken the spirits and drive away melancholy."

Harvesting and uses

Leaves

These can be picked all year round, but the best seasons for harvesting are spring and early autumn (after the summer growth has been cut hard back to encourage the plant to produce new growth). Mature leaves are bitter and drying to the mouth and not of much culinary merit. Use young leaves in salads, with egg dishes, with cream or cottage cheese and in drinks. One of the best dishes I ever created with this herb was poached salmon dressed with salad burnet leaves, which I made for my mother's 60th birthday.

Properties

Salad burnet reputedly gives relief from indigestion simply by eating a few leaves after a meal or when one has indigestion. It is known to be a carminative, digestive and antioxidant; it also contains vitamins A, B and C and is rich in calcium, potassium, iron and magnesium.

Other varieties

None.

SALAD BURNET EGG SALAD

A delicious weekend lunch or light supper, as suggested by my wonderful Aunt Kate, who loves simple food served well. The cool, dry cucumber flavor of the salad burnet leaves combines well with the eggs and mayonnaise. Serve with some fresh chunky whole wheat bread.

Serves 2

6 eggs
2/3 cup (150 ml) mayonnaise
7 tbsp (105 ml) plain yogurt
2 tbsp (30 ml) salad burnet leaves, finely chopped
Salt and freshly ground black pepper
1 crisp green lettuce, broken into whole leaves

Place the eggs in a large saucepan, fill it with water and place it on the stove over high heat. When the water comes to a boil, turn the heat down to medium and cook the eggs for 8 minutes.

Remove the pan from the stove, drain the water and run cold water over the eggs until they have cooled down. Remove the shells, chop up the eggs and place them in a large bowl. Add the remaining ingredients and mix well. Serve on a whole piece of crisp lettuce.

SALAD BURNET AND SWEET CICELY SPRING SALAD

This should be made at the start of the season, when you can go out into the garden and pick young salad burnet and sweet cicely leaves. The flavor combination of cool, dry cucumber with sweet anise is magic.

Serves 2

4 young sweet cicely sprigs
8 salad burnet sprigs
1 endive, radicchio, chicory or chicory frisée, leaves separated, washed and dried
4 strips bacon, cut into small squares
1 tsp (5 ml) pine nuts
2 tbsp (30 ml) olive oil
1 tsp (5 ml) balsamic vinegar
Salt and freshly ground black pepper

Mix the sweet cicely and salad burnet with the endive, radicchio, chicory or chicory frisée leaves in a large serving bowl.

In a large frying pan, dry-fry the bacon pieces, then add the pine nuts and cook until golden.

Mix together the olive oil and vinegar to make a dressing, check the seasoning and add salt and pepper to taste, then add the bacon and nuts.

Sprinkle the dressing over the salad leaves, toss and serve.

SALAD BURNET AND DILL BUTTER

The cool, dry, nutty flavor of salad burnet with the unique aromatic taste of dill is a wonderful combination.

Use this versatile butter in sandwiches filled with fish, cold ham or grated carrot and apple. Alternatively, you can use it to cook baked fish or simply serve dotted over steamed asparagus.

Makes 1 cup (250 ml)

6 salad burnet sprigs
6 dill sprigs
1 cup (250 ml) unsalted butter, slightly softened

Remove the leaves from the stems of the salad burnet, then chop them with the leaves and stems of the dill and the unsalted butter to release their oils. Finish the blending with a fork.

When the herbs and butter have been thoroughly mixed, pack the butter into a roll of waxed paper or plastic wrap and place in the fridge for up to 24 hours before use. The longer you leave it, the better the flavor.

This butter can also be frozen in a freezerproof container. It will keep for up to 3 months.

SALAD BURNET SUMMER COCKTAIL

Here I have gently converted an old recipe to suit today's tastes.

Makes approx. 1 quart (1 L)

12 whole salad burnet leaves
1 bottle of German white wine
1¼ cups (300 ml) amontillado sherry
1 lemon, cut into slices
2 qt (2 L) soda water
Crushed ice

Bruise the salad burnet leaves, then place them in a large pitcher and add the wine, sherry and lemon slices. Cover and leave to stand for 2 hours.

Just before serving, add the soda water and crushed ice.

Excess salad burnet

Salad burnet vinegar

This is a useful vinegar for salad dressings and mayonnaise and a great way to use lots of new growth, which will encourage the plant to produce more.

Makes 2 cups (500 ml)

¾ cup (175 ml) chopped salad burnet leaves
2 cups (500 ml) white wine vinegar

Crush the salad burnet leaves using either a mortar and pestle or a wooden spoon and a bowl.

Bring the vinegar to the boiling point in a saucepan and pour a small amount over the burnet in the mortar; pound together for a minute or two, then allow to cool.

Add the cooled infused vinegar to the remaining vinegar and pour into a sterilized (see page 12) bottle or jar with a nonmetallic lid. Keep for 2 weeks, shaking thoroughly every few days. After the 2 weeks, strain the vinegar through an unbleached paper coffee filter and rebottle. This will keep for at least 2 years.

SAVORY

(also known as Winter Savory, Mountain Savory, Timo,
Sajolida, Throumbi, Sarriette)
Satureja montana

My mother only grew summer savory, *Satureja hortensis*, an annual savory that she used liberally with fava beans to make an excellent summer dish. It was not until I started the herb farm that I found out there are many other varieties that are all just as delicious to cook with.

Description

Winter savory is a southern Mediterranean herb that in cool climates becomes a partial evergreen, which means that some leaves can be picked in the winter months. It has attractive small white flowers that are similar to those of thyme, and small dark green oval, pointed leaves that are highly aromatic when crushed and taste strong, with pepper overtones, when eaten straight from the bush.

All types of savory prefer to be planted in a sunny position in well-drained poor soil that has not been fed with manure or compost the previous autumn. Winter savory can be used as a low edging plant, as it is pretty in the summer, especially when in flower. However, it can look a bit sparse in winter.

As winter savory grows naturally in hot climates in rocky conditions, in cold or damp climates it makes an ideal container plant. Use a mix of equal parts soil-based compost and coarse horticultural grit, and place the container in a sunny, dry, sheltered spot.

History in cooking

This ancient herb has been used as a food flavoring for more than 2,000 years. The ancient Romans used it to flavor sauces and vinegar. Traditionally in southern Italy, where it grows wild, it has been used not only with grilled fish and lamb but also to swill out wine barrels before refilling with the new season's harvest. Bunches of winter savory were attached to each barrel to deter fruit flies from entering the barrels while the grapes fermented.

Harvesting and uses

Leaves

Harvest leaves from early spring until late autumn. However, the best leaves from all the varieties come from new tip growth, as they are the most pungent and succulent. Savory, being known as the "bean herb," combines well with all forms of bean from green vegetable beans such as fava beans to dried legumes. The leaves have a sweet aroma and pungent flavor and can be used as a substitute for black pepper. Note, though, that the flavor is lost when the herb is boiled.

Flowers

Pick as they appear throughout the summer. The small flowers pack a powerful flavor that goes well with cheese, salads and plums and pears.

Properties The leaves aid and stimulate digestion and they also ease colic, flatulence and feelings of fullness.

Other varieties

Summer Savory, Bean Herb
Satureja hortensis
This is an annual herb with small white, mauve-tinged flowers in summer and mid-green/olive linear, pungent small leaves. This is a favorite in Europe and North America, where it is widely used in bean dishes.

Savory Illyrica, Dwarf Winter Savory
Satureja montana subsp. *illyrica*
This semi-evergreen perennial has small mauve flowers in summer and dark green linear, pungent leaves. Like winter savory, this has a strong flavor, which makes it excellent for marinades, grilled meat, vegetables and legumes.

Creeping Savory
Satureja spicigera
This variety is an herbaceous perennial with tiny white flowers in late summer and bright green linear, highly pungent leaves. This can be found growing wild in Sardinia, where it is used as one of the ingredients in salami.

Greek Savory
Satureja thymbra
This is a semi-evergreen perennial with lovely small purple flowers and dark green linear leaves that are very aromatic. This herb has had many names and has even been grouped with thymes. It is excellent with grilled fish, lamb and mushrooms.

African Savory
Satureja biflora
This semi-evergreen perennial has small white flowers and mid-green linear leaves that have a spicy lemon flavor. African savory goes well with legumes and vegetable dishes.

FAVA BEANS WITH SUMMER SAVORY CREAM

Peppery savory is delicious with fava beans. This is my mother's recipe. I have changed only one ingredient: she used heavy (whipping) cream and I prefer crème fraîche. If you have the time and patience you can remove the bean skins after cooking, as the vivid green underneath looks striking and the flavor is sweeter. Serve with cold ham.

Serves 2 as a main course, 4 as a side

12 oz (340 g) young fava (or lima) beans, shelled
2 summer savory sprigs
2½ tbsp (37 ml) unsalted butter
1 tbsp (15 ml) summer savory leaves, finely chopped
2/3 cup (150 ml) crème fraîche
1 egg yolk
Salt and freshly ground black pepper

Bring a pot of water to a boil but do not add salt at this stage, as it will toughen the skins of the fava beans. Add the beans and the summer savory sprigs. Cook until tender, then drain and remove and discard the savory.

Melt the butter in another pan, turn the heat to low, then add the beans and the finely chopped savory leaves. Mix the crème fraîche with the egg yolk and add to the pan. Cook, stirring all the time, over moderate heat, for a few minutes, until the cream thickens. Do not allow the sauce to boil or it will curdle. Season to taste.

Pour into a warmed serving bowl and serve straightaway.

JERUSALEM ARTICHOKE HAM AND SAVORY BAKE

Jerusalem artichokes are renowned for causing flatulence. By cooking them with savory you will find that not only is the flavor enhanced but they are much easier to digest.

Serves 4–6

1 cup (250 ml) crème fraîche
Juice of 1 lemon
2 cloves garlic, finely chopped
1 good handful savory (winter, creeping or summer), leaves picked and chopped
3 handfuls grated Parmesan
Salt and freshly ground black pepper
4 slices cooked ham, cut into squares
2 lb (1 kg) Jerusalem artichokes, peeled and cut into long, thin slices
2 good handfuls fresh bread crumbs
Olive oil

Preheat the oven to 425°F (220°C).

In a bowl, mix together the crème fraîche, lemon juice, garlic, half the savory and three-quarters of the Parmesan and season well to taste. Throw in the ham and sliced Jerusalem artichokes. Mix well and place everything in an ovenproof baking dish.

Mix the bread crumbs with the remaining savory and Parmesan and some salt and pepper. Sprinkle the flavored bread crumbs over the artichokes and drizzle with a little olive oil.

Bake in the oven for around 30 minutes, until the artichokes are tender and the bread crumbs are golden.

BRAISED RED CABBAGE WITH WINTER SAVORY

Red cabbage is something I have grown to love. As a child I found the flavor too strong, but my palate has matured. I really enjoy this dish and find it useful, as it can be served hot or cold and will keep well in the fridge for several days.

Mum used to add raisins to encourage us to eat it; I have added savory, as I find that the piquant pepper flavor combines well with the caraway and cabbage.

Serve hot with cold meats and roast chicken, or cold with Cheddar and fresh crusty bread.

Serves 4–6

1 medium red cabbage
2–3½ tbsp (30–52 ml) butter
1 large cooking apple, peeled and sliced
2 medium onions, peeled and sliced
2 cloves garlic, crushed
Zest and juice of 1 orange
3 winter savory sprigs
1 bay leaf
1 bunch flat-leaf parsley
1 tsp (5 ml) caraway seeds
¼ tsp (1 ml) freshly grated nutmeg
¼ tsp (1 ml) ground cinnamon
Salt and freshly ground black pepper
2 tbsp (30 ml) brown sugar
1 glass red wine (preferably from the night before's bottle)

Preheat the oven to 300°F (150°C).

Remove the large, damaged outer leaves of the cabbage. Quarter it, discard the central core, then shred as finely as possible. Melt the butter on the stove in a heatproof casserole dish, add the cabbage, cover and cook gently for 5 minutes. Add the apple, onions, garlic, orange zest and juice, savory sprigs, bay leaf, parsley, spices and salt and pepper to taste. Mix everything together, add the sugar and wine, stir again, then cover and put in the oven for 3 hours. Check halfway through that it is not drying out; if it is, add a little hot water.

MUSHROOM, GARLIC AND SAVORY BAKE

In Greece savory is often combined with mushrooms. Here is a simple recipe for a light lunch or supper that highlights the flavor of this herb.

Serve with a mixed herb salad and some fresh crusty bread to mop up the mushroom juices.

Serves 2

2 tbsp (30 ml) unsalted butter, plus extra for greasing
12 large field mushrooms (preferably freshly picked), or cap mushrooms
2 tbsp (30 ml) olive oil
7 tbsp (105 ml) coarse dry bread crumbs
2 cloves garlic, finely sliced
1 heaped tsp (6 ml) savory leaves, finely chopped
Salt and freshly ground black pepper
Nutmeg (if using store-bought mushrooms)

Preheat the oven to 325°F (170°C). Grease an ovenproof baking dish.

If you have been lucky enough to pick field mushrooms in mid-autumn, these will need to be washed, peeled, then sliced and patted dry. Alternatively you can use cap mushrooms, which will need to be washed, dried, then sliced in half; there is no need to peel.

Heat the olive oil in a frying pan, add the bread crumbs and stir. As soon as they start to brown, add the garlic, savory leaves, salt, pepper and nutmeg (if you are using fresh field mushrooms, omit the nutmeg). Cook until the garlic becomes translucent but not brown.

Place the mushrooms in the prepared dish, sprinkle over the herby bread crumbs, place in the oven and bake for 25 minutes.

Excess savory

Summer savory butter

Since it's an annual herb, you can have a glut of summer savory, so this is a good way of preserving it for use later in the season. I use this butter for grilling fish or lamb instead of rosemary.

Makes ½ cup (125 ml)

½ cup (125 ml) unsalted butter, slightly softened
Handful savory leaves

Remove the savory leaves by gently rubbing your fingers up and down the stems. Once removed, gently chop to release the oils, then mix the chopped leaves with the butter. (The easiest way of blending the herb and butter together is to use a fork.)

When thoroughly mixed, pack it into a roll in waxed paper or plastic wrap and place in the fridge for up to 24 hours before use. The longer you leave it, the better the flavor.

This can also be frozen – put into a labeled freezerproof container. It will keep for 6 months.

SHISO

(also known as Perilla, Chinese Basil, Wild Sesame,
Rattlesnake Weed)
Perilla frutescens

Until recently this Asian herb was relatively unknown as a culinary delight in Western countries. Even in the early 1980s, purple perilla was being used in the UK as a spectacular spot bedding plant rather than in the kitchen.

I discovered its culinary prowess about 15 years ago while I was exhibiting it at one the Royal Horticultural Society's London flower shows. News of perilla's presence at the show obviously spread throughout the Japanese community. During the two days of the show, I sold out of plants and I learned from my customers all about this unique and delightful herb. Interestingly, it is now a chef's designer herb, being served as a cress herb – as seedlings – where the flavors of the leaves are more concentrated and intense.

Description

Shiso is a hardy annual with pale pink/mauve flowers in summer and large, deeply cut, textured aromatic cumin-flavored leaves. This herb is grown from seed sown in late spring when all threat of frost has passed. When growing in the garden, plant in fertile well-drained soil that has been prepared with well-rotted compost or leaf mold in the previous autumn, in sun or partial shade. One word of warning, though: do not plant near where horses or cattle might eat it, because it can cause respiratory failure in such animals.

History in cooking

The leaves and seeds of shiso have been widely used in China since AD 500, both in the kitchen and medicinally. It has also been used in Japanese cuisine for hundreds of years.

Historically the oil extract from the seeds was used across Asia as a waterproof container, and this practice continues today in rural areas of Korea. In Nepal and parts of India, traditionally the seeds were ground with chiles and tomatoes to make a savory dip or side dish. They are still prepared this way in rural parts now.

Harvesting and uses

Leaves

The leaves can be picked fresh as required from spring until the first frosts. Picking the growing tips will keep the plant more productive than taking the side leaves. Also the growing tips have the most intense flavor, so they can be eaten raw or are ideal for stir-fry dishes. If using mature leaves, they should be cooked.

Flowers

Pick the flowers as they appear in summer. They have a sweet flavor and are great added to all forms of salad or scattered over cold fish dishes.

Seeds

Harvest seeds from late summer until early autumn. The seed has an interesting, rather sweet flavor. I have not cooked with it but I do know that perilla is grown as a seed crop in Japan and northern India. It is then crushed and the oil is extracted, which is said to be rather similar to linseed and is used equally for both culinary and medicinal purposes. However, in parts of Asia perilla oil is valued more for its medicinal benefit than its flavor, as it is a very rich source of omega-3 fatty acid and alpha-linolenic acid.

Properties

This herb is one of the strongest natural antioxidants; it has been under research at Osaka University in Japan, where they have found that it is more powerful than ascorbic acid. Another noteworthy benefit is its ability to dissolve cholesterol.

Varieties

Zi Su, Egoma

Perilla frutescens var. *frutescens*

A hardy annual with mauve flowers in summer and large aromatic green leaves with a hint of brown and a deep purple underside. It is an important culinary and medicinal herb from Korea.

Green Shiso, Aoshiso

Perilla frutescens var. *crispa*

This hardy annual has pink flowers in summer and aromatic anise-flavored deeply cut bright green leaves with crinkled edges. Green shiso is the variety most commonly seen in Japanese markets, and it is used there as a vegetable. The leaves can also be used as a wrapping for rice cakes and in salads and tempura. The seeds from this variety are used as a condiment and with pickles. The essential oil extracted from the leaf and flowering parts contains a substance that is a thousand times sweeter than sugar and which is used in confectionery.

Purple Shiso, Akashiso, Beefsteak Plant

Perilla frutescens var. *purpurascens*

This is a hardy annual with pink flowers in summer and deeply cut aromatic dark purple leaves with crinkled bronzed edges. There can be considerable variation among seed-raised plants; the flowers can be red and the leaves smoother. Purple shiso is used as a dye for pickling fruit and vegetables, as a dried powder in a side dish with rice, as an ingredient in cake mixes and as flavoring in beverages. The flower heads are used as a condiment with sushi.

VEGETABLE AND SHISO TEMPURA

Shiso is wonderful cooked this way, as you keep all its unique, cumin-like flavor, which combines so well with the other vegetables.

The art of good tempura is to have everything ready before you make the batter; aside from the ingredients, have next to you a bowl of flour for dipping the vegetables, a wire draining rack and paper towels, plus a couple of serving bowls so that as soon as a batch is made it can be served.

Cook the vegetables in small batches and have everyone ready to eat as soon as the vegetables are cooked.

Tempura is a very sociable dish, as it is eaten in batches rather than all in one go. However, if you would rather serve it all at once, preheat the oven to 350°F (180°C) and place a serving bowl in the oven once it has heated up. Put the batches of tempura in the bowl as they are removed from the oil.

Serves 4

3½ oz (100 g) mushrooms, cut into bite-sized pieces
3½ oz (100 g) zucchini, cut into bite-sized pieces
3½ oz (100 g) red bell peppers, seeded and cut into chunks
3½ oz (100 g) broccoli, broken into small florets
20 shiso leaves (red, green or a mixture), stems removed

For the dipping sauce
3 tbsp (45 ml) soy sauce
3 tbsp (45 ml) dry sherry
1 tbsp (15 ml) sugar
Zest of 1 lemon

For the batter
¾ cup + 2 tbsp (200 ml) all-purpose flour, plus extra for dusting
1 tbsp (15 ml) cornstarch
1 tsp (5 ml) sea salt
¾ cup + 2 tbsp (200 ml) ice-cold sparkling mineral water
Ice cubes
Vegetable oil, for frying

First wash and prepare the vegetables and the shiso leaves.

Make the dipping sauce by combining all the ingredients. Pour into a serving bowl.

Make the batter in two batches – that way it will not have to stand before using. Mix quickly; it does not matter if you have a few lumpy bits, for if you overmix the batter will be heavy.

Heat the oil in a wok or wide frying pan to 325–350°F (170–180°C). Test by dropping a small amount of batter into it: if it sinks, then rises to the surface, the temperature is right.

Do not overcrowd the pan; just fry a few pieces at a time. Dip the vegetables in the flour, shake off any excess, then coat them in batter and slide them into the oil. The shiso leaves do not need to be dunked in flour first; simply dip in the batter, shake off the excess, drop into the oil and cook for 1 minute, then remove from the oil and drain. Cook the vegetables for 2 to 3 minutes, turning frequently with long chopsticks or a slotted spoon until the batter turns a light gold and the pieces rise to the surface.

Remove the cooked vegetables from the oil and place on the draining rack or paper towels and serve immediately with the dipping sauce.

Repeat until all the vegetables and shiso leaves are cooked.

STIR-FRIED CUCUMBER AND SHISO

The combination of the cool cucumber and the cumin sweetness of the shiso is delightful, and this makes a tasty (and quick) light supper. Serve with boiled rice.

Serves 2–3

1 cucumber, peeled to make stripes
3 tbsp (45 ml) light olive oil
1 fresh red chile pepper, seeded and finely chopped
2 cloves garlic, finely chopped
1½ tsp (7 ml) light soy sauce
1 tsp (5 ml) white wine vinegar
6–8 leaves purple or green shiso, finely chopped
1 tsp (5 ml) sesame oil

Cut the cucumber in half lengthwise. Holding the knife at an angle, slice each half into 1/8-inch (3 mm) thick semicircles.

Heat a flat-bottomed wok or deep frying pan over high heat until it smokes, then add the olive oil. Add the cucumber, stir and spread the slices out so they cover as much of the surface of the pan as possible. Turn them carefully from time to time until they brown slightly on both sides. Add the chile pepper and garlic and stir-fry until fragrant. Pour in the soy sauce and vinegar and mix well. Add the shiso leaves and stir. Remove from the heat, stir in the sesame oil and serve immediately.

SPICY TUNA AND SHISO BURGERS

Fish, especially tuna, combines well with the spicy flavor of shiso. These burgers are delicious and very spicy – so go easy on the wasabi paste.

Serves 6

1½ lb (700 g) fresh skinless tuna steaks or 2 x 7-oz (200 g) cans tuna steak
6–8 green shiso leaves
2 green onions, trimmed
1 tsp (5 ml) wasabi paste or mustard
1-inch (3 cm) piece fresh gingerroot, grated
Salt and freshly ground black pepper
4 tbsp (60 ml) teriyaki sauce
2 tbsp (30 ml) honey
1 tbsp (15 ml) vegetable oil
3 ciabatta or burger buns
2 tbsp (30 ml) sweet chili sauce, plus extra to serve
1 cucumber
1 crisp lettuce, washed and dried
Pickled ginger, to serve

Break up the tuna, then chop it and place it in a mixing bowl. Finely chop the shiso and green onions and add to the tuna with the wasabi or mustard and gingerroot. Mix thoroughly, check the seasoning and add salt and pepper to taste, if needed. Alternatively, use a food processor: add the tuna, shiso, green onions, wasabi and gingerroot to the mixing bowl and pulse to mix all the ingredients together; do not overprocess.

Shape the mixture into 6 burgers and put on a plate or baking sheet. Cover with plastic wrap and chill in the fridge for 1 hour.

Mix together the teriyaki sauce and honey and set aside.

Heat the vegetable oil in a nonstick frying pan. When the pan is hot, add the tuna burgers and cook for 3 to 4 minutes each side, brushing with the teriyaki-and-honey glaze as you go.

Preheat the broiler. Cut the bread or buns in half and lightly toast the cut side under the broiler. Cut the cucumber into ribbons using a vegetable peeler and shred the lettuce. Spread the bread halves with the chili sauce and top with the cucumber ribbons and shredded lettuce. Add the burgers and spoon over them the juices from the pan. Arrange on a serving plate alongside small bowls of pickled ginger and sweet chili sauce.

Excess shiso

Shiso marinade for raw fish

This marinade is lovely with many forms of meaty white fish. You do need a good crop to be able to harvest 2 tbsp (30 ml) growing tips. Serve with a crisp green salad with vinaigrette or sticky rice.

Makes approx. 1 cup (250 ml)

1 lb (500 g) cod fillet or other meaty white fish

For the marinade:
¾ cup + 2 tbsp (200 ml) white wine vinegar
2 tbsp (30 ml) shiso growing tips (green or purple)
Juice of 1 lemon
Juice of 1 lime
1 tbsp (15 ml) sea salt
2 cloves garlic, sliced

Mix together all the ingredients to make the marinade. Slice the fish into 1-inch (2.5 cm) pieces and place in a shallow dish. Pour over the marinade, cover the dish with a lid or foil and refrigerate for 3 hours, turning the fish every half-hour so that it is completely saturated in the marinade. Leave for a further 24 hours, covered, in the fridge.

Remove the fish from the marinade and slice very thinly to serve.

The marinade on its own will keep in a sealed container in the fridge for 48 hours prior to use without losing flavor.

SORREL

(also known as Bread and Cheese, Sour Leaves, Tom Thumbs,
A Thousand Fingers, Sour Sauce)
Rumex acetosa

When my children were at the local primary school, their class used to walk over to the herb farm, where we would talk about plants relevant to what they were learning at school. One year they came over and I had been talking about how the Romans, as they marched along, used to eat a sorrel leaf to stop themselves feeling thirsty, as they did not have bottles of water. One little boy asked if he could eat a leaf. I gave him one and he ate it and proclaimed, "It's like a Granny Smith apple." After that remark I was deluged with requests for leaves.

One word of caution: You should not eat fresh, raw sorrel (cooked is fine) if you suffer from gout or have kidney stones. Equally, avoid overeating this herb in its fresh form while breastfeeding.

Description

This herb looks very like its cousin dock; the leaves are longer and lance-shaped but the dull and inconspicuous flowers are similar. The difference comes in the taste of the young leaves, which have a refreshing lemony flavor. It is an herbaceous perennial, meaning that it dies back into the ground during winter, reappearing in the following spring.

Sorrel prefers a rich, acid soil that retains moisture, although it will happily adapt to any soil that does not dry out in summer. If you want to crop this herb for use in the kitchen, I recommend planting it in partial shade, because once the heat of summer sets in, the leaves become tough, bitter and inedible. A leaf or bark mulch keeps the soil cooler, and once the temperature falls, the flavor will improve. In the summer the plant tends to run to flower and seed quickly; therefore, to keep the leaves fresh, succulent and productive for the early autumn, remove the flower heads as they appear.

History in cooking

The historical use of sorrel as a food dates back to 3000 BC. It is said that eating sorrel leaves cured Julius Caesar's soldiers of scurvy.

The ancient Egyptians and Romans ate sorrel to offset their rich food. The Tudors considered it to be one of the best vegetables, and in Lapland sorrel juice has long been used instead of rennet to curdle milk.

Harvesting and uses

Leaves

Young leaves are tender and not as sour or tough as mature leaves, so pick these from spring until early autumn. A few young leaves added to salads give a refreshing sharp flavor, and they make great sauces that can be served with fish or meat. The leaves can also be used as a natural meat tenderizer by wrapping them around tough meat while it is cooking, or can be added to stews and casseroles or combined with eggs and cheese.

Properties

Sorrel is high in oxalic, tannic and tartaric acid as well as vitamins A, B$_1$ and C and the minerals calcium, potassium, iron and sulfur. Sorrel leaves stimulate the salivary glands, and for this reason eating a small leaf is beneficial to the digestion.

Other varieties

Sheep's Sorrel
Rumex acetosella
This variety has small, inconspicuous flowers that turn greenish brown as the fruit ripens in early summer. The mid-green leaves are shaped like a barbed spear. It grows wild on heaths and grassy places, and where it grows indicates that the soil is acid. Use young leaves in salads and sauces.

Buckler Leaf Sorrel, French Sorrel
Rumex scutatus
This has small, inconspicuous flowers that turn greenish brown as the fruit ripens in early summer. The mid-green leaves are shaped like squat shields. Use the young leaves in salads and sauces.

GRANDMOTHER'S SORREL SOUP

I have reproduced this recipe for *potage a l'oseille* just as my grandmother Ruth wrote it, including her notes, which were written under each recipe. It is a lovely way to use sorrel. This is taken from her book *Food for Pleasure*, published in 1950. Inside my copy is written: "To Clare, with love from Mummy." Clare was my mother.

If you don't grow sorrel or can't buy it, let someone who knows what it is gather the tiny leaves from wild sorrel, as it is easy to make a mistake and get the wrong leaves. Sorrel has a bitter, lemony taste and makes a smooth soup. I use chicken stock instead of water.

Serves 2

3 large handfuls sorrel
Butter or margarine
Salt and freshly ground black pepper
1¼ cups (300 ml) chicken stock or water, previously warmed
4 very thin slices bread (stale bread is excellent)
2 egg yolks
1 tbsp (15 ml) milk

Preheat the oven to 300°F (150°C).

Clean the sorrel leaves, remove the stalks and center ribs and wash them well. Wilt them in a pan with a piece of butter the size of an egg; add the salt and pepper and sufficient water or stock to make a good soup.

Toast the slices of bread in the oven. Using this method rather than a toaster means the bread becomes hard and crisp rather than just toasted on the outside.

Beat the egg yolks with the milk and add to the cooked sorrel and stock. Stir well. Break 2 slices of toast into a few pieces, divide these between 2 bowls, then pour the soup over and serve, putting the remaining dry toast on a plate so that it can be eaten with the soup.

BATAVIA FRAPPÉ

This is another wonderful soup made by my grandmother that appears in two of her books, *What's Cooking?* and *Food for Pleasure*. I have only slightly adapted it to suit today's ingredients. The combination of cucumber and peas with sharp sorrel is great; it is difficult to believe that this recipe was written more than 60 years ago.

Serves 4

2 handfuls peas in their pods
2 handfuls sorrel
2 cucumbers, peeled and grated, then left to drain for 30 minutes
1¼ cups (300 ml) cold water
3½ cups (850 ml) vegetable stock
1¼ cups (300 ml) white wine
Salt and freshly ground black pepper
Table (18%) or half-and-half (10%) cream, to serve

Bring two small saucepans of water to a boil. Add the peas to one and the sorrel to the other and cook until tender. Drain, saving the pea cooking water to use with the vegetable stock. Purée the peas and sorrel. Drain and remove as much of the liquid as possible from the cucumbers and combine with the 2 purées.

Put the water, vegetable stock and white wine together in a saucepan and bring to a boil to remove the alcohol from the wine. When cool, stir in the purées and drained cucumber. Stir well, then pass through a sieve – do not be tempted to liquidize, as this will give the wrong texture.

Check the seasoning. Pour the soup into a container and place in the fridge for at least 2 hours before serving. To serve, add a dash of table (18%) or half-and-half (10%) cream.

SORREL AND ANCHOVY TART

The sharpness of the sorrel with the saltiness of the anchovy fillets makes this tart delicious. Serve with a fresh tomato salad and new potatoes.

Serves 4–6

6½ oz (185 g) ready-rolled plain shortcrust pastry
12 oz (350 g) sorrel, washed and stalks removed
2 tbsp (30 ml) butter
2 tbsp (30 ml) olive oil
3 onions, thinly sliced
10–12 anchovy fillets, chopped
½ tsp (2 ml) freshly grated nutmeg
Freshly ground black pepper
2 eggs, plus 2 egg yolks
1½ cups (350 ml) whipping (35%) cream

Preheat the oven to 400°F (200°C).

Line a shallow 9½-inch (24 cm) loose-bottomed flan pan with the pastry, prick the base with a fork and bake blind in the oven for 20 minutes. (For those of you not sure of the term "bake blind," this is when you line your pastry with a circle of parchment paper slightly larger than the pastry shell. Then place some ceramic baking beans, or in my case some dried pasta, on top to weigh the pastry down.)

Take out of the oven, remove the baking beans and parchment paper, then return the tart shell to the oven and bake for a further 5 minutes. Remove from the oven and allow to cool slightly while you cook the sorrel.

Put the sorrel in a saucepan with a little water. Put the lid on and let it simmer over the lowest possible heat for 5 minutes. Drain in a colander, using a saucer to squeeze out as much liquid as possible. Set aside.

Melt the butter and oil in a frying pan and gently fry the onions for about 10 minutes or until they are soft and beginning to caramelize, stirring occasionally. Remove the pan from the heat and stir in the drained sorrel, anchovies, grated nutmeg and pepper.

In a large bowl, beat the eggs, egg yolks and cream together, then add the sorrel mixture to the egg mixture and give it a really good stir. Pile the mixture into the prebaked pastry shell and bake in the oven for 25 to 30 minutes or until the filling looks set and the edges are turning golden brown. Remove the tart from the oven and allow it to cool before serving.

RHUBARB AND SORREL SAUCE

This is an early summer recipe for when the rhubarb is at its best and the sorrel is young and tender. The combination of the fruit and the sour leaf of the sorrel is very good and goes well with all smoked fish, especially mackerel.

Serves 4

1 lb (450 g) rhubarb, cut into 1-inch (2.5 cm) pieces
²/₃ cup (150 ml) melted butter
½ tsp (2 ml) grated ginger
½ tsp (2 ml) lemon zest
Pinch of grated nutmeg
2 tbsp (30 ml) fruit (superfine) sugar
2 handfuls sorrel, washed and chopped

Boil the rhubarb in a saucepan with a splash of water until tender, then pass it through a sieve.

Return to the pan, add the melted butter with the heat on low and bring to the simmering point. Add the ginger, lemon zest, nutmeg and sugar, stir well and cook very gently for about 10 minutes, then fold in the sorrel and cook for a few more minutes, until the sorrel has broken down. Serve.

Excess sorrel

The best way to cope with a glut of this herb is to pick the young leaves, wash and dry them, then put them in a freezer bag, seal and freeze. Once removed from the freezer, the leaves become very limp as they thaw, but they do retain their flavor so are great for making sauces and soups.

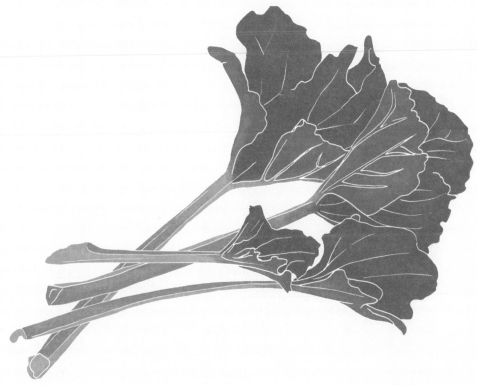

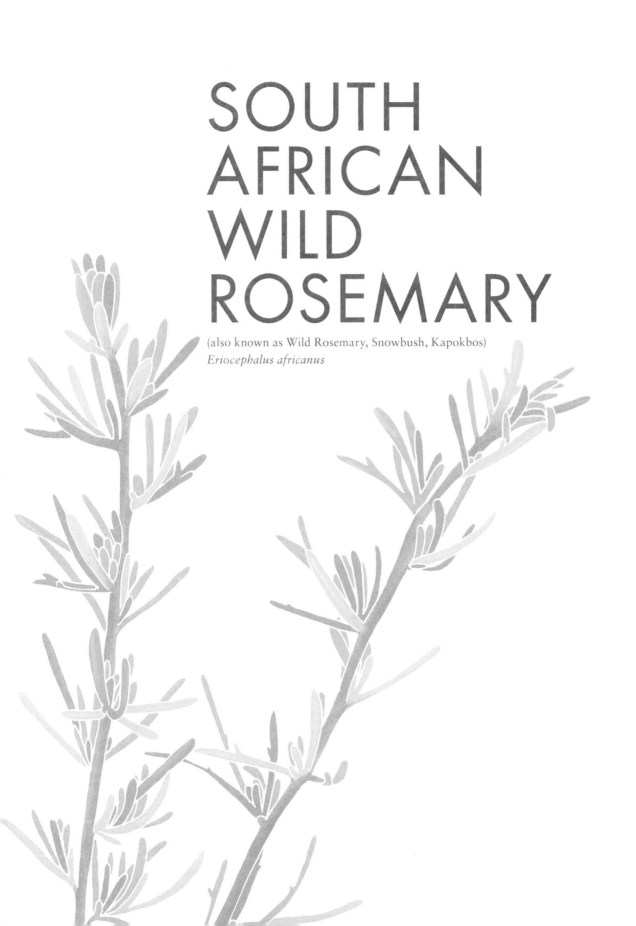

SOUTH AFRICAN WILD ROSEMARY

(also known as Wild Rosemary, Snowbush, Kapokbós)

Eriocephalus africanus

I am lucky enough to have seen this graceful plant growing wild in South Africa, although, to be honest, it does not stand out, as it is surrounded by hundreds of other fantastic flora and fauna. It is not until you rub the leaves that you realize the culinary potential of this herb. I am surprised that it is little known or used, as I find it a great alternative to standard rosemary.

Description

This herb was much used by the early Cape people and the Khoi. It is a half-hardy evergreen with small, needle-like, silver-haired oval, slightly succulent aromatic leaves that grow in tufts along the branch. The attractive clusters of small white flowers with magenta centers are followed by seeds covered in masses of tiny white hairs that make them look fluffy. The whole plant has a spreading, arching habit, so when the plant is in seed it looks rather like a wave crashing in to shore.

South African wild rosemary can be raised from seed, but that can be a bit hit-or-miss, so it is much easier to take cuttings in late spring. Amazingly drought-tolerant, it will adapt to most soils, with the exception of heavy, cold clay and marshy types of soil. The ideal conditions are full sun and well-drained soil, and it is a good coastal plant, as it likes the sea spray and wind. In warm climates it can be grown as a hedge or clipped into ball shapes. In cool climates it is a tolerant and attractive container plant. Protect from frost.

History in cooking

I do not know of any recorded history of this herb being used in cooking. However, I am sure that the indigenous South African Khoi have recipes and uses dating back for hundreds of years.

Harvesting and uses

Leaves

As an evergreen the leaves are available all year round. They have two distinct flavors: mild in the spring from the new growth, and intense after the long, hot summer, when the leaves are small and the flavor is more concentrated. These leaves should be cooked and not eaten raw, making them ideal for dishes that require a long cooking time, such as stews and casseroles with both meat and vegetables.

Properties

Wild rosemary has traditionally been used as a medicine for many ailments, such as coughs and colds, flatulence and colic, and also as a diuretic and diaphoretic. It is said to have similar qualities to rosemary (*Rosmarinus officinalis*).

Other varieties

There are different forms of *Eriocephalus*; however, I can find no record of their being used in the kitchen.

SOUTH AFRICAN WILD ROSEMARY POT-ROASTED CHICKEN

A simple dish that can be quickly prepared and is a pleasure to eat. The flavor of the wild rosemary combines so well with the chicken, and the cooking juices produced make the most lovely flavored gravy or sauce.

Delicious served with mashed potatoes.

Serves 6–8

3-lb (1.5 kg) whole chicken
1¹/₃ cup (330 ml) cider
2 large onions, sliced
4 leeks, white bits only, sliced and well washed
4 South African wild rosemary sprigs, leaves removed from the stems
Salt and freshly ground black pepper
²/₃ cup (150 ml) whipping (35%) cream

Preheat the oven to 325°F (170°C).

Put the chicken in a large casserole dish, pour the cider over and stir in the onions, leeks and wild rosemary sprigs. Season, cover and roast for 45 minutes.

Uncover the chicken and roast for a further 45 minutes, until it is golden on top and cooked through. Transfer the bird to a plate to rest for 5 minutes.

Put the casserole on the stove over low heat and pour in the cream to warm through. Season to taste.

Carve the chicken and serve with the leeks and creamy pan juices.

SPECIAL LAMB STEW WITH SOUTH AFRICAN WILD ROSEMARY

This flavorsome autumn meal was the first dish I cooked with this herb. I included it in *Jekka's Complete Herb Book*, and as it has proved so popular, it had to be included in this book too. We all know that standard rosemary goes well with lamb, but this wild version adds another dimension. Serve with rice and a salad or green beans.

Serves 4–6

½ cup (125 ml) dried chickpeas (or canned)
¹/₃ cup (75 ml) light olive oil, divided
1 large onion, finely chopped
1 lb (500 g) lean lamb, cubed
Salt and freshly ground black pepper
Juice of 2 lemons
2 bay leaves
3 South African wild rosemary sprigs, roughly 4 inches (10 cm) long
3 leeks, cleaned and chopped
8 oz (250 g) spinach
7 oz (200 g) flat-leaf parsley
1 lime, sliced

Soak the dried chickpeas overnight. The next day, drain, then cook them in fresh unsalted water for 15 to 20 minutes. Drain, rinse under fresh cold water and set aside. Alternatively, drain the contents from the can, rinse and set aside.

Heat 2 tbsp (30 ml) olive oil in a large, heavy pan and slowly sauté the onion. Add the lamb and brown on all sides, then season with salt and pepper. Pour on the lemon juice, add enough boiled hot water to just cover the meat, then add the bay leaves and the wild rosemary. Cover and simmer for 30 minutes.

Heat the remaining olive oil and sauté the leeks, spinach and parsley until just cooked. Add this to the meat with the chickpeas and lime slices. Check that the liquid just covers the lamb and add extra if needed. Simmer all the ingredients for a further hour, checking from time to time that nothing is sticking.

Just before serving, remove the wild rosemary sprigs and the lime slices, which can be used to decorate the serving plate.

WILD ROSEMARY TORTILLAS

These tortillas are exceedingly versatile; they can be served with soups, filled with spicy ground meat or cheese and salad, or served for lunch filled with tomatoes, cheese and lettuce. Wild rosemary is more subtle than standard rosemary, so when baked in these breads it adds a delicate flavor.

Makes 6–8

2½ cups (625 ml) all-purpose flour, plus extra for dusting
2 tsp (10 ml) salt
2 tsp (10 ml) finely chopped South African wild rosemary leaves (or you can use standard rosemary)
4 tsp (20 ml) baking powder
2 tbsp (30 ml) lard, margarine or shortening
2/3 cup (150 ml) warm water (more if needed)

In a large bowl, stir together the flour, salt, wild rosemary leaves and baking powder. With your hands, gradually work in the lard, margarine or shortening until it is all incorporated. Add enough warm water to make a soft but not sticky dough. Leave to rest, covered with a clean dish towel, for 30 minutes.

Turn out onto a lightly floured board and knead for 5 minutes. Divide the dough into 8 and shape into round balls using your hands. Roll each one out to a 1/8-inch (2–3 mm) thickness.

Place a heavy frying pan or grill pan over medium-high heat and add the tortillas one at a time. Cook each one for 30 seconds, until brown patches form, then turn over and cook on the second side. Place the cooked tortilla in a clean dish towel to hold the steam in. Repeat until all are cooked.

Serve warm.

Excess South African wild rosemary

I have yet to have a glut of this herb and, since it's an evergreen, I can pick it fresh when required, so there has been no need to preserve it.

STEVIA

(also known as Honeyleaf, Caá-ehe)
Stevia rebaudiana

This is a truly amazing herb. Take the smallest piece of leaf and put it on the end of your tongue and you will realize that the claim that it is 30 times sweeter than sugar is true. In fact, records show that a quarter of a teaspoon (1 ml) of dried leaf is equivalent to half a pound (225 g) of sugar!

I have read many arguments regarding the safety of stevia, all of which leave me confused. The Japanese, who have banned all artificial sweeteners, have used stevia as a commercial sweetener for more than 30 years with no adverse reactions. However, agencies in the United States and Europe have banned it for sale as a food or food ingredient; it can be sold as a dietary supplement, not as a sweetener, in the US. Research is ongoing, with no definitive conclusions as yet drawn. So it is up to you. I will always adhere to science when a fact is proven, but so far nothing has been proven, so for now I will continue to cook with it.

Description

Stevia is a subtropical evergreen herb often grown as an annual in cold climates. It has clusters of small white flowers and green oval, serrated leaves with an intense sugary taste with a hint of licorice.

You can grow stevia from seed but germination is erratic, so I recommend growing it from cuttings taken in early summer. This herb can be grown outside only in the tropics but will happily grow in a container elsewhere, if put in a frost-free position over winter.

History in cooking

This herb has been used in South and Central America for hundreds of years. In the 16th century the invading Spaniards noticed that the Guarani Indians of Paraguay were using this herb not only to sweeten their drinks but also to make herbal remedies and snacks.

Harvesting and uses

Leaves

Outside the tropics the leaves can be picked from late spring to mid-autumn. Young leaves provide the best flavor, and stevia truly does mean that you can cook without sugar. The most important point to remember is not to use too much, or you will ruin your dish. Stevia is excellent with any recipe using fruit, juices or dairy. It can withstand high temperatures, which will not destroy its sweetness, but it is not good for home baking, with a few exceptions such as carrot cake (see page 301). This is because it lacks sugar's abilities to add texture, caramelize or feed the fermentation of yeast.

Properties

Stevia is a digestive tonic and a natural sweetener. The leaves contain vitamins B and C and the minerals calcium and potassium.

Other varieties

None.

TO MAKE A STEVIA SOLUTION FOR EVERYDAY USE

Many factors can alter the sugar content of the leaves of this herb; for example, it could be the time of year or the temperature or soil conditions in which it is grown, so there is no exact way to know the sweetness of what you are picking. To overcome this I have devised a general all-purpose way of making a stevia solution that is good for everyday use.

Always start with just a few leaves, because you can add but you cannot take away sweetness once you have created the solution.

Stevia leaves
1¼ cups (300 ml) boiled water

Take one leaf and place it in a glass measuring cup. Add the boiled (not boiling) water and leave to stand for 10 minutes.

Taste the water with a spoon; if it is not sweet enough for your taste or recipe, add another leaf.

Pour the water and leaves into a small pan and reheat to just below boiling point. Let it stand, covered, for a further 10 minutes, then taste again. If it is not sweet enough, keep adding leaves one by one and heating until you achieve the flavor you require.

STEVIA LEMONADE

A lovely cold, refreshing drink for the summer, in which stevia sweetens the lemon perfectly.

Makes 3½ cups (825 ml)

Zest of ½ lemon
1 cup + 2 tbsp (275 ml) freshly squeezed lemon juice
2¼ cups (550 ml) cold water
2 tsp (10 ml) stevia solution (see recipe above), or to taste
3 lemon slices, plus extra to garnish
2 mint sprigs, plus extra to garnish
1 lemon verbena sprig
Ice cubes

Combine all the ingredients in a large pitcher and stir well.

Place an ice cube in each glass, pour the lemonade over and garnish each with a slice of lemon and a sprig of mint.

CARROT CAKE

Stevia works well in this cake because it is used with ripe bananas, meaning that the caramelizing action of the sugar is not missed.

Serves 8–10

Butter, for greasing
2¾ cups (675 ml) all-purpose flour
1 tsp (5 ml) salt
1 tsp (5 ml) baking soda
2 tsp (10 ml) baking powder
1 level tsp (5 ml) dried stevia leaves, crushed to a powder
¼ cup (60 ml) walnuts, finely chopped
¼ cup (60 ml) blanched almonds, finely chopped
5¼ oz (150 g) carrots, grated
3 large eggs
¾ cup (180 ml) vegetable oil
2 ripe bananas, peeled and mashed

For the topping

1/3 cup (75 ml) unsalted butter, softened
2/3 cup (150 ml) full-fat cream cheese
½ level tsp (2 ml) dried stevia leaves, crushed to a powder
½ tsp (2 ml) vanilla essence

Preheat the oven to 350°F (180°C). Grease a an 8-inch (20 cm) round cake pan.

Into a large mixing bowl, sift together the flour, salt, baking soda and baking powder. Add the crushed stevia leaves, the walnuts, the almonds and the carrots and stir well so that everything is amalgamated.

In a separate bowl, beat the eggs, add the oil and the mashed banana and whisk again. Then, slowly stirring all the time, add this mixture to the flour mixture.

Turn the mixture into the prepared pan and bake in the center of the oven for about 65 minutes, until golden brown and slightly shrinking away from the sides of the pan and a skewer pierced into the center comes out clean. Turn out onto a wire rack to cool.

Make the topping by mixing together all the ingredients. Unlike when you use powdered (confectioners') sugar, this topping will not set hard, but it is still delicious.

Once the cake is cold, spread the icing over the cake and use the prongs of a fork to make a pattern in the icing.

BANANA CAKE

This is an old, trusty family favorite that I have adapted to include dried stevia, as this herb combines so well with bananas. If you have a food processor this recipe takes seconds; alternatively, it is a good workout for your beating arm.

Serves 8–10

2 bananas
7 tbsp (105 ml) soft margarine
1 level tsp (5 ml) dried stevia leaves
2 eggs
2 cups (500 ml) self-raising flour
4 level tsp (20 ml) baking powder
1 tsp (5 ml) salt
2 tbsp (30 ml) milk

Preheat the oven to 350°F (180°C). Grease an 8-inch (20 cm) round cake pan.

If you are using a food processor, add the bananas and process for 10 seconds, then remove the cover and add the margarine, stevia, eggs, flour, baking powder, salt and milk. Replace the cover and mix for 10 seconds.

Alternatively, for those making this recipe by hand, in a large mixing bowl, mash the bananas until fine, then add the margarine and stevia and mix well. Beat the eggs in a small bowl and gradually mix them into the banana, margarine and stevia mix. Slowly add the flour, baking powder and salt and mix carefully so as not to get lumps. Add the milk and stir to combine.

Pour the mixture into the prepared cake pan and bake in the center of the oven for about 1 hour, until well risen and golden brown.

Turn out of the pan and cool on a wire rack. Serve just as it is or with unsalted butter.

Excess stevia

Dried stevia leaves

The object of good drying is to completely eliminate the water content of the plant and, at the same time, to retain its essential oils and flavor. These leaves will be three to four times sweeter than the fresh leaves, so do use them carefully and sparingly. The dried leaves can be used ground or in a liquid solution.

Spread out the leaves in a thin layer on a wooden rack covered in cheesecloth or nylon screening and place in a warm, dark, dry and well-ventilated room. If you have a spare room, this is ideal with the curtains closed; alternatively, use a cupboard with the door left ajar.

Turn the herbs over by hand several times during the first week. When the leaves are totally dry and crumble easily when crushed, they can be stored.

Put the leaves in a dark glass jar with a screw top and label with the name and date. The shelf life of the dried herb is approximately 1 year.

SWEET CICELY

(also known as Anise, Myrrh, Roman Plant, Sweet Bracken,
Sweet Fern, Switch)
Myrrhis odorata

I did not discover sweet cicely until I started the herb farm. I found it growing at one of the herb gardens I was restoring and became fascinated by its history and by the fact that it is hardly used today. With the current culinary trend for eating what our ancestors ate, I foresee this herb coming back into vogue.

Description

This attractive hardy perennial herb is one of the first to emerge after the winter. In spring you can literally sit and watch it grow. The finely divided, fern-like green leaves smell of sweet anise when crushed, and it bears clusters of small white flowers. The attractive long seeds start green and ripen to black in the autumn, and they too have an anise flavor when eaten in the green.

Sweet cicely prefers a humus-rich, well-drained soil in light shade. It is renowned for self-seeding, so if the seed is not wanted either to reproduce the plant or for winter flavoring, the whole plant should be cut down immediately after flowering. This will encourage a new batch of leaves to develop that are great for late summer salads or desserts. The plant can be raised from seed, sown in the autumn, as it needs a frost to germinate, or from division of well-established plants in autumn when the plants start to die back.

History in cooking

An ancient herb, sweet cicely can be found growing wild throughout Britain. There are records of the herbalist John Gerard, in the 16th century, enjoying the roots boiled like parsnips. The seeds are known in the countryside as a wayside nibble.

Harvesting and uses

Leaves

Pick the leaves from spring until early autumn. The flavor of the leaf is sweet aniseed. Chop finely and stir into salads, dressings and omelets. Add to soups, stews and boiling water when cooking cabbage. Add to cream for a sweeter, less fatty taste.

Flowers

The whole flower is edible and can be harvested as it appears from early to mid-spring. Detach each individual flower from the cluster, making sure all green bits are removed. The sweet anise flavor is lovely with tart fruit dishes, or try it mixed with apple purée or in plum fool or rhubarb tarts.

Seeds

Harvest ripe seeds from late summer. Toss unripe seeds, which have a sweet anise flavor and a nutty texture, into fruit salads or chop into ice cream. Ripe seeds have a nutty anise flavor and can be used whole in cooked dishes such as apple pie or crushed to flavor soups and sauces.

Roots
Dig up from early autumn. The roots can be cooked as a vegetable and either served with butter or a white sauce or allowed to cool, then chopped up and added to salads. Alternatively they can be eaten raw, peeled and grated and served with French dressing. The best description as to the flavor is to think of parsnip with an added hint of aniseed. The root, I know from first-hand experience, makes a very good wine – so good it won first prize for a root wine at the local wine circle.

Properties
Sweet cicely contains a volatile oil that includes anethole, which is also found in fennel. This produces the sweet anise flavor of the leaves, flowers and seeds, which aids the digestion of acid, spicy and fatty foods.

Other varieties
None.

PASTA WITH SPRING HERB SAUCE

The most wonderful spring meal: fresh pasta tastes delicious with the anise flavor of the sweet cicely, the sourness of the sorrel, the onion aroma of the chives and the fresh flavor of the parsley.

Serves 4

½ cup (125 ml) extra-virgin olive oil, divided
1 onion, finely chopped
1/3 cup (75 ml) fresh bread crumbs
6 sweet cicely leaves, washed, dried, thick stems removed and coarsely chopped
6 baby sorrel leaves, washed, dried, thick stems removed and coarsely chopped
Handful of chives, cut with scissors
Handful of parsley leaves, finely chopped
1 lb (500 g) fresh pasta
Salt and freshly ground black pepper
Parmesan, grated, to serve

Heat 2 tbsp (30 ml) oil in a deep frying pan and fry the onion and bread crumbs until crisp.

In a large bowl, add all the herbs to the remaining oil.

Fill a large saucepan with salted water and bring to a boil, then add the pasta. Once the pasta is al dente, drain well, then toss it in the oil and fresh herb mixture. Season with pepper, fold in the onion and bread crumbs, and serve immediately with the Parmesan.

RHUBARB AND SWEET CICELY DESSERT

This dessert is based on an old Yorkshire recipe. Historically the county was famous for its rhubarb. For those of you who have walked the Yorkshire dales, you will have seen sweet cicely growing in profusion along the sides of the roads and at the edges of the fields, so this dessert is a true Yorkshire celebration. Traditionally this is served with custard sauce; however, whipped cream is also great.

Serves 4–6

4 egg whites
1 cup + 2 tbsp (280 ml) all-purpose flour
¾ cup (180 ml) milk
½ cup (125 ml) raisins
12 oz (350 g) young rhubarb stems
3 tbsp (45 ml) butter, divided
1 tbsp (15 ml) light oil (grape or sunflower)
4¼ oz (120 g) sweet cicely leaves, finely chopped
2 tbsp (30 ml) brown sugar

Preheat the oven to 400°F (200°C).

Lightly beat the egg whites, then incorporate the flour, milk and raisins. Leave the batter to settle while you prepare the other ingredients.

Wash the rhubarb, remove the leaves and the white part at the end of the stem, then slice into 1-inch (2.5 cm) lengths. Place the rhubarb in a bowl, cover with boiling water and leave for 5 minutes. Drain.

In a deep-sided roasting pan, put 1 tbsp (15 ml) butter with the oil. Place the pan in the oven until the oil is bubbling but not brown. Pour the batter with the raisins into the hot pan. Immediately sprinkle the rhubarb and sweet cicely into the center of the batter, leaving a 1-inch (3 cm) border around the edge. Return to the oven and bake for 20 minutes or until the top has browned.

Melt the remaining butter in a saucepan and stir in the sugar. Allow to cook until syrupy, then drizzle overtop of the dessert.

SWEET CICELY SODA BREAD

As a child I visited Ireland regularly, as my father was brought up in Tipperary. There we often had soda bread; it was the first bread I was taught to make because, unlike standard bread, you do not have to knead it for hours.

Many herbs can be added to soda bread, but sweet cicely imparts a lovely anise flavor that, when eaten with a good potato soup, is superb.

Makes 1 large or 2 small loaves

3½ tbsp (50 ml) butter, plus extra for greasing
2/3 cup (150 ml) rolled oats
1 tsp (5 ml) baking soda
1 tsp (5 ml) cream of tartar (don't skip this, it is important)
2½ cups (625 ml) all-purpose flour, plus extra for dusting
1 cup (250 ml) whole wheat flour
1 tsp (5 ml) salt
2 tbsp (30 ml) sweet cicely leaves, removed from the stems, finely chopped
1 cup, approx. (250–275 ml) buttermilk

Preheat the oven to 425°F (220°C) and grease a baking sheet or line it with nonstick baking parchment.

Combine the oats, baking soda, cream of tartar and both flours in a large bowl. Add the salt and rub in the butter until it resembles bread crumbs. Add the sweet cicely, mix, then pour in the buttermilk, adding just enough to form a soft but not sticky dough. If you have made it too wet, add a tiny bit more flour.

Combine the ingredients, then turn out onto a lightly floured board and knead gently, and I mean gently, for a few minutes. Shape into a round and place on the baking sheet. Flatten slightly with your hand and then, using a sharp knife, mark a cross in the surface of the dough. Bake for about 25 to 30 minutes, until cooked.

Remove from the oven, place on a wire rack, cover the hot bread with a clean dish towel and allow to cool. Serve barely warm. This bread only keeps for a day, but on the plus side it does freeze, in an airtight freezerproof container, for 1 month.

Excess sweet cicely

The seeds are the most prolifically produced part of this plant, and they are ideal for drying. Once dried, they can be used throughout the autumn and winter to add a light, nutty, anise flavor to soups, stews, sauces and apple pies.

Harvesting sweet cicely seeds

The seeds are ripe for harvesting when they turn black and start falling from the plant. It is important to harvest seeds on a dry, still, sunny day. Always collect seeds after midday so that any morning dew has dried off.

The seeds are easily large enough to handle, so take a paper bag or a seed tray lined with newspaper so that you can collect as much as possible and prevent it spreading around the garden. Also, especially if you intend to collect other seeds, take a plant label to put in with the seeds so you do not forget what you have collected.

Once you have collected enough seeds, clean them by removing them from the stems. Spread them out thinly on some cheesecloth or paper towels, place in a dry, airy room and leave for a few days until totally dry. Check them before storing, as there is no point in keeping damaged or eaten seeds.

Store the seeds in a labeled dark glass jar, cardboard box or paper envelope for up to 2 years.

TARRAGON

(also known as French Tarragon, Estragon, Little Dragon)
Artemisia dracunculus

Both my grandmother and mother used this herb profusely in the kitchen and, it is fair to say, it was this herb that was the key to my starting the herb farm. It all came about because a girlfriend of mine asked me for some tarragon, as she was cooking an Elizabeth David recipe. I realized that it was not possible to buy fresh French tarragon anywhere in the UK, so I started propagating it, then selling it to stores and garden centers. The demand for French tarragon and other fresh herbs we were growing meant that we quickly grew out of our garden in Bristol, so, 23 years ago, we moved to our present site.

Description

French tarragon is an elegant hardy herbaceous perennial that dies back in early winter, reappearing in early spring. It has tiny yellow flowers in summer but it rarely flowers in cool climates. The long mid-green aromatic leaves are smooth in texture and have a lovely anise flavor when eaten.

This form of tarragon can only be raised from cuttings taken from growing tips or roots in spring. Russian tarragon, on the other hand, also a hardy herbaceous perennial with vigorous growth, can be grown from seed sown in spring. When planting French tarragon in the garden, choose a well-drained site in a sunny position and protect from excessive wet and cold in winter. Russian tarragon will grow in any conditions. Either tarragon will grow well in containers; use a soil-based substrate and protect the herb from excessive wet and cold. Cut down watering in the winter to minimal and place the container in a frost-free environment.

History in cooking

In ancient times the mixed juices of tarragon and fennel made a favorite drink for the kings of India. This Rolls-Royce of the kitchen has been attributed with causing the divorce of Henry VIII from Catherine of Aragon, because of her excessive use of it in cooking.

Harvesting and uses

Leaves

Pick the leaves from early spring to early autumn. Their flavor varies as the season progresses. The sweetest anise flavor comes in early spring, so this is the ideal time for making tarragon vinegar, as one can use both the leaf and stalk. In summer the leaves become coarser and have a more intense, slightly bitter anise flavor, so these are well suited to long cooking, such as stews, casseroles or baking.

Properties

Tarragon is a very good digestive, antioxidant, diuretic and sedative. It also contains vitamins A, B and C and calcium, magnesium and potassium, so it is beneficial for the liver as well as for easing heartburn and gastric upsets.

Other varieties

Russian Tarragon
Artemisia dracunculoides

A hardy herbaceous perennial that has tiny, insignificant yellow flower heads in summer. The long, narrow mid-green leaves are slightly coarse in texture and the flavor is similar to grass with a hint of anise. This plant originates in Siberia, hence the name Russian tarragon; this also explains why it is so hardy.

Winter Tarragon, Mexican Tarragon
Tagetes lucida

This variety is a tender herbaceous perennial with marigold yellow flowers in late summer and narrow, lance-shaped aromatic, mid-green toothed leaves, which have a strong aniseed/licorice scent and flavor. In cool climates this herb dies back in early spring, reappearing in early summer, hence one of its common names, winter tarragon.

CONSOMMÉ À L'ESTRAGON

One of my grandmother's friends, Lady Jekyll, whose sister-in-law was the famous gardener Gertrude Jekyll, gave this recipe to my grandmother. Apparently when Lady Jekyll made this soup, the tarragon would have cost sixpence (about one dollar today) from the market. My grandmother recommends this soup for those who are trying to lose weight. Personally I think it is simply a great summer soup, and the French tarragon in it makes it a good digestive at the start of a dinner party.

The soup is by far the best when prepared with homemade stock made from a chicken carcass or clear stock made from vegetables.

Serves 6

6 cups (1.5 L) good chicken or vegetable stock (see page 13)
8 French tarragon sprigs (approx. 6 inches/15 cm long)
2 egg whites
1 tbsp (15 ml) French tarragon leaves, finely chopped
Salt and freshly ground black pepper

Pour the stock into a large saucepan, add the tarragon sprigs and simmer over very low heat for 30 minutes.

Ten minutes before serving the soup, fill a deep-sided frying pan with water, place on the stove and bring to a boil. In a bowl, whisk the egg whites to stiff peaks and fold into the tarragon leaves. Drop 6 small tbsp (15 ml each) whipped egg whites into the boiling water to poach for 3 minutes. Turn each one over after 1 minute to cook on the other side.

Pour the hot soup into individual mugs or bowls. Drain the poached egg whites and let them float like islands on the top of the soup. Serve.

RUTH'S VERSION OF PANNA (1931)

This recipe is taken from my grandmother's cookbook *Lovely Food* (1931). She suggested cooking this as "short dinner for people one really likes, who often come to one's house, and whose conversation is too good to allow it to be disturbed by many courses." Serve with fresh toast.

Serves 6–8

1 handful spinach leaves
1 onion, finely chopped
1 French tarragon sprig
1 bunch flat-leaf parsley
2 hard-boiled eggs
3–4 sardines from a can
Some anchovies, from a can
2½ tbsp (37 ml) butter
Salt and freshly ground black pepper

Place the spinach, onion, tarragon and parsley in a large saucepan over medium heat and, using a wooden spoon, gently stir until the spinach has wilted.

Press out all the water from the boiled vegetables and herbs. Have ready the eggs, sardines, anchovies and butter. Pound everything together and pass through a sieve.

Season well and spread on a baking sheet. Place this on ice until you are ready for it to be sent to the table.

To serve, the panna should be cut with a cookie cutter into round pieces about 1½ inches (4 cm) thick. Give 1 piece to each person.

Serve on crushed ice in a silver dish.

MY VERSION OF PANNA (2008)

My mother inherited this dish from her mother and then passed it on to me. Until I wrote this down I have never followed a particular recipe; it is one of those dishes that once you have the main ingredients – fish, spinach, egg and French tarragon – you can adapt to suit your palate or to work with what's in your cupboards. If you prefer, you can use 5¼ oz (150 g) smoked mackerel instead of the sardines and anchovies. The French tarragon goes so well with the fish that it is the one ingredient I would not leave out.

This is a versatile dish that can be served as a first course with toast or some oatmeal cookies or is great for lunch served with salads. Or, if there is any left over (which is rare), it can be used in sandwiches.

10½ oz (300 g) spinach leaves
1 onion, finely chopped
2 French tarragon sprigs
(approx. 6 inches/15 cm long),
leaves removed and chopped
1 bunch flat-leaf parsley, chopped
2 hard-boiled eggs,
peeled and quartered
1 can sardines in olive oil
(3 oz/88 g drained weight)
1 can anchovy fillets in olive oil
(1 oz/30 g drained weight)
5 tbsp (75 ml) unsalted butter
Freshly grated nutmeg

Place the spinach in a large saucepan over medium heat and, using a wooden spoon, gently stir until the spinach has wilted.

Remove from the heat, put in a colander and press out all the excess moisture.

Add all the remaining ingredients, except the nutmeg, to a food processor, then add the warm spinach. Mix, stop and mix again. Do not overprocess, as this is much better if it is not too fine.

Once mixed, grate in the nutmeg to taste, stir well, then put into a small dish. Cover and keep in the fridge until needed.

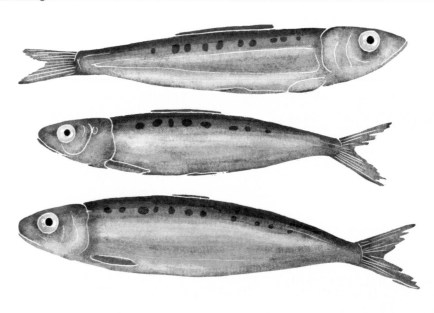

CHICKEN AND TARRAGON ROULADE

The first time I cooked this recipe from my Aunt Anthea, I was serving a cold lunch to the Fruit, Vegetable and Herb Committee of the Royal Horticultural Society; I had been told 18 were coming but 26 turned up. This amazing roulade managed to stretch magnificently.

The French tarragon makes this dish; the anise flavor combines well with the cream cheese and chicken, which is then offset by the smoked bacon. A great combination. Serve with a fresh, crisp green salad and new potatoes covered in mint.

Serves 6–8

6 boneless chicken breasts
10 slices smoked bacon
¾ cup + 2 tbsp (200 ml) cream cheese
1 tbsp (15 ml) French tarragon leaves, finely chopped
1 lb (500 g) spinach, cooked and well drained

Preheat the oven to 325°F (170°C).

Place a large rectangle of plastic wrap on a board and cover with the chicken breasts, their thicker bits opened out. Don't overlap them and don't worry if there are small gaps. Cover with another sheet of plastic wrap and bash with a wooden kitchen hammer or a rolling pin.

Take off the top layer of plastic wrap and cover the chicken breasts with the slices of bacon, laying them up and down, not across. On top of the bacon spread a moderate layer of cream cheese, then sprinkle on the tarragon leaves. Finally add a layer of spinach, having squeezed out any excess water.

Then comes the fiddly bit. Lightly oil a baking sheet and put it in front of the board. Take the far edge of the plastic wrap and roll the chicken toward you like a jelly roll, removing the plastic as you go. Roll the chicken straight onto the baking sheet. Cover the roulade loosely with foil just across the top and slightly down the sides, but not so it is airtight. Place in the oven for 50 minutes.

Remove from the heat and allow to cool. Once cool, cover with clean foil and place in the fridge for 1 hour prior to serving. Serve cold, cut into thin slices.

FRENCH TARRAGON CHICKEN BREASTS

This is my mother's recipe, which is very simple and shows off the wonderful flavor of the tarragon. Serve this dish with baked potatoes and a crisp green salad for a lovely summer meal.

Serves 2

2 tbsp (30 ml) unsalted butter
Light olive oil or sunflower oil
2 boneless chicken breasts
1 shallot, finely chopped
1 clove garlic, finely chopped
1 tbsp (15 ml) French tarragon leaves, removed from the stem and finely chopped, plus a few whole leaves to garnish
2 tbsp (30 ml) crème fraîche

Heat a large frying pan with a lid and add the butter and a good glug of olive oil. Once the butter has melted, add the chicken breasts and cook on both sides until golden brown, to seal the meat. Lower the heat, cover and cook for about 10 minutes, until cooked through.

Remove the cooked chicken and add the shallot and garlic to the pan. Increase the heat and cook, stirring, until soft. Add the crème fraîche and cook for 1 minute.

Return the chicken breasts to the frying pan and toss them in the sauce for 1 minute. Serve garnished with some tarragon leaves.

TARRAGON ICE CREAM

Jonray and Peter Sanchez-Iglesias, who with their parents run the Michelin-starred restaurant Casamia in Bristol, gave me this recipe. They are two of the most creative young chefs and use herbs well and originally; they instinctively understand the flavors. This tarragon ice cream is no exception – it is wonderful.

Serves 4–6

1¼ cups (300 ml) whipping (35%) cream
1¼ cups (300 ml) whole milk
1 bunch French tarragon (reserve a few sprigs to garnish)
1 sheet of leaf gelatin or ½ tsp (2 ml) powdered gelatin
6 egg yolks
¾ cup + 1 tbsp (185 ml) sugar

In a saucepan, heat the cream and milk to the simmering point, then add the tarragon. Remove from the heat and leave to infuse for a minimum of 4 hours.

Strain the tarragon cream/milk through a fine sieve and return to the heat until it is just warm.

Add the gelatin to a bowl of cold water and leave to soften. Whisk the egg yolks and sugar until thick and creamy, then pour the milk/cream mixture onto the egg yolks, whisking continuously.

Cook the mixture over medium heat, stirring all the time with a wooden spoon. When the liquid is slightly thick on the back of a cool spoon, take off the heat straightaway, stir in the gelatin, and then pour into a bowl set over iced water to cool it right down.

Once cool, strain through a sieve, then pour it into an airtight container and leave in the fridge for 2 to 6 hours before churning in an ice-cream machine. If you don't have an machine, put the mixture in a freezerproof container in the freezer for 4 hours, removing it every hour to give it a good stir to break up the ice crystals.

CARROT, TARRAGON AND WALNUT BREAD

Soda bread always reminds me of my early childhood in Ireland, where I used to get in the way while helping to make it. This recipe is an adaptation of an Irish soda bread recipe. Tarragon combined with toasted walnuts makes this a tasty loaf.

Makes 1 large loaf or 2 small ones

3½ cups (875 ml) all-purpose flour, plus extra for dusting
1 cup + 2 tbsp (275 ml) whole wheat flour
1 tsp (5 ml) salt
2 tsp (10 ml) baking soda
5¼ oz (150 g) carrots, grated
1 tbsp (15 ml) toasted walnuts, chopped
1 tbsp (15 ml) French tarragon leaves, removed from the stems and roughly chopped
1¼ cups (300 ml) low-fat yogurt
½ cup (125 ml) reduced-fat (2%) milk

Preheat the oven to 450°F (230°C).

Combine the flours, salt and baking soda in a large bowl, then stir in the carrots, walnuts, tarragon, yogurt and enough milk to make a soft and fairly sticky dough.

Remove the dough from the bowl and place onto a floured surface. Form it into a flat ball – there is no need to knead it. Put the dough on a baking sheet lined with baking parchment, slash the top with a cross and bake for 30 minutes, until risen and cooked. To check if it is cooked enough, tap the bottom of the loaf – it should sound hollow.

Excess tarragon

French tarragon vinegar

One of the most useful vinegars, this recipe is also a great way to use a glut of French tarragon leaves in early summer. The vinegar can be used for salad dressings, marinades or mayonnaise.

Makes 2 cups (500 ml)

2 cups (500 ml) white wine vinegar
Enough French tarragon leaves to fill a 1-pint (500 ml) bottle

Fill a clean empty bottle full of French tarragon leaves. Top up with white wine vinegar and seal. (Use a plastic or plastic-lined lid, as vinegar corrodes metal.) Leave on a sunny windowsill for 4 weeks, shaking it gently from time to time. Strain through an unbleached paper coffee filter and return to a clean, sterilized bottle (see page 12). Add a sprig of tarragon for identification and decoration.

If you cannot wait 4 weeks for the vinegar to infuse with the herbs, try this quick method: Put the herbs and vinegar into a covered heatproof china bowl set over a saucepan of cold water. Bring the water to a boil, then remove the bowl from the saucepan. Leave the mixture to cool for about 2 hours before use.

THYME

(also known as Serpillo, Tomillo, Garden Thyme)
Thymus vulgaris

Thyme is one of the great European culinary herbs whose use spread with the ancient Egyptians and Greeks. When it is used in cooking, its wonderful smell fills the kitchen with a mouthwatering aroma. For me, this is particularly noticeable in winter; the smell of thyme as it cooks brings summer into the kitchen. It seems to radiate the warmth and sunlight that it has absorbed over the hot summer months, which is sublimely uplifting on gray winter days.

Description

Thyme is a hardy evergreen that can be found growing wild throughout many countries of the northern and southern hemispheres. It is an attractive herb, not only to the human eye but also to bees and butterflies. It grows in two forms: upright and creeping. Both habits have small aromatic leaves that can vary in color from dark to bright green and tiny aromatic flowers that can also vary in color from white through to deep red and violet.

All varieties of thyme should be planted in well-drained soil in a sunny position. Thymes hate being wet in winter and, even worse, they hate sitting in water. Make sure the soil has adequate drainage and, if necessary, dig in extra horticultural grit. All thymes are ideal for growing in containers; use a soil-based potting compost mixed with extra grit and place in a sunny position.

To maintain a good healthy plant it is essential to trim all thymes after flowering; this not only encourages them to put on new growth but also prevents them from becoming woody and from sprawling in the wrong direction.

History in cooking

Historically thyme was used with meat dishes, especially rabbit (which was traditionally called cony) and to make infusions with either wine or water. A tea was also made by pouring boiling water over wild thyme leaves, and this was drunk as a tonic to revive and refresh people who had been ill.

Harvesting and uses

Leaves

As thyme is an evergreen, the leaves can be picked fresh all year round as long as you are not too greedy. There are two methods for picking leaves for culinary use: as whole sprigs or just leaves. Sprig length is determined by the age and type of the thyme plant. For example, for common thyme a sprig length from the tip would be on average 2½ to 3 inches (6–8 cm) and it will certainly have a woody section. If, on the other hand, it is a creeping variety (for example, 'Jekka's'), the sprig will be shorter, about 1½ to 2½ inches (4–6 cm), and mostly green growth. If you just require the leaves, the simplest method of removing them is to hold the stem at the tip and gently run your fingers down it. The best time for preserving the leaves is before flowering, because they have the strongest flavor then. This is in spring for the early varieties and early summer for the remaining varieties.

Flowers

Pick the flowers as they open from late spring until late summer. All thyme flowers are edible. They are best used sprinkled over cooked vegetables or rolled into pastries prior to cooking.

Properties

A valuable property of thyme is its oil, which is extracted from the leaves. This oil contains a constituent called thymol, which is a strong antiseptic and muscle relaxant. The antiseptic properties help to kill any minor bugs that might be in the food prior to cooking. Thyme oil also helps break down fatty foods like beef, therefore aiding in the digestion of heavier dishes. In the past 10 years research has indicated that thyme is also a strong antioxidant.

Other varieties

All thymes are edible, but in my opinion the following thymes have good culinary flavors that combine well with a range of dishes.

Bertram Anderson Thyme

Thymus pulegioides 'Bertram Anderson'
Mild flavor, good with vegetables.

Broad-leafed Thyme

Thymus pulegioides
Strong, rounded flavor, excellent with meat, especially for roasting.

Caraway-scented Thyme

Thymus herba-barona
Original caraway flavor that goes well with chicken and meat and works well in both marinades and dressings.

Common Thyme, Garden Thyme

Thymus vulgaris
Ideal for bouquets garnis and with meat, chicken, fish and cheese and in sauces.

Compact Thyme

Thymus vulgaris 'Compactus'
The leaf has a stronger flavor than common thyme. Good with meat and duck and in marinades.

Creeping Lemon Thyme

Thymus 'Creeping Lemon'

This has a true lemon scent and flavor. Perfect with chicken, fish and vegetables and for making marinades and dressings.

French Thyme

Thymus vulgaris 'French'

This has the most pungent flavor of the thymes listed here. Use with tomatoes, fish and chicken and in dressings and sauces.

Golden Lemon Thyme

Thymus citriodorus 'Golden Lemon'

This has a pungent flavor and scent that is lemon with a hint of spice. It works well in marinades and dressings and with chicken dishes.

Golden Thyme

Thymus pulegioides 'Aureus' AGM

This has a lovely warm flavor and is good with vegetable dishes and tomatoes.

Jekka's Thyme

Thymus 'Jekka'

Well, what can I say? This is a seedling that appeared on the farm and grew and grew. It has a wonderful robust habit, surviving all weathers. It is great with vegetable and meat dishes.

Lemon Thyme

Thymus citriodorus

This has a strong lemon flavor and scent. Delicious with fish and chicken and in dressings and marinades.

Orange-scented Thyme

Thymus 'Fragrantissimus'

I am a real fan of this thyme. The flavor is warm and spicy with a hint of orange. Excellent with strong meats and adds flavor to spicy desserts. It is also good in sauces, marinades and dressings.

Pine-scented Thyme

Thymus longicaulis

This thyme has a unique flavor and should be used sparingly. Ideal for marinades.

Porlock Thyme

Thymus 'Porlock'
An early-season thyme that has a warm, mild flavor in comparison to French thyme. Goes well with all forms of food, meat and vegetables alike. Excellent in bread too.

Silver Posie Thyme

Thymus vulgaris 'Silver Posie'
This has a mild flavor reminiscent of garden thyme but softer. Good with vegetables and chicken and in sauces.

Silver Queen Thyme

Thymus x *citriodorus* 'Silver Queen'
An interesting lemon-flavored and -scented thyme. Good with fish, vegetables and desserts as well as in pastry.

THYME SOUFFLÉS

I always thought soufflés were for sophisticated cooks, so I was delighted to find that they were not. I vividly remember creating this dish with much pride when we lived in our first house. My tips are to whisk the egg whites until they form stiff peaks, not to open the oven door while the soufflé is rising, and to have everyone sitting at the table before you take the soufflé out of the oven.

The fresh thyme leaves combined with the cheese makes these little soufflés extra-special.

Serves 6

3½ tbsp (50 ml) unsalted butter, plus extra for greasing
⅓ cup + 2 tbsp (95 ml) all-purpose flour
1¼ cups (300 ml) milk
Pinch of cayenne pepper
¼ tsp (1 ml) mustard powder
Freshly grated nutmeg
1 heaped tbsp (20 ml) French, common or compact thyme leaves, removed from the stems and finely chopped
Salt and freshly ground black pepper
2⅔ oz (75 g) Parmesan, freshly grated, or any other strong-flavored cheese (it needs to be strong to balance the thyme)
3 medium eggs, separated, plus one extra egg white

Preheat the oven to 375°F (190°C). Butter 6 x 3-inch (8 cm) ramekins.

Melt the butter in a saucepan and stir in the flour. Cook for 1 minute, stirring all the time. Remove from the heat and gradually blend in the milk. Return to the heat and cook for a few minutes, stirring constantly until the mixture thickens and is very smooth.

Remove from the heat and stir in the cayenne pepper, mustard and nutmeg. Add the thyme, salt and pepper and mix vigorously until blended. Allow this mixture to cool a little before stirring in the Parmesan. In a bowl, beat the egg yolks thoroughly, then stir them in. Set aside.

In an immaculately clean bowl, whisk the 4 egg whites until they are stiff. They should be glossy and should stand in stiff peaks. Using a metal spoon, fold 1 tbsp (15 ml) at a time of the beaten egg whites into the egg and milk mixture; be careful and gentle to ensure that you do not flatten the egg whites.

Spoon the mixture into the prepared ramekins. Bake in the middle of the oven for 15 to 18 minutes, until well risen and golden brown on top. Serve immediately.

THYME AND CHEESE TOMATOES

This is a lovely summer meal. If you have lemon thyme, the flavor is wonderful with tomatoes; if not, garden thyme is a good substitute. Serve with a crisp green salad and dauphinoise potatoes.

Serves 6

6 large, ripe, firm tomatoes
Salt and freshly ground black pepper
1 tbsp (15 ml) lemon thyme leaves, finely chopped
1 tbsp (15 ml) parsley, finely chopped
1 clove garlic, finely sliced
1 tbsp (15 ml) Parmesan, freshly grated
1 tbsp (15 ml) strong Cheddar, freshly grated
2 tbsp (30 ml) bread crumbs
2/3 cup (150 ml) olive oil, divided

Preheat the oven to 350°F (180°C).

Wash, dry and halve the tomatoes and gently scoop out the flesh and seeds using a teaspoon. Be careful not to break the skins and to leave enough tomato flesh to keep the shape of the fruit. Put the flesh into a bowl and the tomato halves into an ovenproof dish, cut side up. Season with salt and pepper.

To the bowl of tomato flesh add the thyme, parsley and garlic, stir in the grated cheeses, the bread crumbs and 4 tbsp (60 ml) olive oil. Spoon the mixture into the tomato halves. Drizzle the remaining olive oil overtop and cook in the oven for 25 minutes or until the tomatoes are lightly golden on top.

THYME CHICKEN PARCELS

In one of Jamie Oliver's early TV series I watched him creating meals by wrapping the ingredients in foil and then baking them in the oven. I immediately thought, *What a brilliant idea*, and adapted some of my recipes to suit this method of cooking.

Here the flavor of the thyme is enhanced by the light flavors of the leek and the white wine, which all infuse the chicken. This is a great way to cook; all the flavors are locked in and there's also minimal washing up to be done.

Serves 2

1 red or yellow bell pepper, seeded and sliced
1 leek, well washed and sliced
1 large glass white wine
3 tbsp (45 ml) unsalted butter, cut into little pieces
1 tbsp (15 ml) broad-leafed thyme leaves (or you can use compact, lemon- or orange-scented, caraway, French or common)
2 cloves garlic, finely chopped
Olive oil
Sea salt and freshly ground black pepper
2 skinless boneless chicken breasts, lightly scored

For each chicken breast you will need 1 piece of foil 14 x 16 inches (360 x 400 mm) and 1 piece of baking parchment the same size

Preheat the oven to 325°F (170°C).

Mix together the bell pepper, leek, wine, butter, thyme, garlic, olive oil, salt and pepper in a bowl.

Place the pieces of foil on a work surface and on top of each place the parchment paper. Fold in half and then seal the two shorter sides by folding over twice, leaving the top open, thereby creating a bag. Into each bag place a chicken breast and half of the mixture you have in the bowl. Once the ingredients are in, fold over the top twice to seal the bag.

Carefully, so as not to make holes in the bags, place them in a roasting pan and bake in the middle of the oven for 25 minutes. Do take great care when opening the bags as they will release hot steam and hot liquid. I recommend doing this at the table, with any other vegetables or rice that you have prepared already plated, so you can serve the chicken directly.

BAKED LAMB STEW WITH POTATOES AND THYME

This is a form of Irish stew that my mother regularly made from cheap cuts of lamb. The potatoes absorb the fat released from the lamb as it cooks, which in turn makes them delicious. The thyme enhances the flavor of the lamb. You can use stewing lamb or, if you wish to impress, lamb chops. It is a highly aromatic, warming and nourishing all-in-one meal.

Ideally, serve with fresh crusty bread and salad or broccoli.

Serves 6

2 lb (1 kg) stewing lamb, cut into chunks, or 12 small chops
2 large red onions, roughly chopped
2 lb (1 kg) potatoes, peeled and cut into large chunks
Salt and freshly ground black pepper
3 tbsp (45 ml) thyme leaves (a single variety or a mixture of compact, Porlock, French, common or Jekka's)
3 tbsp (45 ml) celery leaf, including the stems, chopped (or use flat-leaf parsley)
½ cup (125 ml) water
½ cup (125 ml) olive oil
6 ripe large tomatoes, cut into thick slices
3½ tbsp (50 ml) butter

Preheat the oven to 350°F (180°C).

Put the lamb, onions and potatoes into a large casserole dish or deep baking dish and season to taste. Add the thyme, celery leaf, water and olive oil.

Mix the ingredients thoroughly with your hands, turning all the vegetables and meat over. Cover the potatoes and lamb with a single layer of sliced tomatoes, lightly salt, then dot butter over the top. Cover with a double layer of parchment paper or foil and bake in the oven for 2 hours. From time to time remove the cover and spoon some of the juices over the top of the dish. When cooked the lamb should be tender and the potatoes soft.

Remove the casserole from the oven amd increase the oven temperature to 400°F (200°C). Remove the waxed paper or foil, return the casserole to the oven and cook for a further 45 minutes. After 20 minutes gently but thoroughly turn the lamb, potatoes and tomatoes. This will brown the potatoes and the meat as well as reduce the cooking juices.

ORANGE-SCENTED THYME IN GOLDEN SYRUP AND ALMOND TART

Here is a family favorite that, when served with Cornish crème fraîche, turns into a treat. More than 20 years ago I had a visitor to the herb farm who introduced me to the idea of using thyme in desserts. Once she had left I went to the cottage and immediately experimented, and I discovered that the sharp, aromatic flavor of thyme offsets the sweetness of sugar or, in this case, golden syrup.

Serves 6

For the pastry
2/3 cup (150 ml) unsalted butter, plus extra for greasing
2 cups (500 ml) all-purpose flour, plus extra for dusting
Pinch of salt
1 tsp (5 ml) finely chopped orange-scented thyme leaves
4 egg yolks
Cold water

For the filling
1/3 cup (75 ml) corn syrup
1/2 cup (125 ml) fresh brown bread crumbs
2 tbsp (30 ml) peeled and flaked almonds
1 tbsp (15 ml) grated zest from an unwaxed lemon
2 tbsp (30 ml) lemon juice
2 tsp (10 ml) finely chopped orange-scented thyme leaves

Preheat the oven to 400°F (200°C). Grease an 8-inch (20 cm) flan dish with butter.

Before making the pastry, measure the butter and wrap it in foil or plastic wrap and place in the freezer to harden.

Sift the flour and salt into a large bowl. Remove the butter from the freezer, fold back the covering and grate over the flour, using the coarsest side of the grater. Once you finish grating, add the thyme leaves and fold in with the butter and flour, using a thin metal spatula. Once the butter and flour are well combined and start to resemble bread crumbs, use a fork to lightly mix in the egg yolks with a little cold water. (I do use my hands for the last bit.)

Having made the dough, remove it from the bowl, place it in plastic wrap or a plastic bag and put it in the fridge for at least 2 hours, until you are ready to use it.

Roll out the prepared pastry on a lightly floured surface to about 1/8 inch (3 mm) thick. Gently lift it from the table and line the prepared flan dish. Cut off any excess pastry, and set aside – this can be used to decorate the top of the tart. Prick the bottom all over with a fork.

Mix together the filling ingredients and spread them gently and evenly over the bottom of the tart. Decorate with the remaining pastry trimmings. Bake for 25 to 30 minutes on the middle shelf of the oven, until golden.

Serve hot, or it can be eaten cold if you can keep it that long.

LEMON THYME APPLESAUCE

The citrus flavor of lemon thyme is perfect with the tartness of cooking apples. This sauce is great hot or cold and can be served with pork chops or a roast griskin. A griskin is a special pork cut that I thought was common but have since found is rarely known outside south Gloucestershire and Bristol. It is the cut usually reserved for making back bacon, and it is perfect, as there is absolutely no waste. Buy a large enough bit to do two meals.

A griskin is great roasted and almost better cold, thinly sliced and served with this lemon thyme applesauce, spicy red cabbage and dauphinoise potatoes.

Serves 4–6

3 tbsp (45 ml) unsalted butter
2 cooking apples, peeled and cut into quarters, cored and sliced
2 tsp (10 ml) lemon thyme leaves
Fruit (superfine) sugar, to taste

Melt the butter in a small saucepan. Add the sliced apples and lemon thyme leaves, stir, reduce the heat to minimum, cover and cook very slowly, checking from time to time to make sure it does not stick. The apple will break down but not become totally mushy.

Check for sweetness; if you or your family has a sweet tooth, add sugar to taste and stir well. Cook for a further 2 minutes to dissolve the sugar. Serve hot or cold.

Excess thyme

As thyme is evergreen there are always leaves that can be picked to use fresh, so there is no need to dry or freeze them. However, at certain times of the year, especially during flowering, when there is a profusion of flowers, and just after flowering, when the plant is cut back, you will have a lot of leaves available.

The great thing about thyme leaves and flowers is that they are so versatile; they can be used and preserved in many ways.

Thyme leaf butter
This butter can be used with grilled fish, pushed under the skin of a chicken prior to roasting, rubbed into flour or simply put on cooked vegetables.

Makes ½ cup (125 ml)

Handful of thyme leaves, from any of your favorites
½ cup (125 ml) unsalted butter, slightly softened

Gently chop the thyme leaves to release the oils. Then mix the chopped leaves with the unsalted butter. (It is important to use unsalted butter because it has a mild flavor compared to its salted counterpart, and the added herbs will provide enough flavor.) I have found that the simplest and easiest way of blending the herb and butter together is to use a fork.

When it has been thoroughly mixed, place it on some waxed paper or plastic wrap, bringing the wrapping right over the butter, then roll the soft butter inside it to make a sausage shape; this makes it easy to cut the required amounts.

Place this in the fridge for at least 24 hours before use. The longer you leave it, the better the flavor. Use within 2 weeks. Alternatively, it can be frozen for use within 3 months.

Thyme leaf vinegar

This is a useful vinegar to use in marinades and mayonnaise.

Makes 2 cups (500 ml)

Thyme leaves
2 cups (500 ml) white wine vinegar

Fill a clean empty bottle with fresh thyme leaves. Top up with white wine vinegar and seal. (Use a plastic or plastic-lined top, as vinegar corrodes metal.) Leave on a sunny windowsill for 4 weeks, shaking gently from time to time. Strain the liquid through an unbleached paper coffee filter into another clean, sterilized bottle. Put a sprig of thyme in the bottle for identification and decoration.

If you cannot wait 4 weeks for the vinegar to infuse with the herbs, try this quick method, which is good for emergencies, although the longer method produces better-flavored vinegar: Put the herbs and vinegar into a covered heatproof glass or china bowl and set it over, but not touching, a pan of cold water. Bring the water to a boil, remove the bowl from the pan and leave it to cool for about 2 hours before using the vinegar. Being vinegar, this will keep for a number of years in a dark cupboard.

VIETNAMESE CORIANDER

(also known as Rau Ram, Laksa Plant, Vietnamese Hot Mint)
Persicaria odorata

I was given this herb by John Carter, who is one of the most erudite men I have met and also an extremely good plant collector, specializing in water plants. He was given this herb by a nursery in Australia, which was given it in turn by some Vietnamese boat people. In Australia it is called Vietnamese hot mint, which is a misnomer, as it is not a member of the mint family but a member of the knotweed family.

Persicaria odorata is the only one of the *Persicarias* that is edible, so please be careful. The first time I ate its leaves I was totally taken by surprise. To begin with the taste is mild, with a hint of lime and spice, then as the flavor develops it becomes hot and peppery.

Description

Vietnamese coriander is a subtropical evergreen perennial. It has attractive creamy white flowers in summer that are rarely produced in cold climates, even when it is grown as a houseplant. The highly aromatic leaves have a narrow brown/maroon V shape near the base. In cold climates this herb happily adapts to being grown as a houseplant. Position it in a window that does not get the midday sun, as this will scorch the leaves. You will find that it does grow fast, so it will need repotting twice a year. In the tropics it is a rampant grower and will spread happily around the garden.

History in cooking

This native Vietnamese wild plant is considered a traditional herb in Thai, Malaysian and Vietnamese cooking, where its hot, pungent flavor with a hint of lime is used to flavor soups and fish dishes.

Harvesting and uses

Leaves

As this is an evergreen herb there is little need to preserve it, as the leaves are available all year. However, it does make good oils and vinegars, and the best leaves for this are the new, young leaves rather than the tougher old leaves.

Properties

Throughout the Far East Vietnamese coriander is used to treat indigestion, flatulence and stomachaches. It is reputedly eaten by Buddhist monks to suppress sexual urges. This herb is never cooked; it is used as a fresh leaf condiment and is always added at the end of cooking. In Asia it is usually eaten raw as a salad or herb accompaniment. It combines well with meat, vegetables and fruit. It is important in Vietnamese cooking, being used copiously with noodle soups (pho), where large heaps of the leaves are dipped into the soup with chopsticks.

Other varieties

No other member of this plant family is edible, so please be careful.

MELON À L'INDIENNE WITH VIETNAMESE CORIANDER

My mother always made this first course when she was in a hurry and had a house full of people who had to be fed fast. I had no idea until I was reading my grandmother's cookbooks that she was the origin of this amazing dish. I have added the Vietnamese coriander to this recipe because the flavor of the leaf, with its hint of limes, heat and spice, combines so well with the cool sweetness of melon.

If you have a food processor the flavor of homemade mayonnaise is wonderful, but for speed you can buy good ready-to-eat mayonnaise from many stores. However, in case you wish to make your own, I've included here a reliable recipe. Use enough of it to coat the fruit and reserve the rest for sandwiches, potato salads or other dishes. Store in the fridge and use within 48 hours.

Warning There can be an increased risk of salmonella poisoning when eating raw or lightly cooked eggs. Pregnant women, the elderly and young children should take particular care, and such dishes are not recommended.

Serves 4–6

For the mayonnaise
2 egg yolks
½ tsp (2 ml) Dijon mustard
2 tbsp (30 ml) white wine vinegar, divided
1 cup + 2 tbsp (275 ml) olive oil
Salt and freshly ground black pepper

1 melon (I would normally choose a honeydew or similar; it doesn't work with watermelon)
2 tsp (10 ml) curry powder (preferably a mild korma spice blend made with coriander, cumin and turmeric)
2 Vietnamese coriander leaves, very thinly sliced, plus one left whole to decorate

First make the mayonnaise. Place the egg yolks and mustard in the food processor bowl with 1 tbsp (15 ml) vinegar. Process until all is well mixed. With the machine switched on, very slowly add the olive oil in a steady stream through the feed tube until all the oil has been used up and the mayonnaise is thick and shining. With the machine still on, very slowly add the remaining vinegar.

Switch the machine off, add salt and pepper to taste and give it a quick mix, then place in a bowl and cover and refrigerate until needed.

Cut a thin slice off the bottom of the melon so it will stand up. Cut the top off the melon and reserve it. Remove the seeds from the center and put them into a sieve over a bowl so you can save the juice. Use a serving spoon to remove the flesh from inside the melon and place this in another bowl. Go as deep as you dare but try not to break through the bottom or the sides.

Mix the juice from the seeds in the bowl with 2 tbsp (30 ml) mayonnaise, the curry powder and sliced Vietnamese coriander and all the melon pieces. Once combined, check it for flavor.

Put the melon pieces back into the melon skin and decorate with one leaf of Vietnamese coriander. Replace the reserved top of the melon as a lid and put it in the fridge for at least 2 hours before serving.

GREEN BEAN, MUSHROOM AND VIETNAMESE CORIANDER STIR-FRY SALAD

The pungency of the Vietnamese coriander with vegetables is excellent, as it adds another dimension to the tangy soy-based flavor of the dressing. This simple dish is lovely served with noodles as a light supper or lunch.

Serves 2

7 oz (200 g) green beans, topped and tailed
3 tbsp (45 ml) sunflower oil, divided
3½ oz (100 g) mushrooms, sliced
2 tbsp (30 ml) light soy sauce
2 tbsp (30 ml) white wine vinegar
Salt and freshly ground black pepper
2 Vietnamese coriander leaves, finely sliced

Cook the green beans in a saucepan of boiling water until just tender, then drain.

Heat 2 tbsp (30 ml) oil in a deep frying pan or wok, add the mushrooms and stir-fry quickly. Add the beans and fry for 1 minute.

Whisk together the remaining oil and the soy sauce and vinegar and add seasoning to taste.

Turn the cooked vegetables into a bowl, scatter the Vietnamese coriander overtop and then pour on the dressing, making sure all is well coated. Serve.

SPICY FISH CAKES

Here Vietnamese coriander is in its element, as it goes so well with fish and lemon grass. The wonderfully flamboyant Nancy Lam cooked this herb for me at a Chelsea Flower Show. She created a fish curry with it, and the memory of her calmly dominating the kitchen has stayed with me. Serve with homemade tomato sauce (see page 12) or a chili dipping sauce and plain rice.

Serves 4

1 lemon grass stalk
10½ oz (300 g) skinless cod, bream, John Dory or sea bass fillets, chopped
1 tbsp (15 ml) desiccated coconut
¾ cup (175 ml) coconut milk
1 tbsp (15 ml) cornstarch
2 egg whites, whipped to soft peaks
1 tsp (5 ml) ground turmeric
3 Vietnamese coriander leaves, finely sliced
1 tsp (5 ml) salt
1 tsp (5 ml) sugar
Flour, for dusting
Butter and olive oil, for frying

Grind the lemon grass stalk in a blender or food processor. In a large bowl, mix together the fish and lemon grass, then add all the other ingredients except the flour, butter and olive oil.

Take handfuls of the mixture and form individual little cakes. Roll the cakes in the flour, shaking off the excess.

Heat a little butter and oil in a large frying pan and cook the fish cakes, turning them so that both sides are cooked and golden brown. Remove from the pan and drain on paper towels before serving.

Excess Vietnamese coriander

The leaves of this herb are excellent for making chile oil or vinegar, and a lot easier to use. These oils and vinegars are extremely good for use in marinades, dressings and sauces.

For more information about preserving and the risks of using herbs in oils, see page 36.

Vietnamese coriander oil
Makes 1 cup (250 ml)

3 good handfuls Vietnamese coriander leaves
1 cup (250 ml) light olive oil or sunflower oil
2 tsp (10 ml) lemon juice

Wash and dry the leaves on paper towels. Finely chop the leaves (this can be done in a food processor), add the oil and the lemon juice and mix well. Pour into a container with a sealing lid and place in the fridge. Use within 5 days; shake well before use as the lemon juice will separate.

Alternatively, after 2 days strain the oil through an unbleached paper coffee filter, pour into a clean, dry container with a sealing lid and keep in the fridge. Use within 3 days; shake well before use.

Vietnamese coriander vinegar
This vinegar is ideal for use in pungent sauces or stir-fry dishes.

Makes 1²/₃ cups (400 ml)

¾ cup (175 ml) young Vietnamese coriander leaves, sliced
1²/₃ cups (400 ml) white wine vinegar

Put the leaves into a jam jar, pour in the vinegar and seal with a non-metallic top. Place on a sunny windowsill and shake the jar every so often.

After 2 or 3 weeks, test the vinegar for flavor. If satisfactory, strain through an unbleached paper coffee filter and return the vinegar to a clean bottle with a single leaf as decoration. Label and date the bottle.

This will keep happily for a year or even longer, as vinegar does not age like oil.

VIOLET

(also known as Garden Violet, Sweet Violet)
Viola odorata

This herald of spring can also be found flowering over winter, when you can catch the perfume of the flower wafting on the cold air of a crisp morning. My grandmother used these flowers to decorate food; however, she was fairly scathing if they were used in profusion. To her food was about texture, flavor and platefuls rather than being dainty and decorous with works of culinary art.

Description

The scent of the sweet-smelling white or purple flowers transports me back to my childhood. The heart-shaped leaves, which are edible, are great for early spring salads, ideal for mixing with salad burnet, sorrel and mustard leaves in particular. All *Violas* are edible, but the small-flowering species have a far better flavor than the large ones. The best of the lot for flavor and scent are sweet violets.

Sweet violets are fully hardy and can be easily grown in a semi-shaded position. They thrive in moderately heavy rich soil. If you have a light or gravelly soil, some texture should be added; a mulch of well-rotted manure the previous autumn is a good idea, which can be dug in in the spring. You can raise this plant from seed sown in early autumn, but it is much easier to propagate from the runners of an established plant, removed in spring, or by division of an established plant in early summer after it has finished flowering.

History in cooking

This charming herb has been much loved throughout the ages and, having been around for more than 2,000 years there are many myths about it. The one I am particularly fond of is a Greek legend. Zeus fell in love with a beautiful maiden named Io and he turned her into a cow to protect her from his jealous wife, Hera. The earth grew violets to be Io's food, and so the flower was named after her. Historically crystallizing the flowers dates back to the 13th century, at which time they were boiled in sugar and sold by the French apothecaries.

Harvesting and uses

Leaves
The leaves are available all year round, but they have their best flavor in late spring. They have a mild flavor that is good in salads, but the mature leaves are tough, so it is best to use new growth.

Flowers
Pick the flowers as they appear from late winter to mid-spring. Harvest them in the late morning when the dew has dried and the flower is fully open.

<table>
<tr><td>Properties</td><td>Traditionally the flowers were used in cough medicine and as a breath freshener, so from a culinary point of view, sweet violet has few digestive benefits beyond fresh breath. Medicinally the flowers and leaves are used to treat various skin conditions from eczema to acne.</td></tr>
</table>

Properties

Traditionally the flowers were used in cough medicine and as a breath freshener, so from a culinary point of view, sweet violet has few digestive benefits beyond fresh breath. Medicinally the flowers and leaves are used to treat various skin conditions from eczema to acne.

Other varieties

All the *Violas* are hardy perennials and all are low-growing.

Wood Violet
Viola reichenbachiana
This variety has pale lilac/blue flowers in early spring and heart-shaped green leaves. The flowers have little scent.

Common Dog Violet, Blue Mice, Hedging Violet, Horse Violet, Pig Violet
Viola riviniana
Pale blue/lilac flowers in early summer and heart-shaped green leaves.

Field Pansy
Viola arvensis
This herb has predominantly white or creamy flowers in early summer. The green leaves are oval with shallow, blunt teeth.

Mountain Pansy
Viola lutea
The flowers vary in single colors from yellow to blue and violet. The green leaves are oval near the base of the stem and narrower further up.

Heartsease
Viola tricolor
This variety has attractive small tricolor flowers that appear in many different combinations, including yellow, violet, blue, purple and white. The green leaves are deeply lobed.

VIOLET SPRING SALAD

This is a pretty salad that is also very tasty. It can be made with any green salad leaves, and for those of you lucky enough to live in or near the countryside, you can make a true spring salad with young dandelion leaves, hawthorn shoots and primroses.

Serves 4

1 lettuce (butterhead or romaine)
4 oz (115 g) lamb's lettuce mâche
1 tbsp (15 ml) flat-leaf parsley, finely chopped
1 tbsp (15 ml) chervil, finely chopped
½ cucumber, peeled and chopped
1 tbsp (15 ml) young sweet violet leaves, finely chopped
10–15 each sweet violet, heartsease and common dog violet flowers

For the salad dressing
3 tbsp (45 ml) olive oil
1 tbsp (15 ml) lemon juice or white wine vinegar
Salt and freshly ground black pepper
Pinch of fruit (superfine) sugar

Wash and shake dry the lettuce, discarding the outer leaves, and put into a large bowl. Add all the other ingredients except the flowers and the dressing, and gently mix.

Make the salad dressing by combining the oil and lemon juice or vinegar in a bowl and whisking thoroughly. Season with salt and pepper to taste and add the smallest pinch of sugar.

Add the flowers to the salad, reserving a few to add just before serving. When you are ready to serve the salad, add the dressing, toss well and decorate with the remaining flowers.

SWEET VIOLET JELLY

This is a great way to use up apples stored over winter. Violets make this jelly so delicious that you will treasure it or, alternatively, give it to friends as a special present.

Makes 2 x 12-oz (350 g) jars

2 lb (1 kg) cooking apples, washed, cored and chopped
3¾ cups (900 ml) water
1 lb (450 g) sugar
¾ cup (175 ml) sweet violet flowers, stems and green removed (reserve 1 tbsp (15 ml) to decorate, if you wish)
2 tbsp (30 ml) lemon juice
2 tbsp (30 ml) white wine vinegar

Put the apples in a large saucepan with a lid. Add the water and bring to a boil, then simmer until the apples become soft and pulpy. This takes anywhere from 20 to 30 minutes, depending on the variety of apple. Pour carefully into a jelly or cheesecloth bag and leave for a day or overnight to drain into a large bowl.

When the draining has finished, measure the juice and add 1 lb (450 g) sugar for every 2½ cups (600 ml) juice. Put into a large pan and bring to a boil, adding the flowers tied in a piece of cheesecloth. Boil for about 20 minutes, until setting point is reached. At this point remove the flowers in the cheesecloth and spoon off the surface scum. Stir in the lemon juice, vinegar and the reserved flowers, if you wish, and pour into 2 warmed sterilized glass jars (see page 12). Seal when cool and date and label the jars.

VIOLET APPLE CAKE

This is the best dessert you can make to use up apples from winter storage. The delicate flavor the violets add is beautiful.

My father gave me a food processor in 1975; it transformed my cooking, and this is one of those recipes that really benefit from being made with one.

This cake is best served warm with lots of whipped cream. Alternatively, you can serve it cold at coffee time.

Serves 6–8

1½ lb (675 g) cooking apples
(before peeling and coring)
2 cups (500 ml) all-purpose flour
4½ tsp (22 ml) baking powder
1 tsp (5 ml) salt
1 cup + 2 tbsp (275 ml) fruit
(superfine) sugar
2 eggs
1 tsp (5 ml) almond extract
½ cup (125 ml) unsalted butter
Powdered (confectioners') sugar, for
dusting
2 tbsp (30 ml) sweet violet flowers,
divided

Preheat the oven to 350°F (180°C). Grease and line a 10-inch (25 cm), removable-bottom, round cake pan with baking parchment or waxed paper.

Peel, core and quarter the apples, then either slice by hand or use the slicing disk on a food processor. Once sliced, keep them in cold water to stop them going brown until the cake mixture is made.

Sift the flour, baking powder and salt into a large mixing bowl, add the sugar, then beat the eggs lightly with the almond extract and add to the bowl. Melt the butter and pour into the bowl. Either beat well by hand or mix in the food processor for roughly 10 seconds. Remove the cover, scrape down the sides of the bowl, then mix for a further 5 seconds.

Put half the cake mixture into the prepared cake pan, spreading it evenly over the bottom. Drain and dry the apple slices and lay them over the cake mixture in an even layer. Scatter 1 tbsp (15 ml) violets overtop. Spread the rest of the cake mixture on top of the apples. This mixture is rather thick and not easy to spread, but it honestly does not matter too much if some of the apple is left showing, as it will become covered during cooking.

Bake in the oven for 1½ hours, until golden brown, risen and slightly shrunk away from the sides of the pan. Turn out and serve, thickly dusted with sieved powdered sugar and decorated with the remaining violet flowers.

CRYSTALLIZED VIOLETS

I was bribed with these delightful crystallized flowers to go to dancing classes. At the end of each class Mum used to take me to Carwadine's cake shop, where I always chose a small lilac cake with a crystallized violet on top.

I have mentioned crystallizing flowers before in this book (see Borage, page 55), but this is the quick method, which is useful not only because of its speed but also because the ingredients are easily available. However, it does use egg whites, so I should warn that there can be an increased risk of salmonella poisoning with raw or lightly cooked eggs, so care should be taken, particularly among pregnant women, the elderly and young children. If you are worried about the risk, please follow the crystallizing method mentioned for borage flowers on pages 55–56.

14 wild or sweet violets (including stems), washed (do not use African violet, Santpaulia, which is a houseplant and not edible)
2 egg whites
Fruit (superfine) or powdered (confectioners') sugar

Preheat the oven to 250°F (120°C).

Pick the flowers in late morning, choosing perfect specimens. Dip them first in water to remove any insects or dust, then dry them gently on some paper towels.

In a bowl, beat the egg whites with a wire whisk until just frothy. Place the sugar in another bowl. Taking one violet at a time, pick it up by the stem and dip it into the egg whites, covering all the surfaces. Then gently dip it into the sugar, again being sure that all the petals, top and bottom, are covered.

Place the coated flowers on baking sheets lined with baking parchment and snip off the stems. Using a toothpick, open the petals to their original shape. Sprinkle sugar on any uncoated areas. Use a fine clean artist's paintbrush to remove any lumps of sugar.

Dry the flowers in the oven for 30 to 40 minutes or until the sugar crystallizes. Gently remove the violets to a wire rack with a metal spatula or two-tined fork. Sprinkle again with sugar if the violets appear syrupy. Cool.

Store in airtight containers with waxed paper between the layers for up to 2 weeks.

Excess sweet violet

Sweet violet syrup

This is an excellent syrup that is useful when making fruit salads, sorbets or any dessert needing an aromatic syrup base.

Makes 1½ cups (350 ml)

1½ cups (350 ml) water
1 lb (450 g) fruit (superfine) or granulated sugar
²/₃–1¼ cups (150–300 ml) sweet violet flowers

Bring the water to a boil in a saucepan, turn down the heat and add the sugar, stirring all the time. When the sugar has dissolved, add the flowers, stirring from time to time, and gently simmer the mixture until it turns into a syrup. This can take up to 8 minutes.

Strain the syrup through a fine sieve or some cheesecloth if you want absolutely no flower bits left. Pour the strained syrup into a clean, sterilized (see page 12) glass jar, allow to cool, seal well and store in the fridge for up to 2 weeks.

WILD STRAWBERRY

(also known as Woodland Strawberry, Fraises des Bois, Wild European Strawberry)
Fragaria vesca

This is a herb of my childhood. I remember picking wild strawberries and whortleberries on walks in the forest on Exmoor, bringing them home carefully and then eating the delicious fruit the following morning with our cereal.

Description

Wild strawberry is a low-growing hardy perennial that can spread profusely. The flowers have four or five white petals with a yellow center, which are followed by delectable small red fruit. The leaves are bright green and are made up of three leaflets with serrated edges.

This herb can easily be grown by breaking off a runner (a miniature form of the plant with a tiny root system on a long stem coming off the parent plant), then transplanting it.

Alternatively it can be raised from seed, which takes longer and is a less reliable method. The seed of the strawberry is visible to all, being embedded all around the outside of the fruit. To collect your own seed, leave the fruit in the sun to dry in summer. When fully dry and shrivelled, rub off the seeds and store them in a dry place until you are ready to sow them in early spring. Wild strawberry prefers a good fertile soil that does not dry out in summer, in either full sun or shade. It grows well in woods and hedgerows and makes a marvelous ground-cover plant, as it spreads quickly by means of its runners.

History in cooking

This native wild strawberry is not a direct ancestor of the modern commercial varieties but is a species in its own right. Richard Mabey, in *Flora Britannica*, says that he has seen a 16th-century recipe for a form of strawberry shortcake, made with almond flour and cooked simply by leaving the paste in the hot sun for a couple of hours. In the 17th century, the famous herbalist Nicholas Culpeper said that the fruit is "excellent good to cool the liver or a hot choleric stomach, and to quench thirst," among many other attributes.

Harvesting and uses

Leaves

The leaves can be picked throughout the growing season, but the young ones are the best and have a musky flavor and scent.
The leaves can be used to make teas and infusions.

Fruits

The strawberries can be harvested from early summer until early autumn. They are delicate when ripe and easily bruised if gathered directly into a basket or jar, so take a tray and gently lay them out so they do not touch each other. They can be added to fruit salads, eaten on their own with cream, used in cakes, pies and syrups or to flavor cordials. If you have enough, you can also use them to make vinegar or jam.

Properties   The strawberries are a mild diuretic and have a laxative effect that improves digestive functions. The leaves are included in many blended herbal teas; they were traditionally used to treat stomach upsets. Please note that this does not apply to the cultivated form of strawberry, which is why this plant is an herb.

Varieties   Alpine Strawberry
Fragaria vesca 'Semperflorens'
This hardy perennial looks identical to the wild form, with the exception that it does not produce runners, so it has to be propagated from seed.

WILD STRAWBERRY SHORTCAKE

I make no apology for this recipe. It is gorgeous, and made even more so by using these delightful wild strawberries with their unique sweet, aromatic flavor.

Serves 6–8

⅓ cup (75 ml) unsalted butter, cut into small pieces, plus extra for greasing
2¼ cups (550 ml) all-purpose flour, plus extra for dusting
4¼ tsp (21 ml) baking powder
1 tsp (5 ml) salt
¼ cup (60 ml) fruit (superfine) sugar, plus extra to serve
1 egg, beaten
⅓ cup (75 ml) reduced-fat (2%) milk
½ tsp (2 ml) pure vanilla extract
⅓ cup + 1 tbsp (90 ml) whipping (35%) cream
⅓ cup (75 ml) Greek-style yogurt
1 tsp (5 ml) powdered (confectioners') sugar
12 oz (340 g) wild strawberries

Preheat the oven to 425°F (220°C). Grease a baking sheet with a little butter.

Sift the flour, baking powder and salt into a bowl. Rub in the butter with your fingertips until the mixture resembles fine bread crumbs. Stir in the fruit sugar and make a well in the center.

Mix together the egg, milk and vanilla extract and pour into the dry ingredients. Gradually stir the dry ingredients into the liquid, then bring the mixture together with your hands to form a soft dough. Gently pat the dough into a smooth ball and turn it out onto a floured surface.

Roll out the dough into a 7½-inch (19 cm) round. Transfer it to the prepared baking sheet and bake for 10 to 15 minutes or until well risen, firm and browned on top. Slide the shortcake onto a wire rack and leave to cool.

Using a large serrated knife, slice the shortcake horizontally in half. With a large metal spatula, lift off the top layer, place it on a board and cut into 8 equal wedges. Set aside. (If you like, for an attractive finish, trim a fraction off each cut so that the wedges are slightly smaller.) Place the bottom layer on a serving plate.

Whip the cream to soft peaks, then fold in the yogurt and the powdered sugar, followed by three-quarters of the strawberries. Spoon the cream over the shortcake base. Place the 8 wedges on top, sprinkle lightly with a little fruit sugar and add the remaining strawberries. Serve.

WILD STRAWBERRIES WITH STRAWBERRY LEAF SABAYON

This is a delicate summer dish. There is something magical about these small wild delights that makes this dessert so special.

Serves 6

For the sabayon
10 strawberry leaves
¼ cup (60 ml) water, boiled and allowed to sit for a couple of minutes
3 egg yolks
½ cup (125 ml) fruit (superfine) sugar
2/3 cup (150 ml) white wine

8 oz (250 g) wild strawberries, reserving 6 for decoration

Infuse the strawberry leaves in the boiled water until it is cold, about 40 minutes, then strain and reserve the water.

Whisk the egg yolks and sugar together in a large bowl until thick and pale. Put the bowl over a pan of hot, but not boiling, water so that the bottom of the bowl is immersed in the hot water. Keep whisking and add the wine. After more whisking the mixture should become frothy and mousse-like. Make sure that during all the whisking the water does not boil; this is critical, as the mixture will separate.

Remove from the heat once you achieve a mousse texture, then whisk in the strawberry-leaf water. Set the bowl over a bowl of ice cubes and continue whisking until the mixture is cold.

Serve by placing the strawberries in 6 small individual bowls, drizzle 1 tbsp (15 ml) of sabayon over the fruit, then decorate each with one of the reserved strawberries.

WILD STRAWBERRIES WITH BALSAMIC VINEGAR

The first time I ate this I could not believe how simple it was. My mother found the recipe in Tuscany and I have reproduced it. It is essential to get the best thick balsamic vinegar for desserts or for dipping bread, not the one used for salad dressing.

This dessert is delightful served with vanilla cookies. I have included the cookie recipe (see page 346), as it is worth the effort; alternatively, if you do not have the time, serve it with vanilla ice cream.

Serves 4

½ cup (125 ml) red wine
½ cup (125 ml) water
1 lb (500 g) wild strawberries, rinsed and allowed to drain
1/3 cup + 1 tbsp (90 ml) fruit (superfine) sugar
1 tbsp (15 ml) balsamic vinegar

Put the wine and water in a glass or china bowl, add the strawberries and sprinkle with the sugar and balsamic vinegar. Mix gently then put into the fridge for at least 45 minutes before serving.

VANILLA COOKIES

Makes approx. 30 cookies

½ cup (125 ml) unsalted butter, softened
¾ cup (175 ml) fruit (superfine) sugar
1 tsp (5 ml) vanilla extract
2 eggs
2½ cups (625 ml) all-purpose flour, sifted, plus extra for dusting

Preheat the oven to 350°F (180°C).

In a large bowl, mix the butter with the sugar and vanilla extract until it is light and fluffy, then add the eggs one at a time and beat well. Add the flour, using a wooden spoon, to make a soft sticky dough.

Remove the dough from the bowl and place on a sheet of plastic wrap. Wrap it up and place in the fridge for at least 1 hour.

Lightly flour the work surface and your hands, remove the dough from the fridge and roll it out to about ¼ inch (5 mm) thick using a floured rolling pin. If necessary add extra flour, but not too much, as this will make the cookies hard.

Cut shapes, stars, rounds – whatever takes your fancy – and, using a flat knife, lift the cookies onto a greased baking sheet or one that is lined with nonstick baking parchment. Leave a small space around each one to allow for spreading. Bake in the oven for about 10 minutes, until they are lightly golden.

Remove and cool on a wire rack before storing in an airtight container.

Excess wild strawberry

Wild strawberry vinegar

I doubt that you will ever have a glut of this herb, but if you do ever have too many, wild strawberry vinegar is a must. You can use this with fruit and in salad dressings, sauces and marinades.

Makes 2 cups (500 ml)

1 lb (500 g) wild strawberries, washed
2 cups (500 ml) white wine vinegar
2 tbsp (30 ml) fruit (superfine) sugar

In a glass or china bowl, add all the ingredients, stir well, cover and allow to infuse for 2 to 3 days.

Strain first through a colander to remove the strawberries, then through an unbleached paper coffee filter. Pour into clean, sterilized (see page 12) bottles with nonmetallic lids.

This vinegar will keep well for a number of years.

GLOSSARY

BOTANICAL

Acid soil
Soil with a pH value of below 7 –
from 1 to 7 on the pH scale.

Alkaline soil
Soil with a pH value above
7 – from 7 to 14 on the pH scale.

Annual
A plant that completes its life cycle in
one year.

Aromatic
A plant with high levels of volatile
oil.

Biennial
A plant that completes its life cycle in
two years; in general it produces leaf
in the first year and flower and seed
in the second year.

Bulbils
Small bulb-like structures that form
in the flower heads, such as in chives.

Crown
The upper part of the rootstock from
which the roots arise, at or just below
soil level, such as in chicory and
horseradish.

Deciduous
A plant that drops its leaves
in the winter/cold months.

Evergreen
A plant that bears leaves all
year round.

Frost-hardy
A plant that needs protection when
temperatures fall below 23°F (-5°C).

Half-hardy
A plant that needs protection when
temperatures fall below 32°F (0°C).

Hardy
A plant that needs protection when
temperatures fall below 5°F (-15°C).

Herbaceous
A perennial plant that dies down at
the end of each growing season,
reappearing in the spring.

Monocarpic.
A plant that flowers only once,
produces seed, then dies. This can
take three or more years, such
as with angelica.

Perennial
A plant that lives for at least three
growing seasons.

pH value
This is the number that describes
how acid or alkaline your soil is.
A pH of 7 is considered neutral;
an acid soil has a pH value below
7, whereas at above 7 the soil is
alkaline.

Rhizomes
Swollen underground stems. As the
rhizome grows it often develops
segments with buds that break into
growth. Mint is a classic example of
a rhizomatous plant.

Tender
A plant that needs protection when
temperatures fall below 41°F (5°C).

Umbels
These are umbrella-like clusters of
flowers with all the flowering stems
arising from the same point, such
as from a single stem.

MEDICINAL

Antifungal
A substance that combats
fungal infections.

Antioxidant
A substance that prevents oxidation
and the breakdown of tissues.

Antiseptic
A substance that destroys or inhibits
microorganisms that cause infection.

Antispasmodic
A substance that relieves muscle
spasm or reduces muscle tone.

Carminative
A substance that relieves digestive
gas and indigestion.

Decoction
A water-based preparation of bark,
roots, berries or seeds that have been
simmered in boiling water.

Infusion
A water-based preparation in which
any of the following are brewed in a
similar way to tea: flowers, leaves,
stems or bark.

Stomachic
A substance that eases stomach pain
or increases stomach activity.

Topical
The application of an herbal
remedy to a specific place on the
body surface.

Vermifuge
A substance that expels intestinal
worms.

Vulnerary
A substance that heals wounds.

ACKNOWLEDGMENTS

There are so many people I wish to thank for helping me create this beautiful book. My family – past and present – especially my husband, Mac, my son, Alistair, and my daughter, Hannah, for her enthusiasm and beautiful illustrations. My friends for their contributions, either by eating and commenting or by letting me use their recipes. And a big thank-you to Jamie for finding the time in his hectic life to write the glowing foreword to the book – he is always an inspiration.

Thank you to all the Ebury team, especially Imogen, who has magic eyes for seeing the missing link; to the wonderful team at Jekka's Herb Farm, who kept going whatever the weather; to Will for creating a beautiful book; and to my agent Martine, for making sure all the dots were in the right place. And finally to my dog, Hampton, for making sure the trash got emptied.